Picking
Winners

Linus O'Connell

Picking Winners

A Horseplayer's Guide

ANDREW BEYER

With a new foreword
by Pete Axthelm

Houghton Mifflin Company / Boston

Library of Congress Cataloging in Publication Data
Beyer, Andrew.
  Picking winners.

  1. Horse race betting. I. Title.
SF331.B45   798'.401   74-34311
ISBN 0-395-39379-5 (pbk.)

The charts appearing on pages 17, 18, 20, 23, 26, 29, 30, 32,
33, 35, 36, 38, 39, 42, 43, 44, 53, 57, 58, 59, 78, 79, 81, 82, 83, 97,
98, 99, 102, 151, 152, 154, 155, 156, 161, 163, 166, 167, 170,
192, 193, 195, 196, 197, 199, 200, 201, 203, 204, 205, 206, 208,
209, 210, 211, 212, 213, 214, 216, 217, 218, 219, 220, 221,
222, 224 of this book are reprinted by special arrangement
with Triangle Publications, Inc. (Daily Racing Form).
Copyright © 1972, 1973, 1974 by Triangle Publications, Inc.
Reprinted with permission of the copyright owner.

To my mother

Contents

Foreword by Pete Axthelm

IN THE PADDOCK AREAS of Hialeah Park or Saratoga, horseplayers often recognize Andrew Beyer and tell him that they have followed the strategies that he offered them in *Picking Winners*. I have witnessed a number of these meetings, and I am happy to report that almost every one of Andy's followers comes equipped with both shirt and shoes. Many even boast that they still possess bus fare to their homes.

We fellow racetrack regulars have always enjoyed kidding Beyer. When a horse with an "omni-figure" plods home fifth, or one with a cherished "hidden figure" decides to hide somewhere near the eighth pole, we love to chide the man who sometimes celebrates victories by declaring himself King of the World. But if needling is a healthy part of track routine, so is profit. And on the tenth anniversary of the landmark publication of *Picking Winners,* I can cheerfully attest to the enduring success of Beyer's methods and his special brand of fine madness. A man who modestly states, as he does in these pages, that his handicapping is without equal, is clearly burdened with a large ego. Readers should also know that on most days, he has a bankroll to match it.

In the hyperbolic spirit that governs Beyer's approach to racing, I think it is fair to liken his role to those of Muhammad Ali in boxing, Joe Namath in pro football, George Steinbrenner in owning a baseball team. All have their flaws and their detractors. All issued bold predictions, some of which proved embarrassingly wrong. But all changed the entire concept of the business in which they have thrived.

For a man who has never shuffled in a ring, thrown a touchdown pass, or hired a free agent, Beyer has been an enormous force in his sport. For centuries, a benighted public has viewed racing as a hopeless puzzle. Only a handful of brave and witty souls have come up with solutions that make sense of it all. Early in this century there was Pittsburgh Phil. A few decades ago, Jule Fink and the Speed Boys had similar impact. Our generation of bettors is fortunate to have Beyer. The reader who takes the time and effort to absorb his approach, his speed figures—and his all-important philosophies of money management—takes a significant step toward that elusive grail known as beating the races.

For the novice or the nonbeliever, let me step back and repeat that point: yes, thoroughbred racing can be "beaten." The horseplayer is heavily, sometimes unconscionably, taxed. But under the parimutuel betting system, he is still wagering against a large body of fellow players, many of whom are woefully uninformed. The handicapper who takes the trouble to become one of the best-informed people at the track should eventually extract his share of gains from the casual, misguided, or whimsical folks at the windows alongside him. This is not to suggest that there are any short-term sure things, or systems that will guarantee great wealth. Winning is a long-term matter of overcoming the percentages, and it involves an invigorating mix of work, creativity, and exhilarating fun. That blend is what *Picking Winners* is all about.

Before all this praise makes Beyer sound like Spend a Buck romping home in the Kentucky Derby, here are a few qualifications. (They're allowed, because I picked Spend a Buck and he didn't.) I do not share Andrew's religious belief that his speed figures are "the way, the truth, and the light." I believe that these figures should be combined with a thorough study of horses as Beyer puts forth in *The Winning Horseplayer*. Watch them warm up and make note of which ones appear sore or particularly eager to run. Watch them run and note which ones encounter trouble that might give them excuses to run much better the next time. But before doing all that—or as a decent replacement if you are not among the fortunate few who can attend the races regularly—establish a good base of knowledge by learning the Beyer method.

As a Yale graduate, I remain unconvinced that Harvard is the ideal proving ground for handicappers. I am also certain that such honors are not hotly debated among the scholars presiding at either school. But Beyer's Harvard education probably contributed to the logical and concise manner in which this book leads even a beginner through the preliminary stages of handicapping and on to the complexities and rewards of speed figures. Perhaps it also had something to do with the entertaining columns that have long graced the *Washington Post*—and the colorful writing that will make this book enjoyable even for the reader without the dedication to become a disciple of the figures.

In some ways, *Picking Winners* is an autobiography. Its pages burst with the engaging personality of Beyer at the track: a slightly disheveled, lean man with a purposeful stride and a hand clutched firmly to the briefcase bulging with the figures. Years ago, Andrew and I decreed a rule of track etiquette: no one is allowed to drop to his knees and proclaim himself King of the World unless he has made a score equal to ten percent of his annual income. This experience is rare, but it is also unparalleled on the emotional scale of any red-blooded horseplayer. As one who has enjoyed it a few times, I can only applaud the author, who has enjoyed it with remarkable frequency over the years.

Of course, Beyer has also been known to punch holes in walls or stumble groggily into the night when photo finishes go wrong or stewards disqualify his horses. As you read him, remember that losses will go with the dreams, and a well-placed deuce on a trifecta can be every bit as thrilling as a major wager. In fact, one of the charms of this book is that it offers none of the quick-buck schemes that are all too common in the handicapping genre. Instead, it provides the intelligence and spirit of fun that make us all go racing in the first place.

One bright morning a few years ago, Beyer arrived at Gulfstream Park in Florida with a horse whose speed figures were virtually jumping off the page. With characteristic bravado, he announced, "God placed us on earth to bet on horses like this one."

The horse ran a bad third and provided a lesson for all who will enjoy this book. Learn Beyer's method, have a great time, and remember that there will occasionally be days when the Deity bets only to show.

Picking
Winners

1

The Joy of Handicapping

FROM TIME TO TIME, every confirmed horseplayer is racked by doubts about what he is doing with his life. He is playing the toughest game in the world, one that demands a passionate, all-consuming dedication from anyone who seriously wants to be a winner. Even a winner will necessarily experience more frustrations than triumphs, and when the frustrations come in rapid succession he may wonder if the struggle is worth it.

As I drove to Liberty Bell Race Track on the morning of December 9, 1970, I was beset by more than the usual doubts about my obsession with betting. For months I had been suffering through an unbroken series of racetrack disasters — a worse losing streak than most horseplayers will ever endure. I was beginning to question the assumptions that had encouraged me to devote so much of my energy to studying the *Racing Form:* Can the races be beaten consistently? And even if the game can ultimately be beaten, is it worth spending years of effort to reach a goal that most members of society would view as a trivial achievement? I remembered a conversation I had once had with a seventy-year-old horseplayer who felt he had wasted his life at the racetrack. "Son," he told me, "if I'd spent the time studying law books that I've put into the *Racing Form,* I'd probably be on the Supreme Court now."

I would be better able to answer my own questions after the second race at Liberty Bell that afternoon. It was an ordinary maiden-claiming race — for cheap horses who had never been able to win — but it was the most important race of my life. A week earlier I had been riding the Gray Line bus to Laurel, studying the *Racing Form* intensely. The past performances for the ninth race at Laurel happened to appear next to those for the first race at Liberty Bell, and the record of a horse on the also-eligible list at the out of town track leaped out of the page at me. His name was Sun in Action. His record was superficially dismal: In the only two starts of his career, he had finished fifth and seventh while competing at the rock-bottom level of horsedom. But Sun in Action had done something very unusual in those two races. In his debut he had broken slowly and rallied strongly, passing six horses and making up nine lengths in the last quarter mile. The next time he showed a burst of early speed and then tired. This change of running styles had produced many winners for me — including a 148-to-1 shot — but I had never seen a horse embody the pattern as clearly as Sun in Action.

Sun in Action was scratched from the race in which I

discovered him; he would not be entered again until the next week. During that week I scrutinized every aspect of his record a hundred times. I became obsessed. I could neither think nor talk of anything else. I did not merely hope or suspect that he was going to win his next race. I knew. Sun in Action was going to be my salvation.

When his name finally appeared in the entries for a mile-and-one-sixteenth maiden race, I could not contain my excitement. Three months earlier I had been hired to write a horse-racing column for the Washington *Daily News.* On the day of the race I wrote about Sun in Action, unconditionally advising the paper's readers that he was "the betting opportunity of the year." If I was going to go broke that day, I might as well be publicly humiliated, too.

I took all of my dwindling bank account to Liberty Bell. Sun in Action was 23 to 1 when I walked to the $50 window a few minutes before post time. He was 20 to 1 when I left, after betting $200 to win for myself and another $200 for friends who had been infected by my enthusiasm for the horse. Sun in Action broke quickly and he was running second when the field reached the first turn. But then he started dropping back. And back. And back. After three-quarters of a mile he was fourteen lengths behind the leader. I lowered my binoculars with resignation and told the friend who had accompanied me on the trip, "No chance. Sorry."

As I conceded defeat, Sun in Action was beginning to gain some ground on the last turn, running so wide that his jockey had to lean left in the saddle to prevent him from going to the outside fence. As he reached the stretch he was still an impossible eight lengths behind the leader, Birchcrest. Sun in Action continued gaining momentum through the stretch, but with only a sixteenth of a mile to run he still didn't seem to have a chance. In those final yards, however, Birchcrest began to tire perceptibly, and Sun in Action was flying at him. The finish was too close to call.

During the agonizing minutes while the photo was being developed I consoled myself with the thought that, even if Sun in Action had lost, I had not been disgraced. My judgment and my confidence in the horse had been vindicated. But who wants a moral victory? Put up number five!

They put up number eight, Birchcrest, the winner by a nose. And a few seconds later they put up a red sign that said OBJECTION. It was a stewards' inquiry, against the winner. Moments later the track announcer said that Sun in Action's jockey, Martin Fromin, had also claimed foul against the winner.

I sat hypnotized by the tote board, where the numbers eight and five were blinking as the stewards pondered their decision. A man near me was holding a $2 ticket on Birchcrest and he looked very unhappy. "There's no chance," he said. "They'll take him down." He was right. Birchcrest was disqualified for crowding Sun in Action on the first turn, forcing Fromin to check his horse sharply so he wouldn't stumble over Birchcrest's heels. The result was now official and the tote board said Sun in Action paid $43.20 to win. I had won more than $4000 for myself, the same amount for friends who had given me their money, and an unknown sum for readers who had wagered with their bookmakers that morning. I was a minor celebrity when I got back to Washington.

Sun in Action's victory meant more to me than $4000. It convinced me, for the last time, that the races could be beaten. And the exhilaration of that triumph persuaded me that mastering the art of handicapping was a goal worth pursuing, no matter how much time and energy it required. The mental attitude with which a man approaches gambling can determine whether he will succeed or fail. I did not have all the necessary skills yet, but I now had the self-confidence and determination to become a winning horseplayer.

This was not exactly the life's calling for which I had been programmed. I had once been destined to be respectable. The son of a college professor and product of a good middle-class upbringing in Erie, Pennsylvania, I was a model student in high school and went off to Harvard, where I expected to become a scholar and write learned essays on the poetry of T. S. Eliot. I was diverted.

Even in my early childhood I displayed a natural affinity for games of chance that my father and mother noted with some chagrin. My first gambling experience came at the age of five when I hit the jackpot on a slot machine. When I was twelve I persuaded my parents to take me to Randall Park in Cleveland, where I caught my first glimpse of that wonderful, esoteric set of statistics known as the *Daily Racing Form*. I was hooked. By the time I was fifteen I was buying the *Form* every weekend, studying it from cover to cover and placing $2 bets with an indulgent bookmaker. My fondest memory of Strong Vincent High School was sitting in the physics class of grim-faced, humorless Mr. Armagost when a messenger came into the room and handed the student council president a note reading, "Your parlay at Aqueduct paid $74." Mr. Armagost was not impressed.

When I went to college my resolution to become a diligent scholar was undermined by the discovery that four racetracks lay within easy commuting distance of Harvard Square. I managed to dabble at both academic and equine pursuits for the better part of four years, until an irreconcilable conflict arose two weeks before graduation. My final examination in Chaucer was scheduled on the same day that Kauai King would be trying to win the Triple Crown at Belmont Park. I knew nothing about the *Canterbury Tales* but I did know something about Amberoid in the Belmont Stakes. So I went to the track. Although I blew a $12,000 education, I did collect a $13 payoff on Amberoid, cutting my losses for the day to $11,987.

Having been reared to become an intellectual, I was seduced by horse-race betting because it offers more mental challenge and stimulation than any subject in the formal academic world. Few people ever master it. Men who are successful in every other facet of their lives — in school, in their jobs, in their financial affairs — can tackle racing and be frustrated, bewildered, or even ruined. It is maddening to serious students of handicapping that society confers its blessings on traditional academic pursuits but views the study of horse racing as utter frivolity. If you are writing a thesis on religious symbolism in the poetry of Sir Thomas Wyatt the elder, you are a respectable scholar. If you are studying the symbolism in the *Daily Racing Form*, you're a bum.

Horseplayers have to be content with the private satisfaction that comes from mastering the art of handicapping. The gratification is especially great because success at the racetrack is completely unambiguous. A man who writes a book may have to wait a lifetime for the judgment of history; a man who studies the stock market may have to wait for months or years to learn if a particular investment was a good one. A horseplayer can see his opinion validated — or contradicted — in a matter of seconds. At the end of a race meeting or a calendar year he can total his results and measure the extent of his success or failure. If there is a plus sign on the bottom line he will know unequivocally that he has achieved a goal that eludes almost everyone who pursues it. Even the money is secondary to that satisfaction.

The cerebral stimulation of handicapping, and the ego gratification that comes from doing it well, are only part of the attraction of playing the horses. The act of betting itself, as the legendary plunger Nick the Greek once said, "improves the flavor of living." Most solid citizens think gamblers are in the same psychological league as dope fiends and child molesters, but they don't understand and they don't know what they're missing.

A friend of mine from Boston was obsessed by playing the horses. He would awaken at dawn so he could study the races all morning, spend the afternoon at the track, and devote his evening to a stack of yellowing *Racing Forms*, searching for new handicapping techniques. He didn't have much money but his life was a joy. Every day was a new challenge, a new adventure. My friend didn't think there was anything abnormal about his passion. "I am thankful," he said once, "that God gave me the capacity to enjoy. And let's face it: there's nothing more enjoyable than gambling."

The capacity to enjoy: so few people have it. Most citizens live lives of such routine and drudgery and are so concerned about security that they cannot imagine how delicious uncertainty is. A gambler may have as many periods of pain and frustration as he does of exhilaration, but at least he knows he's alive.

I remember a day when I fell in love with a horse named Sandlot at Bowie Race Track. He was shipping in from New York, where in his most recent race he had encountered an astounding amount of bad luck but still managed to finish second in excellent time. I went to the track in a state of high excitement, prepared to make a killing. As the seventh race approached and the tension increased, it occurred to me that most people are completely reliant on external forces for this sort of stimulation. They fall in love, they get a promotion, they inherit money — but they must wait for these momentous events to happen. A horseplayer can will them. I bet Sandlot at 5 to 1 and watched ecstatically as he broke from the gate quickly, took the lead, and steadily increased his advantage. With a sixteenth of a mile to go, he was four lengths in front and I shouted, "Mark him up!" The words had barely escaped my lips when a gray horse named Zadig came streaking from out of nowhere and caught Sandlot in the last stride to win by a nose. I was stunned and silent for the rest of the day, and as I left the track a friend asked me how I felt. I thought of a scene in the movie *Patton* in which George C. Scott walks through a battlefield where fighting has raged all night long. He sees that many of his men are dead, hears the moaning of the wounded, and says, "God help me, but I love it so."

To reach this advanced state of lunacy, most horseplayers travel down similar paths. They are initially lured to the racetrack by greed, perhaps believing the blandishments of tipsters, system peddlers, and glib how-to-beat-the-races books that say there is easy money to be made at the track. They may be further encouraged by a stroke of beginner's luck. But all horseplayers soon learn that it is enormously difficult to win at the track consistently. In casino games, players are destined to lose and the house will get rich because it has a 1 or 2 percent advantage in its favor. In racing, the state and tracks extract more than 17 percent of every betting dollar. So the vast majority of horseplayers will inevitably be losers. It is a testimony to the unique lure of racing that once a man has discovered it and starts losing money — as he surely will, for a while at least — he usually doesn't abandon the sport and put his capital into municipal bonds. His appetite will be whetted by his initial failures.

Some people who become addicted horseplayers remain

dilettantes all their lives. They do not truly believe that the races can be beaten so they do not make a determined effort to learn. They live not for the day when they will be expert handicappers but for the one big lucky hit that will change their lives.

Serious students of handicapping are driven by the desire to learn so that someday they will have the skills to win consistently. In most areas of human knowledge a reasonably intelligent person with the will to become an expert can become one. If he wants to learn about Byzantine history or ancient philosophy or Elizabethan drama, he can spend years reading every book in the library, assimilating all the accumulated worldly wisdom on the subject. But in the field of horse racing this kind of intense study probably won't turn a horseplayer into a winner.

Most published material on handicapping is based on the assumption that horseplayers are looking for an easy, untaxing way to beat the horses and make a fortune overnight. The pages of racing magazines used to be filled with advertisements for systems that virtually assured the reader he would be able to retire to a life of ease by sending $25 for the secret of beating the races. These systems all consisted of a few simple rules: "Bet only horses who have finished out of the money in their last race while finishing within 5¼ lengths of the winner, and are racing within nine days of their last start." They all had exotic names: the Trainer's Overlay Profit System, the Investor's Dependable Earnings Accumulator. And they were all advertised with powerful pitches. I will confess that I succumbed to the come-on for something called the Master Key System. The brochure advertising it described the life of J. K. Willis, a telegraph operator who devoted years of effort to understanding the mysteries of handicapping. "Month after month," he wrote, "I studied, investigated, analyzed and experimented. Time after time it seemed as if I had solved the riddle, only to have my hopes dashed by some incurable flaw. And then, when I was almost convinced that I was wasting my time, I discovered the long-sought solution, the secret of beating the races — a simple wonder-working formula of figures . . . that provided the surest thing in Turfdom." Not long after making this momentous breakthrough, Willis was stricken and crippled by an acute form of rheumatism and ordered by his doctors to an area of the country where there was no racing. "Killing time is a problem," he wrote. "To help pass the slowly moving hours and divert my mind from my physical condition, I decided to teach my system to others." Who could resist? I raced for the nearest mailbox with my check for $25. I did not subsequently retire to a life of ease.

In the last few years systems have become passé and have been displaced by gadgets — nifty plastic slide rules like the Smart Money Detect-O-Meter, the Harvard Concentric Selector, and the Kel-Co Calculator. I succumbed to the propaganda for the latter device, which was said to have been developed by an aerospace scientist who is an expert on statistics and probabilities, and tested it on paper during a two-week period at Hialeah. It produced a 42 percent loss.

The systems and the gadgets are all based on the same assumption: that the complexities of horse racing, which have baffled men for centuries, which involve hundreds of factors, can be resolved by the application of a few simple rules or calculations. The assumption is a seductive one. I spent many hours tinkering with systems and once even created one that worked spectacularly. Armed with the Beyer Miracle System, I looked for horses who had shown early speed and tired in their next to last race, then ran at a longer distance, showed early speed again and tired less drastically. During one month at Bowie Race Track, system horses were winning nearly 50 percent of the time, at odds as high as 71 to 1. And then, just as abruptly as it had started working, it stopped. There is probably a time and place where any simple system will be profitable, even if it consists of betting horses with three-syllable names that begin with the letter *A*. But in the long run there is no way to circumvent the complexities of handicapping. A bettor who wants to win must come to grips with them.

When a horseplayer recognizes the shortcomings of systems and slide rules, he will probably turn to books to learn the art of handicapping. But he will find that most writers display the same mentality as the system peddlers. They try to make winning at the track sound as easy as possible. They present their readers either with a compilation of systems or with a set of inflexible rules to guide them when they handicap.

This approach is epitomized in *Lawrence Voegele's Professional Method of Winner Selection*, a book that was made a spectacular financial success by a nationwide advertising blitz. Voegele bases his "method" on a statistical study of 5000 races. It tells him, for example, that 84.3 percent of winners run within fourteen days of their last race. So Voegele turns this statistic into a dictum: Never bet a horse who has not started within the past fifteen days. Even though this is a sound guideline — a recent race suggests that a horse is in decent physical condition — there are many cases in which a layoff is a positive sign. If a horse has been racing frequently and his form begins to deteriorate, his trainer may give him a rest to revivify him. Then he brings the horse back into racing condition with a series of good workouts. If the trainer is competent the animal may be ready to run his best race after a layoff. But Voegele would summarily dismiss this or any other exception to his rule. He knows it will be much easier for his reader to operate with an inflexible method that dictates what he should do rather than with an approach that calls for him to use his intelligence and judgment at every stage of the handicapping process.

I read most of the literature on handicapping and it didn't make me a winner. Nor do I know any consistently successful bettor who acquired most of his knowledge from books. After recognizing the limitations of writings on the subject, a horseplayer who is still hungering for knowledge may try to discover the truths of handicapping through his own research. I know one Harvard-educated horseplayer, dubbed by a *Look* magazine article as "the Wizard of Odds," who plans to feed into an IBM 360 Model 65 computer the past performances for every race run in New York over a two-year period — some 30 million digits of information. His problem is finding $100,000 to finance the project. It would require an undertaking of this magnitude for a single person to unravel many of the mysteries of horse racing. Most of us are fortunate to have a few small but original insights into handicapping during the course of our careers as horseplayers.

Many aspiring handicappers, unable to master the game after reading all the books and conducting their own research, give up the quest in despair without realizing that there is a body of knowledge that could show them how to win at the track. This knowledge is transmitted not by the printed word but by an oral tradition.

Good horseplayers learn from each other. Contrary to the popular image of them as close-mouthed loners, serious bettors like to talk, argue over theories, and exchange ideas with people who share their obsession. They don't possess great secrets of handicapping any more than the system peddlers do. But winning horseplayers do know the areas of handicapping that are important and worth study, ones that the majority of bettors overlook because the handicapping books ignore them.

Without exception every successful horseplayer I know is keenly aware of the importance of the trainer when judging a horse's record and his chances in a race. He knows he must familiarize himself with the trainers at the track where he operates. He must learn who is competent and who is not. He must learn the specific strengths and weaknesses of individuals. A handicapper in New York, for example, ought to know that Frank Whiteley wins a high percentage of the time with horses making the first start of their careers; Elliott Burch, a trainer of comparable stature, seldom wins with them. But a horseplayer who has acquired his knowledge from books would be only dimly aware that this is a vital part of handicapping. The trainer factor does not lend itself to simplistic rules or dogmatic assertions. The writers don't want to tell their readers that the only way to learn about trainers is to sit down with a stack of *Racing Form*s and analyze their records. So they ignore the subject.

Because my job with the Washington *Star-News* brings me into contact with many fellow horseplayers, I have been fortunate enough to meet other serious handicappers who contributed greatly to my own knowledge. Sheldon Kovitz, a college classmate, taught me how to evaluate, with remarkable precision, the real meaning of horses' times. Clem Florio, probably the best handicapper for a newspaper in America, showed me how to relate a horse's speed figures to his current physical condition. Steve Davidowitz, an editor of *Turf and Sport Digest*, convinced me to view all handicapping factors in light of the racing surface over which the horses are competing.

There was no dramatic flash of insight, accompanied by a lightning bolt from the heavens, by which I learned how to beat the races. I began to study in the uncharted areas that these successful handicappers had suggested to me. At first I used these new techniques in a somewhat disorganized fashion. I finally ordered them, in my mind, to form a logical, coherent method of handicapping. And then I took the most important step of all. Frustrated by the realization that I was still not maximizing my winnings, I formulated a betting strategy and learned how to manage my money and my emotions. The process took years and it is still continuing, because no serious horseplayer ever stops learning. But I can now say, with much satisfaction and with no equivocation, that I beat the races. I do not claim that my method is the one and only true path to enlightenment, but I do know that it works.

I would like to be able to suggest that the reader will be able to finish this book, proceed directly to the nearest racetrack, and amass a fortune. But he can't. This book is only a shortcut to mastering the art of handicapping. The reader will not have to spend years, as I did, simply learning which directions to pursue so he can understand the game, but he will have to study so he can apply the important principles of handicapping to the track at which he operates. And he will need experience and judgment to use the principles properly. There are no neat lists of "dos and don'ts" in this book, no dogmatic pronouncements to make handicapping sound easy. If a man is looking for easy money, he is horribly misdirected if he looks for it at the racetrack.

2

A Handicapping Primer

I HAVE STOOD on street corners in the midst of blizzards and rainstorms waiting for the *Daily Racing Form* to be delivered to the corner newsstand. I have burst into paroxysms of rage because a friend or loved one inadvertently wrinkled a copy of my precious newspaper. I have accumulated thousands of old *Racing Forms* in my basement because I cannot bear the thought of throwing them away, even after they have yellowed and mildewed with age and the horses whose records they contain have long since retired or died.

The *Racing Form* occupies the place in the existence of a horseplayer that a Bible does in the life of a fundamentalist. It is the source of our knowledge, the basis of our decisions, the repository of our memories. Although bettors are fond of criticizing it for its high price and its occasional inaccuracies, the *Form* is the best publication of its type in the world. An American horseplayer who visits England and tries to handicap with that country's comparable publication, the *Sporting Life*, will inevitably return home with a renewed appreciation for the vast quantities of information jammed into every line of the *Form*.

For the benefit of uninitiated readers I have included in this chapter an explanation of the symbols in the *Racing Form* and the handicapping principles that underlie them. Learning how to analyze the data in past performances is an absolutely essential skill, though it alone is rarely enough to make a horseplayer a consistent winner. Handicapping is a competition among bettors. Because the betting dollar is so heavily taxed, only a small percentage of the people at a racetrack can possibly win. They are usually the people with superior knowledge.

A horseplayer who relies solely on the information in the past performances will know only what everybody else does. So the emphasis in this book will be placed upon the areas of handicapping that the *Form*'s past performances do not cover explicitly and that most bettors therefore ignore: the methodology of trainers, the influence of the track on the outcome of races, the importance of horses' physical appearance, and the accurate measurement of the times of races. But before a reader can venture into these uncharted areas, he must first master the fundamentals.

CONSISTENCY

The figures in the upper right-hand corner of a horse's past performances summarize his record for the last two years and paint an overall picture of his ability and reliability. In 1973 Jacques Who raced twenty times. The letter *M*

ques **Who** ✳   **117** Gr. c (1970), by Grey Dawn II.—Lady D...
Breeder, J. D. Wimpfheimer (Ky.).

1973	20	M	13	1		$26,470
1972	10	M	0	0		$960

r, J. D. Wimpfheimer.   Trainer, W. Sedlacek.

-73²Bel	7 f 1:24⅖ft	4½	120	64½	5⁴	3¹½	2½	VasquezJ⁷	Mdn 79	P'ceMissi...
-73¹Bel	⊤ 1⅛ 2:03⅕fm	3¾	115	2¹½	3¼	3ⁿᵏ	5¹¾	VasquezJ¹	Mdn 92	Harbor Pilot 105 Pistolet WaltherF. 9
-73¹Sar	⊕ 1⅛ 1:49⅗fm	6-5	▲115	6⁷	4⁴	3³	23½	BaezaB³	Mdn 79	Getthru 115 JacquesWho Pistolet 10
-73³Sar	1 1-8 1:52⅖ft	2½	115	4⁵	4⁶	53½	43¾	BaezaB⁸	Mdn 73	Noble Indian108 Pistolet B.W.'sL'rk 8
-73¹Sar	⊕ 1⅛ 1:48 fm	2¾	115	8⁵	86½	65½	44	BaezaB⁹	Mdn 87	Remagen122 B.W.'sLark NobleIndian 11
-73³Aqu	1 1:38⅖sy	7-5	▲113	51¾	1ʰ	2½	2¹	BaezaB⁵	Mdn 72	R'lR's'n113 J'cq'sWho G'tl'm'n'sWord 7
7-73²Aqu	1 1:36 ft	3½	113	55½	4⁶	32½	2ʰ	VeneziaM¹	Mdn 87	Y'wH'wJ'nct'n113 J'cq'sWho Reasoric 12
-73²Aqu	1 1:35⅖ft	3	111	4²	2³	2⁵	2⁸	VeneziaM⁵	Mdn 82	PleaseDon't111 JacquesWho Pistolet 8
3-73¹Bel	1 1:43⅗ft	3	111	4⁶	2¼	2ʰ	24	VeneziaM⁷	Mdn 80	K'y to theK'gd'm112 J'sWho Br'yBeau 8
-73²Bel	⊕ 1 ₁⁶ 1:43⅗fm	6¾	111	44½	1¼	2ʰ	2¾	VeneziaM⁸	Mdn 83	Mist'rF'nt'y122 Jacq'sWho SkyK'gd'm 10

Aug 20 Sar trt 3f ft :38b

means he is a maiden, a horse who has never won a race. He finished second thirteen times and third once, compiling earnings of $26,470.

Jacques Who's record made him a legend in his own time with New York bettors and a source of utter bewilderment to his trainer, Woody Sedlacek. After the colt suffered through a dismal season in 1972, Sedlacek straightened out his physical problems, prepared him for what he thought would be a winning effort, and presumably made a bet. Jacques Who broke slowly, rallied, opened a lead in mid-stretch, and looked like a winner. But when another horse challenged him, he gave up entirely and lost by a head. He kept behaving like this throughout the year, establishing a remarkable record of futility.

Jacques Who was the classic embodiment of the type of animal known as a "sucker horse," one who seemingly refuses to win under any conditions. This behavior is usually inexplicable, but Jacques Who's bad tendencies may have been hereditary. His half sister, La Basque, was also running during the 1973 season; she finished third seven times in the first nine starts of her career but was unable or unwilling to win.

Most horseplayers seem to have a fatal weakness for sucker horses. The betting public at the New York tracks sent Jacques Who to the post at odds of 3 to 1 or less almost every time he ran, reasoning, no doubt, that he was overdue to win a race. The reasoning always proved to be wrong.

Handicappers should view with skepticism any horse who displays a chronic inability to win, no matter how strong his credentials may appear otherwise or how weak his opposition may be. In maiden races that are teeming with sucker horses, a bettor can sometimes hit extreme longshots by the process of elimination — by disregarding all the perennial losers and taking a chance on a lightly raced horse who has shown virtually nothing but has not yet proved himself to be a hopeless case.

Just as persistent losers are bad bets, horses with excellent winning percentages are often good bets. A handicapper cannot play consistent horses blindly, because their successes will eventually propel them to a level of competition where they are overmatched. But when such horses fulfill all the important handicapping requirements, they will usually find a way to win because they possess the determination and competitive spirit that animals like Jacques Who do not have.

BREEDING

Exemplary								115	B. g (1967) by Fleet Nasrullah—Sequence, by Count Fleet.					
Owner, W. L. Miller. Trainer, W. L. Miller.									Breeder, L. Combs II. & D. Combs (Ky.)	$4,250		1973 2 0 0 0		
Apr23-74¹Kee	6 f 1:13⅕ft	23	112	55½	55½	33½	2¾	Patt'sonG³	4000 75	Mark'sRing113	Exemplary	TaulH
Apr17-74¹Kee	6½ f 1:18 ft	19f	¹12	89³10¹⁵12¹⁹12¹⁷				Valdiz'nF⁴	6250 71	F'rm'lCount114	Mr.Ex'c't'n'r	G'l'tF
Mar12-74⁶Lat	5½ f 1:09 sy	7¾	117	111¹108	10¹²	98¾		BeechJJr¹	5000 64	Allur'gLady112	AlibiFella	Pressitba
Mar 5-74⁸Lat	5½ f 1:08⅗gd	14	117	94½	97	86½	86	BeechJJr²	7500 69	Bay Do Do 110	Perennial	Misty T
Feb21-74⁶Lat	5½ f 1:08 ft	9-5	⁴117	3¹	53½	68½	6¹⁴	WeilerD⁴	7500 64	Andy'sM'yC'p122	E'b'y'sT'in'	R'd'sB
Jan31-74⁶Lat	1 1:42 gd	7-5	⁴117	1¹	1h	2½	36½	WeilerD²	7500 62	HeavenlyHero113	BBsPride	Exempla
Jan26-74⁸Lat	6 f 1:15⅗m	8¾	117	2h	3¹	4³	4¹³	WeilerD⁴	Alw 57	Big Spade 124	Gray Page	Nadar
Jan12-74⁷Lat	6 f 1:11⅘ft	3¼	115	3½	1h	2h	3½	BrambleC²	Alw 88	NativeSh's109	T'sBigGem	Exempla
Jan 7-74⁸Lat	6 f 1:10⅕ft	11	112	1⁵	11½	22	2¹	Ten'b'mM¹	Alw 96	Maj'sticN'dle109	Exempl'ry	Mike'sP

The breeding line in a horse's past performances identifies his sire, dam, and maternal grandsire. Exemplary is a son of Fleet Nasrullah, out of the dam Sequence, who was a daughter of Count Fleet. Though this information may be largely academic to horseplayers, it is the basis of the highest-stakes gambling in the racing world.

The owners and breeders who pay astronomical prices for unraced one-year-old horses on the basis of pedigree and conformation are taking what the man who runs the Saratoga Yearling Sales concedes is "a crapshooter's gamble." Exemplary was a roll of the dice that came up craps. He was sold at Saratoga in 1968 to the Ada L. Martin Stable for $280,000, which at the time was the highest price ever paid for a yearling colt. He wound up running in $4000 claiming races, unable to win.

If even the breeding experts can make mistakes of such proportions, horseplayers are fortunate that they do not have to pay much attention to bloodlines when they are handicapping. Once a horse has acquired a racing record, his pedigree matters very little. When a man encounters Exemplary in a $4000 claiming race, it doesn't matter whether he is an ill-bred plug or a horse who was once destined to be great.

There are, however, a few circumstances in which bettors may be helped by a rudimentary knowledge of breeding. In two-year-old-maiden races, bloodlines can provide clues about the ability of first-time starters. Certain sires, like the great Bold Ruler, consistently beget precocious sons and daughters. Other sires, like Sea-Bird, usually produce offspring who are late bloomers, if they bloom at all.

When a sprinter attempts to run a mile or more for the first time, his breeding may determine his capability at the longer distance. A horse would probably perform well at a route if he were a son of Gallant Man, who usually transmits stamina to his offspring. A horse would not be likely to fare so well if he were a son of Loom, whose progeny are usually gasping for breath after they have run three-quarters of a mile.

Of all the characteristics of thoroughbreds, the one that seems to be carried most often from generation to generation is the ability to run well on the grass. The following sires were all excellent turf runners who usually pass on this talent to their sons and daughters:

Assagai	Round Table
Herbager	The Axe II
Mongo	Tom Rolfe
Prince John	Vimy Ridge

When a scion of one of these horses makes his debut on the grass, I will give him serious consideration no matter how dismal his record on the dirt may be. But even this application of breeding will at best produce only a few winners for a handicapper during the course of a year. A horseplayer trying to learn the game would be advised to concentrate his study in more productive areas.

SEX

Laughing Bridge	**120**	Dk. b. or b. (f) 1972), by Hilarious—Brookbridge, by Ambehaving.
		Breeder, N. Hellman (Fla.). 1974. 7 4 1 1 $5

Owner, N. Hellman. Trainer, A. A. Scotti.

Aug12-74⁸Sar	6 f 1:10⅖ft	1-3 ▲120	3½	11½	13	15	Pin'yLJr⁴	ScwS 86	(F)	augh'gBr'ge120 Stulc'r S'eSwin
Jly 29-74⁸Sar	6 f 1:09⅖ft	3-5 ▲117	1½	15	18	1¹³	BaezaB¹	AlwS 9	(F)	'gh'gB'dge117 M'yB'l'tine FairW
Jly 10-74⁸Aqu	5½ f 1:02⅖ft	3½	115	2¹	23	26	29	BaezaB¹	AlwS 9	(F)	uff'n118 L'gh'gB'dge OurD'c'gG
Jun20-74⁴Bel	5½ f 1:04⅖ft	2¼	117	11	12	12½	14¼	BaezaB⁴	Alw 9	(F)	aughingBridge117 Suzest ACha
Jun 3-74⁶Bel	5½ f 1:04⅛gd	7-5	117	11½	1½	24	37	TurcotteR⁵	Alw 8	(F)	opernica117 ACharm L'hingBr'
Apr16-74⁴Aqu	6 f :58⅘ft	2-3 ▲116	13	1⁴	17	17¾	Turc'tteR³	Mdn 9	(F)	'gBr'ge116 Wh't's theR's'n B'dV
Mar22-74³Hia	5 f :59 ft	2½ ▲117	1½	13	13	12½†TurcotteR²	Mdn 94	(F)	'gh'gB'ge117 M't'yM'd F'rY'gM

†Disqualified from purse money.

Aug 19 Sar 5f gd :59⅛h   Aug 10 Sar 3f ft :33⅖h   Aug 5 Sar 5f ft :59⅖h

The sex of a thoroughbred is indicated in the breeding line of his past performances. A male is a colt (c) until he reaches the age of five and becomes a horse (h). A castrated male of any age is a gelding (g). A female is a filly (f) until she turns five and becomes a mare (m). The symbol Ⓕ describes races limited to fillies and mares.

Most horseplayers consider this to be important handicapping information, perhaps because sexism is so deeply ingrained in the American racing scene. Female jockeys are held in low esteem; female trainers are practically nonexistent; and female horses are considered the natural inferiors of their male counterparts.

The folly of the latter notion was demonstrated during the 1974 racing season, when the crop of two-year-old fillies was vastly superior to the colts. Ruffian was one of the greatest two-year-olds in history. The fillies she was beating, Laughing Bridge and Hot N Nasty, would have been champions in a normal year.

I saw Laughing Bridge win two stakes at Saratoga during the summer of 1974 and was convinced that she could defeat males in the track's big two-year-old race, the Hopeful Stakes, if she got the chance. I relished the prospect: Laughing Bridge's odds would be generous because of the public's reluctance to bet on fillies against colts. So I sought out trainer Al Scotti and asked him if he planned to nominate Laughing Bridge for the Hopeful.

Scotti looked at me as if I were a madman. "I don't run fillies against colts," he said.

"Why?"

"They're the weaker sex," Scotti said. "A good filly can't beat a good colt."

"That just isn't true," I protested. "The reason fillies don't beat colts very often in this country is because trainers are afraid to run them. But look at Europe. Fillies beat colts all the time over there. Dahlia's a filly, and she's the best horse in Europe now. It's nothing unusual for a filly to win the Arc de Triomphe — the biggest horse race in the world."

"You're right about one thing," Scotti conceded. "Trainers don't like to run fillies against colts because they don't like to be second-guessed. But that doesn't bother me. Hell, I'm not going to get into the Hall of Fame anyway."

I pressed on: "Laughing Bridge ran six furlongs here in 1:09⅘. The last stake for colts was run in 1:10⅖. She'd kill those colts in the Hopeful."

"Well, I don't know," Scotti said. "She might open four lengths out of the gate, get to the head of the stretch, and start thinking that woman's place is in the home."

Laughing at the absurdity of his own argument, Scotti said he wanted to consult an official of the New York Racing Association before deciding on his course of action. He went to the official's office and emerged a few minutes later shaking his head. "He thought I'd be crazy to run a filly against colts," Scotti said.

Scotti did not enter Laughing Bridge in the Hopeful. Instead, he ran her against other members of the "weaker sex" in Saratoga's big filly race, the Spinaway Stakes. Ruffian blew Laughing Bridge off the track, winning by nearly thirteen lengths and running the second-fastest six furlongs in Saratoga's long history. The difference between second-place money in the Spinaway and the winner's share of the Hopeful was $29,000.

Sexism can be costly, and a horseplayer should not let himself succumb to it. He may occasionally cash a bet on a filly who has been competing against colts and is now entered against members of her own sex, because this move is often a signal that the trainer thinks he has his filly ready for a winning race. But most of the time a handicapper should pay little attention to the sex of horses. He should consider them as individuals and try to evaluate their relative merits without letting prejudice against females cloud his judgment.

THE RUNNING LINE

R.'s Pet	122	B. c (1971), by Subpet—Island Fair, by Noor.								

Br., J. J. DiGrazia & P. J. DiVito (Fla.). 1974 5 4 1 0 $135,910
1973 9 2 1 1 $15,575

er, W. C. Partee. Trainer, H. Tinker

6-74⁹OP	1 1-8 1:50⅗ft	2½e▲123	12¹⁷ 66½ 22½ 1h	McH'eD¹¹ AlwS 90 J.R.'sPet 123 SilverFlorin NicksFolly 17
0-74⁸OP	1-70 1:43⅕ft	1-2e▲119	5⁵½ 1h 1½ 1½	McHar'eD⁷ Alw 80 J.R.'sPet119 BoldClarion PerfectAim 7
6-74⁹OP	1-70 1:42⅘ft	4-5e▲121	6⁶ 6⁸ 43½ 2¾	McH'eD¹ HcpO 81 PerfectAim111 J.R.'sPet121 OfficeK'g 11
2-74⁹OP	6 f 1:11⅕ft	6-5e▲118	53½ 41½ 32½ 1h	McH'eD² HcpO 89 J.R.'sPet 118 Satan'sHills Tisab 9
6-74⁸OP	6 f 1:12⅕sl	2¾e 113	64½ 42 12½ 17	McH'eD⁵ HcpO 84 J.R.'sPet113 BigLatch Brunate 10
5-73⁸Haw	6½ f1:15⅘ft	8 110	78½ 67 44 22½	BroganG⁶ AlwS 92 Be aNative114 J.R.'sPet TrojanBr'nze 8
7-73⁸Haw	6 f 1:10⅕ft	6¾ 116	99¾ 88½ 65¾ 55¾	SibilleR⁵ AlwS 89 Be aNative122 PrincelyPl's're Br'sB'l 10
6-73³Haw	5½ f 1:04⅘ft	9¾ 115	79½ 711 65 42½	SibilleR³ Alw 91 Be aN'tive121 Pr'c'lyPl's're BrassBall 7
5-73⁸AP	5¼ f 1:04 ft	8 119	6⁶ 66 35½ 35½	GavidiaW² Alw 89 Beau Groton 122 Hula Chief J.R's Pet 8

April 25 CD 5f ft 1:01h   April 21 CD 5f ft 1:01⅘h   April 4 OP 5f ft 1:03⅖b

The *Racing Form*'s past performances vividly describe the way a horse has run his previous races. They indicate his position in the field and the number of lengths by which he was leading or trailing at four different stages of the race.

In sprints from six to seven furlongs, the *Form* shows a horse's position at the quarter-mile mark, the half mile, the stretch, and the finish. In routes from one mile to one and three-sixteenths, it shows his position at the quarter, three-quarters, stretch, and finish.

The most recent race of J.R.'s Pet — the top line of his past performances — was at 1⅛ miles. After a quarter mile he was running twelfth, 17 lengths behind the leader.

After three-quarters of a mile he was sixth, 6½ lengths behind the leader.

As he came into the stretch he was second, 2½ lengths behind.

At the finish, he was the winner by a head. (A margin of a nose would have been abbreviated "no." A margin of a neck, "nk.")

A horse's running line and finishing position are obviously the crucial part of his past performances. Many handicappers concentrate on it, trying to find patterns and clues in the running line alone that indicate how a horse is likely to perform in his next race. The popular author Tom Ainslie says to discount the chances of an older horse whose last two running lines look like this:

$$3^3 \quad 2^1 \quad 2^{1/2} \quad 1^{no}$$
$$2^1 \quad 1^{nk} \quad 1^{hd} \quad 2^{nk}$$

Ainslie reasons that the horse exerted himself so much in these head-and-head battles that he is likely to go off form the next time he runs.

Almost every handicapping book illustrates the way horses round into form by citing a pattern like this:

$$3^3 \quad 2^1 \quad 1^1 \quad 1^3$$
$$5^4 \quad 4^3 \quad 4^2 \quad 2^1$$
$$6^9 \quad 6^9 \quad 5^8 \quad 4^6$$
$$10^{11} \quad 10^{12} \quad 10^{10} \quad 9^{10}$$

In the bottom line of his past performances, this horse ran a thoroughly dismal race. He came to life in his next start, finishing fourth, and continued to improve. His sharp second-place finish signaled that he was ready for a winning effort.

One of the most positive signs in a horse's running line is an unprecedented flash of speed:

$$2^{nk} \quad 3^5 \quad 6^8 \quad 8^{13}$$
$$9^{10} \quad 10^{12} \quad 10^{13} \quad 10^{16}$$
$$6^7 \quad 8^{13} \quad 8^{13} \quad 8^{14}$$

This brief burst of speed for a quarter mile — after which the horse was running second by a neck — can be a harbinger of a dramatic wake-up. Horses with such records can and do win at enormous odds.

A more reliable sign of imminent improvement comes

when a horse manages to carry his speed to the stretch for the first time:

1^1	1^1	2^{nk}	6^7
2^{nk}	3^4	5^8	9^{13}
$2^{1/2}$	5^7	8^{13}	12^{20}

An animal with a record like this is very likely to lead all the way in his next start.

Every horseplayer has his own notions of what running lines should and shouldn't look like. But whatever his preferences may be, they will cost him money if he views horses' form patterns as phenomena independent of other handicapping factors. The textbook notions about a horse rounding to form or exerting himself too much in previous efforts may be valid in theory. They would be useful if a horse's physical condition never changed, if he ran all his races against the same opposition, at the same distance, over identical tracks. But past performances never take such a conveniently pure form. A handicapper must view running lines in the context of the dozens of factors that influence a horse's performances, not as independent entities that by themselves will reveal how a horse will run in the future.

CLASS

Horses are judged by the company they keep. Most handicappers assess the relative ability of thoroughbreds by observing the quality of the opponents they have faced and beaten. Measuring class demands some fairly sophisticated techniques, which will be discussed in Chapter Ten, but before a horseplayer can use them he must first acquire a basic understanding of the different types of races.

Sharp Gary   **126**   Dk. b. or br. g (1971), by Carry Back—Token of Love, by Prince John
Breeder, E. R. Scharps (Fla.).
Owner, E. R. Scharps.   Trainer, J. T. Diangelo.

		1974	6	3	0	1	$53,9
		1973	8	1	0	1	$7,2

Apr20-74⁷Aqu	1 1-8 1:51⅖ft	23	126	11¹⁷ 9¹² 6⁴½ 3²¼	Vel'q'zJ⁹	ScwS	5	Flip Sal 126 Triple Crown Sharp Gary
Mar23-74⁹FG	1 1-8 1:51⅕ft	15	120	78¾ 73¼ 87¾ 78¾	V'n'ziaM⁹	AlwS	9	Sellout 118 Buck's Bid Beau Groton
Mar 9-74⁸GS	1¹⁄₁₆ 1:46⅗m	8-5	▲121	33⅓ 6⁷ 6¹² 6²¹	MapleE³	HcpS	1	C'p'teH'd'che111 W'gS'th N'bleMich'l
Feb18-74⁸Bow	1¹⁄₁₆ 1:46⅗ft	7	122	53¼ 3² 3½ 1¹	Barrera⁵	AlwS	5	SharpGary122 JollyJohu GroundBr'k'r
Jan26-74⁸Lib	1¹⁄₁₆ 1:47⅗gd	3¾	112	3² 3³ 2½ 1ⁿᵏ	Barrera⁹	AlwS	8	Sh'pG'ry112 W'gS'th M'm'sD's n'Mine
Jan13-74⁶Lib	1-70 1:43⅖gd	2½	120	2¹ 1² 1¼ 1ⁿᵒ	Barrera⁶	Alw	7	SharpGary120 RestlessRoad Ribopeak
Dec26-73⁴Aqu	6 f 1:10⅘gd	8¾	118	68¼ 34½ 3¹ 1⁴	V'ziaM1⁴	M20000	9	SharpGary118 Molt Unanim'sVerdict
Dec 7-73¹Aqu	6 f 1:10⅗ft	11	118	10¹²12¹²41¹16 9¹⁵	V'iaM1⁴	M25500	6	Ev'nSh'r's118 M'reH'p'f'l Un'm'sV'd't
Dec 1-73²Aqu	6¼ f 1:17⅕ft	24	122	119³12¹21¹¹14 8¹⁸	Ven'aM⁴²	Mdn	9	Watersc'pe122 H'v'nF'rbid S'rfC'tch'r
Nov24-73¹Aqu	6 f 1:11⅕ft	12	122	85¼10¹²10¹³109¼	Venezia⁴⁹	Mdn	8	Nostrum122 I'llmakeitup Rube theGr't
Sep15-73³Bel	6 f 1:09⅗sy	7¾	121	5⁹ 5⁸ 5¹⁴ 7¹⁸	C'd'oA⁴¹⁰	Mdn	7	C'm'loN'b's121 H'r to t'eL'e Chr't'f'ro
Sep 8-73³Bel	6 f 1:10⅗ft	11	120	3² 3½ 3² 36¼	RiveraN⁴⁴	Mdn	4	St'n'w'lk120 Sp'rkl'gPl's're Sh'rpG'ry
Aug29-73²Bel	6 f 1:10⅗ft	17	119	75¾ 53½ 65¼ 5⁶	RiveraN⁴²	Mdn	4	TripleCrown119 Accipiter R'ghMarch
Apr23-73³Aqu	5 f :59¾ft	13	117	4² 4³ 3⁴ 4⁷	BaezaL⁹	Mdn	10	WhoD'zit117 Jov'lJudge T'mp't'rSw'n

April 29 CD 5f ft 1:02b   April 13 Aqu 1m ft 1:38⅖h   April 6 Bel 5f sy 1:01⅗b

About two-thirds of all the races run in America are claiming races, in which each entrant is up for sale for a designated price. If a horse is entered in a $10,000 claiming race, any owner or trainer at the track can acquire him for that sum by filling out the appropriate form and depositing it in a box in the racing secretary's office fifteen minutes before post time. After the race the buyers take the horse to his new stable. If the animal drops dead on the track, the new owners are responsible for disposing of the carcass. The claiming system is a wonderfully effective way of insuring that the entrants in most races will be evenly matched. The trainer of a $15,000 horse could, of course, enter him in a $5000 race with a virtual certainty of winning. But he would have to be crazy to do it because no rational man is going to sell a horse for $10,000 less than he is worth.

If a trainer considers his horse too valuable to run in claiming races he can enter him in allowance races — a category that bewilders most beginning horseplayers. In claiming races a handicapper can evaluate class rather easily: an animal who runs for a $15,000 price tag is presumably superior to one who competes at the $8500 level. Although there can be enormous variation in the quality of allowance races, the past performances simply say "Allowance" for all of them.

Every allowance race has conditions limiting the eligibility of the entrants. The conditions may be straightforward: "For 3-year-olds who have never won two races." Or they may be terribly abstruse: "For 3-year-olds and upward which have not won $6800 twice since July 14 other than maiden or claiming."

Sometimes the conditions will suggest the relative quality of allowance fields. An event for "fillies and mares who have never won three races" will usually be superior to one for "fillies and mares who have never won two races." When the conditions are confusing, the purses will usually suggest the strength of allowance fields. Horses running for prize money of $10,000 will usually be better than those who compete for a $9000 purse. Since the past performances indicate neither the conditions nor the purses of allowance races, a handicapper should keep a set of result charts, in which this information is listed.

Stakes races, so named because owners must pay a fee to enter, offer the biggest purses and attract the best horses. Many stakes are handicaps, for which the track racing secretary assigns the weight that the horses will carry, theoretically to give each one an equal chance of winning.

Starter handicaps are an odd breed of race, open to horses who have run for a certain claiming price since a certain date. For example: "For horses who have started for a claiming price of $3500 or less since July 15." These races usually attract horses who have improved greatly since they started for the designated claiming price. A $3500 starter handicap may actually be the equivalent of a $10,000 claiming race.

Maiden races are limited to horses who have never won. Maiden-special-weight events may draw fields of highly regarded young horses; even a little Secretariat has to start his career somewhere. Maiden-claiming races, on the other hand, usually are composed of the dregs of horsedom — animals bad enough that they haven't been able to win and cheap enough that their trainer is willing to lose them. The claiming price on such races is frequently inflated. A horse who wins a $5000 maiden claimer is likely to be over-matched in bona fide $5000 competition.

These are the symbols used by the *Racing Form* to describe different classes of races:

5000	$5000 claiming race
M5000	$5000 maiden-claiming race
H5000	$5000 starter handicap
c5000	Horse was claimed for $5000
Mdn	Maiden-special-weight race
Alw	Allowance race
AlwS and	Stakes races in which weights are
ScwS	determined by various conditions
HcpS	Handicap stakes
HcpO	Overnight handicap: one that is not a stake

Racing's classification system is complex. But when a horseplayer understands and learns to use the class factor, he is equipped to answer the central question of handicapping: who is better than whom?

COMPANY LINE

When a handicapper becomes familiar with the horses who run at a track he can judge their class by recognizing

ay Pierre   **112** Ch c (196?), by Chateaugay—La Bonne Mouche by Bold Ruler.
Breeder Mr. & Mrs. J. W. Galbreath (Ky.).1973 14 2 1 3 $ 31,480
ner, Mrs. L. W. Knapp, Jr.   Trainer, S. Di Mauro.   1972 16 3 1 1 $23,210

18-73⁸Aqu	1 1:35³⁄₅ft	15	114	1¹	3¹¹⁄₂	35	38³⁄₄	MapleE⁵	Alw 80 Onion117 Champ'gneCharlie GayP'rre	5
4-73⁸Aqu	1 1:34⅘ft	2½	119	2¹½	36	39	3¹²	BaezaB¹	Alw 81 Everton 11 116 GentleSmoke G'yP'rre	7
23-73⁸Aqu	1 1:35 ft	11	116	11½	12	11½	14¼	PincayLJr⁶	Alw 92 GayPierre116 PassenM'd Gall'ntKn've	7
16-73⁸Aqu	6 f 1:11 ft	19	111	44½	36	44½	65½	MapleE⁵	Alw 82 Gov'rn'rM'x113 L'tleBigCh'f Cheriepe	7
6-73⁷Aqu	6 f 1:10⅖ft	35	112	81⁵	88½	77	44½	MapleE¹	Alw 86 Cutlass 112 Ang'e Light Busted	8
26-73⁷Aqu	7 f 1:22⅘ft	29	116	55	88½	910	95³⁄₄	MapleE¹	Alw 81 Cutlass 113 Plum Bold Jazziness 11
10-73⁸Bel	6 f 1:08⅘ft	21	112	46¼	66¼	6¹²	41¹	MapleE²	Alw 88 Whatabreeze 118 My Gallant Busted	7
7-73⁷Bel	7 f 1:22½ft	10	112	1¹	1½	32	49¼	Cast'daM⁶	Alw 84 D'deeM'm'l'de118 ZuluTom C'ri'sC'se	7
21-73⁵Aqu	6 f 1:09³⁄₅ft	37	112	1¹	3ⁿᵏ	41	36	Cast'daM⁵	Alw 89 Petrograd 112 Banderlog Gay Pierre	6

Dec 11 Bel trt 4f gd :50⅘b   Nov 22 Bel trt 3f ft :36⅖b   Nov 12 Bel trt 4f ft :50b

the names of the opponents they have been facing. The *Racing Form*'s past performances list the first three finishers in a race. A horseplayer trying to evaluate Gay Pierre's most recent allowance race might not know what its conditions or purse value were, but he could see that the winner of the race was Onion, who had conquered Secretariat in the Whitney Stakes earlier in the year. The second-place finisher was Champagne Charlie, also a stakes-caliber animal. Gay Pierre's loss in this company was no disgrace, and he would have a reasonable chance to win if he were entered against moderate allowance horses.

DATES OF PREVIOUS RACES

ead Table ✳   **116** Ch. c (1969), by Prince John—Birthday Cake, by Swoon's Son.
Breeder, Happy Hill Farm (Ky.).   1973 12 9 1 2 $49,030
ner, J. Miller.   Trainer, E. W. King.   **$22,500**   1972 11 2 2 0 $16,000

5-73⁵Aqu	6½ f 1:16 ft	2³⁄₄	116	1¹	12	12½	12	AmyJ³	16000 96 Head Table 116 Extra Hand Fota	7
1-73⁹Aqu	6 f 1:11⅕ft	2	^116	3ⁿᵏ	1h	12½	11½	C'oAJr¹⁰	c8000 87 HeadT'ble116 WitnessSt'nd B'uReav'r	12
5-73⁴Aqu	6 f 1:10⅘ft	6-5	*116	41½	52	4³⁄₄	1ⁿᵏ	Pin'yLJr²	11000 89 HeadTable116 Messmate IrishMate	12
27-73⁴Bel	6 f 1:10⅖ft	9-5	*120	3¹	3¹½	3ⁿᵏ	3¹½	Tur'tteR⁵	15000 87 DeltaTraffic116 BoldMerit HeadTable	10
20-73⁸Bel	6½ f 1:17⅕ft	6-5	*116	1h	1h	1h	1h	Pin'yLJr⁵	12500 90 HeadTable116 B'g ofWind SilentR'm'r	9
6-73²Sar	6 f 1:11 ft	6-5	*116*	31½	33½	32½	31½	WallisT⁴	c15000 83 Long Hunt 116 Palm Pago Head Table	8
28-73⁴Aqu	7 f 1:22⅖ft	6-5	*124	1h	1½	12	2h	Bel'nteE⁵	16000 89 NavyBlueBl'd114 H'dTable ArcticCh'f	7
13-73³Aqu	6½ f 1:17½ft	1	^121	7h	11½	1½	11	Bel'nteE⁶	18000 90 Head Table 121 Irish Mate Suspected	7
30-73¹Aqu	7 f 1:23⅝ft	2¼	116	12½	12½	14	15	MapleE²	15000 88 HeadTable116 OdieBob JestaDreamer	8
11-73²Bel	6 f 1:10½ft	7-5	*111*	32½	31½	1h	12	WallisT³	15000 93 HeadTable111 RidingTune Span'hFl't	7
1-73⁸Bel	7 f 1:23⅝ft	2¼	*111*	65³⁄₄	34	11½	12	WallisT⁸	c11000 90 H'dT'ble111 N'vyBlueBl'd N'bleVict'ry	12

Nov 8 Bel trt 5f ft 1:02h

A generation ago, one of the most positive signs in a horse's past performances was a very recent race. Horses in that bygone era were handled cautiously and raced sparingly, and when one like Head Table was entered just four days after his previous start it was an almost certain indication that his trainer thought he was physically fit and ready to win.

Since the racing industry has expanded so greatly — with an overabundance of tracks and an undersupply of thoroughbreds — horses are asked to run much more frequently. At cheap tracks, especially, they may run every week until they are so infirm that they cannot walk to the starting gate.

So a recent race isn't as much of a guarantee of a horse's sharpness as it used to be. But it is still a generally positive sign. If a horse ran well a week ago, that evidence is fresh enough to provide a good indication of what he is likely to do today. If a horse has been idle for several months, a handicapper will have to analyze his workouts, his previous performances after layoffs, and his trainer's methods in order to assess his chances.

TRACK CONDITIONS

Riva Ridge ✻   127   B. c (1969). by First Landing—Iberia, by Heliopolis.
Breeder, Meadow Stud Inc. (Ky.).   1973   3   2   0   0 $43,
                                                               1972   12   5   1   1 $395,

Owner, Meadow Stable. Trainer, L. Laurin.

Jun17-73⁹Suf 1 1-8 1:48½ ft 2-5 ⁴125 1¹ 12½ 13 13¾ T'rc'teR⁵ HcpS 100 RivaRidge125 CraftyKhale Loud
May28-73⁷Bel 1 1:35 sy 2½ 127 54½ 58½ 5¹¹ 7¹⁷ Tur'tteR² HcpS 80 Tentam116 Key to theMint K'g'sB'h'p
May12-73³Aqu 6 f 1:08⁴ ft 1-3 ⁴121 2¹½ 1² 1⁴ 1⁴ TurcotteR¹ Alw 99 RivaRidge121 Dr'm ofK'gs Silv'rM'lle
Nov11-72⁷Lrl ⊕ 1½ 2:38 ssf 4½ 120 1ʰ 5¹⁹ 62⁶ 63⁸ Velas'zJ⁸ InvSp Droll Role 127 Parnell Steel Pulse
Oct28-72⁷Aqu 2 3:21¾ ft 2 119 22 3¹⁷ 320 3¹⁸ Vel'q'zJ³ WfaS 71 A't'b'gr'hy124 K'y to theM't RivaR'ge
Sep30-72⁷Bel 1½ 2:28½ sy 7-5 ⁴119 2½ 2ʰ 2³ 46½ Turc'teR⁵ WfaS 85 K'y to theMint119 S'm'rG'st A't'b'gr'y
Sep20-72⁷Bel 1 1-8 1:46½ ft 2-3 ⁴123 1¹ 1ʰ 2½ 2⁵ Turc'teR¹ HcpS 98 Canonero II. 110 Riva Ridge Loud
Aug 5-72⁸Mth 1 1-8 1:50 ft 1-3 ⁴126 33 2ʰ 2³ 46 Turc'tteR³ InvH 84 Freetex117 King'sBishop CloudyDawn
Jly 1-72⁸Hol 1 1-4 1:59½ ft 3-5 ⁴129 1½ 1ʰ 11½ 1ⁿᵏ Tur'teR⁴ AlwS 95 Riva Ridge 129 Bicker Finalista
Jun10-72⁸Bel 1 1-2 2:28 ft 3-5 ⁴126 1¹½ 13 1⁷ 1⁷ Turc'teR¹ ScwS 93 RivaRidge126 Ruritania CloudyDawn
May20-72⁸Pim 1¾ 1:55 sy 2-3 ⁴126 43 22 2⁴ 46 Tur'tteR² ScwS 86 BeeBeeBee126 NoLeH'e K'y to theM'
May 6-72⁹CD 1 1-4 2:01½ ft 3-2 ⁴126 1½ 11½ 13 13½ Tur'teR⁹ ScwS 91 RivaRidge126 NoLeHace H'ldY'rPeace
July 2 Bel 3f ft :33⅘h   June 28 Bel tc 6f fm 1:13h   June 24 Bel 6f ft 1:13b

The condition of tracks can take a variety of forms, but the *Racing Form*'s past performances manage to describe most of them.

Fast tracks (fst) are dry and hard.

Sloppy tracks (sly) have puddles of water on the surface but still may be firm on the bottom.

Good tracks (gd) are the intermediate stage between fast and sloppy, when rain is falling or the racing strip is drying out.

Muddy (my), slow (sl), and heavy (hy) describe conditions when moisture has accumulated and permeated the racing surface, making it progressively more deep, tiring, and messy.

Firm (fm) and soft (sf) describe conditions of a grass course.

Certain types of horses usually do well on certain types of tracks. Front runners win frequently in the slop, because horses who try to come from behind are hindered by mud kicked in their faces. Stretch runners usually have an advantage on deep, tiring tracks. But it is dangerous to generalize too much about the effects of track conditions on horses because individual racetracks differ so much. A sloppy track at Aqueduct is nothing like a sloppy track at Garden State. (The influence of racing surfaces will be discussed in detail in Chapter Four.)

The most important consideration on an off track is simply whether a horse has demonstrated either a fondness or a dislike for running in mud. Riva Ridge was one of the best horses in America from 1971 to 1973 but he never won in the mud. As his past performances show, he was often humiliated on off tracks. Riva Ridge had a stablemate with the opposite tendencies. Spanish Riddle was just a decent allowance-class horse under most conditions, but if a few drops of rain fell on a track there wasn't a sprinter in America who could beat him.

As important as track conditions may be for horses like Riva Ridge and Spanish Riddle, many handicappers pay too much attention to this factor. When they go to the track on rainy days they abandon their normal procedures and bet automatically on mudders or, worse yet, on absurd long-shots, assuming that the results will be wild and unpredictable. This is usually a costly mistake. The fundamentals of handicapping do not become any less important in the mud.

TURF RACES

Court Road	116	Dk. b. or br. h (1966), by Day Court—One Lane, by Prince John.
		Breeder, Elmendorf Farm (Ky.). 1972 .4 1 0 0 $5,40
Owner, Elmendorf Trainer, V. J. Wickerson.		$20,000 1971 .10 3 1 1 $33,45

Aug 9-72⁸Sa	(T)	1:40 fm	6½	112	89	88	56½	58½	C'pedesR⁸	40000	88	Nevado 116	Shadow Brook	Jogging 1
Aug 1-72²Sa	(T)	1:53⅕shd	3½	116	42½	21½	13	14	B'zarC³	17000	116	Court Road 116	Tradesman	Delver
Jly 15-72³Aqu		1 1:35⅖ft	4	115	45½	46½	7¹¹	7¹²	Bal'zarC⁵	30000	78	Proj'ctive120	DanP'tch	NavyL'uten'nt
Jly 6-72⁷Aqu	f	1:21⅗ft	31	112	1h	2h	55½	56½	BaltazarC⁶	Alw	87	Beaukins 112	Accohick	Swift Passage
May 8-71⁶Hol	(T)	2:13⅘fm	7-5	▲120	36½	11	13	13¾	Pin'yJr⁵	A20000	91	CourtRoad120	GrayPower	Twogie
Apr27-71⁶Hol	(T)	1:42⅕fm	2	114	4³	3¹	2½	1²	Pin'yLJr³	20000	88	CourtRoad114	GreatDescretion	Secolo
Apr16-71⁸Hol	(T)	1:42 fm	3¾	▲122	5¹⁰	86½	9⅞	86	Pin'yLJr³	AlwS	83	TheField122	TripleAxe	Aggressively 1
Apr 8-71⁸SA	(T)	2:25⅕fm	3¾	118	55	52½	55	44½	Pin'yLJr³	HcpS	84	Pleas'ntH'rbour115	B'titu	Azinc'rt II.
Mar20-71³⁵SA		1½ 2:02⅖fm	4-5	▲114	43½	2h	1½	1¹	PincayLJr⁴	Alw		Court Road 114	Born Wild	Makor
Mar13-71⁸SA		-4 2:03 sl	19	109	76½	9¹⁵	9²⁰	9²⁵	D'ss'uLJ⁴	HcpS	58	Ack Ack 130	Cougar II.	The Field 1

July 28 Aqu 5f ft 1:02h   June 30 Aqu 1m sy :48b   June 25 Aqu 5f sy 1:01⅕h

Racing on the grass — indicated in the past performances by the symbol (T) — is a game completely different from racing on the dirt. Horses who couldn't win claiming events on the main track can become turf champions. Horses who tire badly in sprints on the main track may become capable distance runners on the grass. And, conversely, many horses with championship credentials on dirt have been utter flops when they have attempted to negotiate a turf course.

A horseplayer trying to pick the winner of a turf race should be guided by a four-word precept: class on the grass. He should almost always prefer horses who have proved their turf ability and ignore, for the most part, their dirt form. A handicapper analyzing the record of Court Road at Saratoga on August 1, 1972, would have observed that the horse had been a very capable turf runner the year before.

He had two races on the main track in 1972 in which he showed some slight signs of life but was beaten soundly. Then he was entered in his proper milieu. The year-old evidence about Court Road's grass-running ability would have made him an excellent wager. He won by four lengths, set a track record, and paid $9.20.

Only in races where no horse has shown any particular aptitude for grass running should a handicapper consider betting an entrant who is making his debut on the turf. Even in these cases a horse's dirt form is not as important as other factors. Certain sires produce offspring who like the turf and certain trainers, such as Mac Miller, T. J. Kelly and Allen Jerkens, are especially adept at developing turf specialists. Workouts on the grass may often suggest that a horse is ready to win in his first try over the different terrain. But none of these indications is unfailingly reliable, and a handicapper should not bet serious money on a horse unless he has already run on the grass and liked it.

DISTANCE

Mio Host   **107** B. g (1970) by Gallant Host—Mia Sorella, by Mr. Hemisphere.
Br., May Stock Farm & E. L. May (Cal.).   1974   9   3   1   0 $8,850
wner, S. Galt. Trainer, P. Briones. $8,500   1973   21   3   2   1 $8,090

```
or19-745Pim  6 f  12⅕ft  23  114 10¹¹ 9¹⁵  8¹²  8¹¹ Marq'zR³ 10500 74 Erezev114     CharlieJr.  BigDevil 10
ar30-749GS  1₁₆  48⅔sy   3  112  3²¼  36   47   5¹¹ FantiniP⁸ H3500 52 Watawopper114  PositivePete   Built 8
ar19-746Pim  6 f  12⅕ft  24  114  76¼  77¼  56¾  25  McC'onG¹  8500 80 RoyalEmperor114 MioHost OsageJac 9
b23-749Bow 1 1-4  08 ft   8  109  1¼   34   5⁸   5¹⁴ WalshE²  H4000 69 Cont'tedCl'wn110 EightEasy Riv'rAb'd 8
b13-747Bow  7 f  25⅗ft   2¼ 114 10⁶¾  86¼  3¼   12¼ HawleyS¹  6500 77 MioHost114  River Idol NoblePromise 11
b 2-749Bow  1₁₆  48 ft    9  108  1h   2h   2h   54  Jim'ezC³ H4000 64 Faber'sChoice111 Riv'rAbroad Magoni 9
n22-743Bow  1₁₆  47⅗m    3¼ 114  2h   1h   4²   67¼ Fel'noBM⁵  6500 63 DaintyDick114 Fo'c'sleFiend Riverld'l 9
n12-741Bow  7 f  26⅖m    2¼ 119  2½   1³   1⁸   1¹⁰ GinoL⁵    c3000 71 MioH'st119 Ch'rgeR't H'ckl'b'ryFr'nd 10
```

How would a handicapper evaluate the chances of Mio Host in a $7500 claiming race? It would depend. Mio Host would be viewed differently if he were entered at six furlongs, seven furlongs, 1¹⁄₁₆ miles, or 1¼ miles. (A furlong is an eighth of a mile.) Like most horses, Mio Host's capabilities vary drastically according to the distance he runs.

If today's race were at six furlongs, a handicapper would note that Mio Host had tried the distance twice without success. He broke slowly and rallied insufficiently. He wasn't completely ill-suited at six furlongs, but he would have to face cheaper opposition to win at the distance.

A seven-furlong race would suit Mio Host perfectly, giving him an extra eighth of a mile in which to continue his rally. He won impressively in both of his starts at the distance.

One might suppose, because of his stretch-running style, that Mio Host would like $1\frac{1}{16}$ miles even better than seven furlongs. But he doesn't. He never managed to finish in the money at a route. On March 30, when he was obviously in form, he showed brief speed and tired at $1\frac{1}{16}$ miles. He would obviously have to be dropped in class to win at this distance.

In a demanding mile-and-a-quarter race, Mio Host could be eliminated at almost any class level. He tried to go that far only once, on February 23, and after taking the early lead he collapsed and suffered the worst defeat in his past performances.

A handicapper should always try to determine whether a horse has been entered at an appropriate distance. The best evidence of his suitability is a victory, or at least a strong performance, at the distance in the past. If a horse has previously tried today's distance and failed when he was in condition and entered at the right class level, he can usually be disregarded.

When a horse is trying a new distance — particularly in the case of a sprinter attempting to go a route for the first time — a handicapper should view him as a risky proposition and realize that his running style in sprints may be very deceptive. Horses who finish powerfully in short races, like

Mio Host, will often show early speed and tire at a longer distance. And some rare horses who habitually tire in sprints will improve when they run farther because they can better cope with the slower, less demanding pace of route races. Generally, however, the sprinters most likely to succeed in routes are the ones who have shown that they can lay within striking distance of the leader and finish strongly, with a running line like this:

$$3^3 \qquad 3^2 \qquad 2^{nk} \qquad 1^3$$

Routers entered in sprints can usually be eliminated, unless they have shown high speed in the early stages of their races, or unless their records show that they have been able to win sprints in the past.

A trainer will sometimes purposely enter his horse at an inappropriate distance in order to prepare him for a future race. The trainer of a faint-hearted sprinter might put him in a route race to build his stamina. The trainer of a plodding router might enter him in a sprint to sharpen his speed. If horses have been prepped in this way, they may be excellent bets when they are entered again at the right distance.

TIME AND SPEED RATINGS

iple Crown ✳   126   Ch. c (1971), by Hawaii—Belle Jeep, by War Jeep.
Breeder, T. Gentry (Ky.).

er, S. Lehrmann Trainer, W. P. King.

							1974	7	2	3	1	$110,132
							1973	6	2	1	0	$18,742

0-747Aqu	1 1-8	1:51⅗f	9-5	▲126	14	1²	2½	21¼	BaezaB¹⁰	ScwS 77	Flip Sal 126 Triple Crown Sharp Gary 11
1-748SA	1 1-	1:48⅘	3	120	4¹	52½	31½	68½	BaezaB⁷	SpwS 79	Destroyer 120 Aloha Mood Agitate 8
7-748SA	1	1:42⅘	4¼	124	52½	62¾	43¼	3¾	BaezaB⁷	Hcp S 89	AlohaM'd118 MoneyLender TripleCr'n 10
3-748SA		1:38⅘	5	122	2½	2ʰ	1ʰ	1ⁿᵒ	BaezaB²	Alw 75	TripleCrown122 AlohaMd M'n'yL'nd'r 9
0-748SA	7	1:22⅗	3½	114	3¹	42½	4¹	1ⁿᵒ	BaezaB⁶	Alw 90	TripleCrown114 El Esp'leto Destroy'r 8
3-748SA	6	1:11⅗d	2	114	2½	3½	3ⁿᵏ	2ⁿᵒ	BaezaB³	Alw 84	Mon'yLend'r122 TripleCr'n ElEspan'o 6
9-748SA	6½	1:20⅗	1	▲120	3½	12½	1½	2ʰ	BaezaB⁹	Alw 71	GoldStand'd 120 TripleCr'n FastP'ppa 10
1-735SA	6	1:10½	1	▲114	5³	42½	2ʰ	2½	BaezaB²	Alw 89	MerryFellow117 TripleCrown ElArish 7
7-738CD		1:36⅘	6½	116	51¾	21½	45½	8¹⁸	BaezaB¹	Alw 67	C'nonade119 S'tan'sHills D'tBeL'eJim 15
3-738Bel		1:36	10	122	1½	1ʰ	3ⁿᵏ	41¼	BaezaB³	Scw 87	Pr't'g'nist122 Pr'ce ofR'son C'nn'nade 10
9-734Bel	6	1:10⅘y	9¾	120	41½	2½	14	15	BaezaB¹	Alw 91	TripleCrown120 Kurt theN'tive Toth'd 10
1-734Bel	7	1:24	9-5	▲121	1ʰ	1ʰ	3³	79¾	BaezaB⁸	Alw 72	Hosiery 119 Flip Sal Cannonade 11
9-732Bel	6	1:10⅗f	13	119	2ʰ	2ʰ	1½	11½	BaezaB⁷	Md 90	TripleCrown119 Accipiter R'ghMarch 11

May 2 CD 4f sy .46⅗h   April 29 CD 6f ft 1:14h   April 26 Bel 6f ft 1:11⅘h

Time is the most precise measurement of a horse's ability. Triple Crown's last race was run in 1:51⅘ for a mile and one-eighth. This is the winner's time; Triple Crown was beaten by a length and a quarter. According to a universally accepted rule of thumb, one length equals one-fifth of a second. So Triple Crown's actual time was 1:51⅗.

If another horse had run a mile and an eighth in 1:52 on the same day and was now meeting Triple Crown, the advocates of speed handicapping would religiously bet on Triple Crown, concluding that he was two-fifths of a second, or two lengths, superior to his rival. Unfortunately, times can seldom be so easily compared, because horses run at many different distances, over racing surfaces that are constantly changing.

To help its readers resolve these difficulties, the *Racing Form* computes a numerical speed rating for each of a horse's previous races. Its Eastern Edition also offers a track variant that purportedly indicates the speed of the racing surface over which he was running. But the *Form*'s figures are too crude for serious handicapping. A sophisticated and accurate method of making speed figures will be discussed, in excruciating detail, in Chapter Seven.

JOCKEYS

Smiling Jacqueline	120	B. m (1969), by Hilarious—Fulfiliole, by Beau Gar.
		Breeder, Hobeau Farm, Inc. (Fla.). 1974 6 1 0 2 $
Owner, Green Mill Farm. Trainer, T. J. Gullo.		$25,000 1973 16 1 0 2 $1

Mar12-746Aqu	1 1-8 1:52 ft	2½	112	2⁶ 2¹ 1⁵ 18½	Vel'sq'zJ²	5000 75	ⒻSmil'gJ'q'line112 Hi-Mimi L'tleT
Mar 5-748Aqu	1 1:35⅗ft	22	107*	7⁹ 7¹⁷ 6¹⁶ 6¹²	SkinnerK5	Alw 77	ⒻKl'pto110 Midni':'M'd'g'l Gr't'nM
Feb20-748GP	Ⓣa1₁₆ₜ1:44⅗fm	6¾	112	7⁸ 8⁹½ 6⁹½ 5⁵	rbasq 25	Alw 86	ⒻInstinctively114 TappedIn W't'rnlo
Feb12-745GP	Ⓣa1₁₆ₜ1:45 fm	2¾	114	5¹² 6¹¹ 6⁷½ 3¹¾	Vel'q'zJ4	35000 87	ⒻW'st'nld'l 116 C't'sV. Smil'gJ'qu'l
Feb 6-748GP	Ⓣ a1 1:38½sfm	8¼	114	8⁹½ 8¹³ 8¹⁵ 8¹³	TurcotteR²	Alw 77	ⒻSh'rw't'r113 Inst'ctiv'ly D'gt'thV'
Jan23-748GP	Ⓣ a1 1:41⅕fm	31	112	9¹⁴ 8⁸ 3⁶½ 3³	C'rd'roAJr¹	Alw 72	ⒻD'eCr'kL'y122 N'th ofV's Smil'gJ
Nov21-737Aqu	1 1:36⅗ft	9¼	115	7⁷ 8¹³ 8¹⁵ 7⁹	BaezaB5	Alw 77	ⒻEv'yEv'g112 M'ke anAt't L'r'neEdr
Nov 6-735GP	7 f 1:24⅖ft	17	109¾	8¹³ 8⁷¼ 5¹⁰ 35¼	Skinn'rK3	30000 74	ⒻJill theQ'n118 M'sNewb'y S'l'gJ'q
Feb 2 Hia 5f ft 1:00h							

When his horse wins a race, a bettor will sing the praises of his jockey, citing him as a master strategist and a paragon of virtue. Half an hour later, the same horseplayer is likely to be denouncing the same jockey as a blind, incompetent little thief. The reactions are understandable — it is easier to pour out one's emotions on a human being than on a dumb animal — but they are often misdirected.

Jockeys usually win races because they are riding the best horses. Not even the giants in the history of the profession, men like Eddie Arcaro and Bill Shoemaker, could magically transform a horse's capabilities. If a great rider can make a horse improve by as much as a length over his performance in the hands of an average jockey, that is a notable achievement.

Yet horseplayers are so obsessed by jockeys that they often bet on them blindly. If the popular Sandy Hawley is riding a legitimate 4-to-1 shot in Maryland or Canada, that horse is likely to go to the post at odds of 2 to 1 or less. Because the superior jockeys attract an enthusiastic following and the odds on their mounts are so depressed, a handicapper will usually get a better value for his money by playing horses that are ridden by average, competent, unpopular jockeys.

I try not to let my handicapping of a race be influenced by any prejudices about riders — not even ones who have lost money for me in the past — unless I am convinced that certain jockeys are hopelessly inept. Every track has a few riders who can be counted on to be left at the post, blocked or boxed, or to commit some similar atrocity whenever they are aboard a horse who has a chance to win. There is no conceivable circumstance, for example, in which I would bet so much as $2 on a horse ridden by Kathy Kusner.

When a horse has been ridden in previous races by an incompetent, inexperienced, or unfashionable jockey and then gets the services of a top jockey, he deserves consideration — as Smiling Jacqueline did on March 12. She had been ridden in her previous start by Kenny Skinner, a little-known apprentice, and now was being ridden by the great Jorge Velasquez. Even though Velasquez couldn't be expected to improve upon Skinner's performance by 10 or 15 lengths, the rider switch was an important signal of the trainer's intentions. When a trainer employs Kenny Skinner, he is probably not taking his best shot to win a race. When he uses Jorge Velasquez, he probably is.

WEIGHT

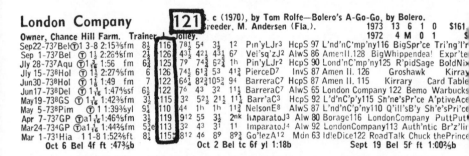

Every handicapper, and every handicapping book, has a theory about weight: Never bet a horse carrying more weight than he did in his last start. Five pounds of added weight slow a horse by one-fifth of a second. Weight is important in routes but not in sprints. The list is endless. It is also worthless.

Weight is a factor that seems to defy generalizations because every individual horse is affected by it differently. For most horses the effect of an increase in weight from 112 to 119 pounds would be imperceptible. In the case of the few who would be hampered by the extra burden, it is impossible to factor out weight from the countless other influences that determine horses' performances so that its effect can be measured.

I will discount a horse's chances when he is carrying very high weight only if his past performances unequivocally suggest that he cannot win with the burden he is now assigned. Such situations arise in handicaps, when good horses are steadily loaded with more weight until they are unable to win. The past performances of London Company indicate that his breaking point is 126 pounds, and I would not bet him carrying that weight.

I have found weight to be important in one other type of situation. When a three-year-old is asked to carry the top weight in a race against older horses, he will not win. Even if the weights by themselves are insignificant — with the younger horse carrying 113 and his elders 112 — the disparity will prevent the three-year-old from winning. The reasons for this phenomenon are utterly inexplicable to me.

WORKOUTS

cretariat X **126** Ch. c (1970), by Bold Ruler—Somethingroyal, by Princequillo.
Breeder, Meadow Stud, Inc. (Va.). 1973.. 3 2 0 1 $63,768
er, Meadow Stable. Trainer, L. Laurin. 1972.. 9 7 1 0 $456,404

1-737Aqu	1 1-8 1:49⅗ft	1-3e▲126	75½	55½	45½	34	T'rc'teR⁶	ScwS 83 Angle Light 126 Sham Secretariat	8
7-737Aqu	1 1:33⅖ft	1-10 ▲126	3¹	1²	1½	1³	T'rc'teR³	AlwS 100 Secret'riat126 Ch'mp'gneCh'rlie Flush	6
7-737Aqu	7 f 1:23½ssy	1-5 ▲126	5⁶	5³	1ʰ	14½	Tur'tteR⁴	AlwS 85 Sec'tar't126 Ch'pagneCh'lie Impec'n's	6
8-728GS	1₁ᵣₑ 1:44⅖ft	1-10e▲122	69½	33	11½	13½	Tur'teR⁶	ScwS 83 Secretariat122 AngleLight StepNicely	6
8-727Lrl	1₁ᵣₑ 1:42⅖ssy	1-10e▲122	6¹⁴	5³	1⁵	1⁸	T'rc'teR⁵	ScwS 99 Secretar't122 St'p t'eM'sic AngleL'ht	6
4-727Bel	1 1:35 ft	2-3e▲122	11¹³	53½	1½	12†	Tur'teR⁴	ScwS 97 Secr'tar't122 St'p theM'sic St'pNic'ly	12

†Disqualified and placed second.

6-727Bel	6½ f 1:16⅖ft	1-5 ▲122	65½	53½	12	11½	Turc'teR⁴	ScwS 98 S'cr't'r't122 St'p t'eMusic Sw'tC'rier	7
6-727Sar	6½ f 1:16⅕ft	1-3 ▲121	96½	1ʰ	14	1⁵	Turc'teR⁸	SpwS 97 Secretariat121 Fl't toGl'y St'p theM'c	9
6-727Sar	6 f 1:10 ft	3-2 121	5⁴	4²	1½	1³	Turc'teR²	SpwS 96 Secr't'riat121 L'da'sCh'f N'thst'rD'c'r	5
1-724Sar	6 f 1:10⅖ft	2-5 ▲118	73¾	3½	1ʰ	11½	TurcotteR⁴	Alw 92 Secretariat 118 Russ Miron Joe Iz	7
5-724Aqu	6 f 1:10⅗ft	6-5 ▲113*	66½	43	1½	1⁶	Felic'noP⁸	Mdn 90 Secret'riat113 M'sterAch'v'r BetOn It	11
4-724Aqu	5½ f 1:05 ft	3 ▲113*107	108¾	75¼	41¼	Felic'noP²	Mdn 87 Herbull 119 MasterAchiever Fl't'nR'y'l	12

(May 2 CD 5f sy :58⅗h)   (April 27 CD 6f sy 1:12⅗h)   (April 17 Bel 1m ft 1:42⅖b)

Secretariat went into the 1973 Wood Memorial Stakes at Aqueduct with a streak of ten straight victories and the reputation of a budding superhorse. He came out of it with his credentials tarnished and his chances to win the Kentucky Derby two weeks later in serious doubt. His loss in the Wood Memorial appeared to be a shocking upset, but an astute student of workouts might have foreseen it.

Secretariat always trained like the champion he was. Before his first two victories of the 1973 season he recorded workouts that left the clockers rubbing their eyes in disbelief — three furlongs in 32⅗ seconds, and a mile in 1:35⅖. But in the two-week period before the Wood Memorial something had changed. Secretariat went a half mile in 49 seconds and a mile in 1:42⅖ — times that would have been unimpressive for a claiming horse. This was a tipoff that something was wrong with Secretariat, and he verified that suspicion by running the dullest race of his life.

Nobody knew whether Secretariat would run another mediocre race in the Kentucky Derby or would revert to his best form. His workouts again provided a clue. Before the Derby he zipped six furlongs in 1:12⅗ and five furlongs in :58⅗, both over sloppy tracks. He confirmed the impression that he was the old Secretariat again by winning the fastest Derby in history.

A horse's condition will often change from race to race, causing many handicappers to moan about his inconsistency or the unpredictability of the sport. But good handicappers can often foresee reversals of form by reading the workout line carefully.

While there are some morning glories who invariably train fast and run poorly in actual competition, most horses who work well are signaling their readiness to run a good race. These workout times would be considered good for a top-class horse:

> Three furlongs in :35.
> Four furlongs in :47.
> Five furlongs in 1:00.

Six furlongs in 1:13.
Seven furlongs in 1:26.
One mile in 1:39.

Workouts slower than these might still be very impressive if the track were dull, if the horse were cheap, if he worked from the gate (indicated in the *Form* by the letter *g*) instead of from a running start, or if he were not urged by his exercise rider. The letter *b* after a horse's workout time indicates that he was breezing, that he was under heavy restraint. *H* means handily: he was being moderately urged by his rider.

Good workouts are especially meaningful if a horse shows something in them that he hasn't shown in his races. When a fast-breaking sprinter works four furlongs in 47 seconds, that does not reveal anything new about his capabilities. But if he works a mile in 1:38, displaying uncharacteristic stamina, that may be a tipoff that his condition is improving sharply.

The best judges of workouts are the people who see them: the clockers. With the possible exception of politicians and television repairmen, no occupation group has a greater reputation for larceny. When a horse turns in a significant, fast workout, the clockers may keep it as their own private information and tell the *Racing Form* that he worked five furlongs in an indifferent 1:03. Horseplayers in Maryland are so justifiably suspicious that the clockers lack integrity that they pay close attention to any horse who has been idle for several months and shows no workouts in his past performances. They figure that the horse must have been training somewhere and that sinister forces are making an effort to conceal his workout information.

At the major league tracks in New York, Florida, and

BELMONT PARK (Track Fast)

3 FURLONGS

Horse	Time	Horse	Time
Arum Lily	:38 b	Path to Peace	:37⅗b
Boston Peggy	:37 bg	PROD	:34⅖h
Blue Cross	:36⅔h	Ravage	:35⅖bg
Blue Bush	:36⅔b	Self Importance	:38 bg
Continuation	:37 b	Set the Style	:37 b
Drollery	:35 h	Sylvan Place	:38 b
Easter Chorus	:36⅔h	Summ'rtime Pr'mise	:35⅖h
Foolish Pleasure	:36 h	Take a Bride	:36 h
French Rule	:37 bg	Weather Well	:36⅕b
Game Tim	:36 b	You Will Like It	:37 bg
Good Marks	:38 b		
Handsome Ghost	:37⅕bg		
Jack Sprat	:35 h		
Let Me Count	:37 b		
Life of the Party	:37⅗b		
Lake Montauk	:38⅗bg		
Magical Lady	:38 b		
Motto	:35 h		
McCorkle	:35⅓h		
Nopalito	:36 b		
Othris	:40 bg		
Parlor Game	:35⅗bg		

4 FURLONGS

Horse	Time	Horse	Time
Amberalero	:52⅖b	Java Moon	:50⅖b
All Stirred Up	:48 h	Lead Line	:48 h
Breezy Gal	:49⅖hg	Mush Mouse	:47⅖hg
Clio Maroon	:48⅗hg	Our Dancing Girl	:47⅖h
Century Gold	:50⅖bg	Old Vic	:50⅖b
Camelford	:47⅕h	On His On	:48 h
Dr. Yana	:47⅕h	Posterity	:50⅖b
El Bailador	:47⅖h	Powerful Minn	:48 h
Fashionable Girl	:50⅖b	PRINCE DANTAN	:46⅕b
Relio Rise	:49⅕h	Pilots Son	:46⅗h
Hello Goodbye	:49⅖h	Rock Music	:49⅖b
Instaneaneously	:50⅖b	Sky Island	:50 b
		Sound of the Bell	:47 h
		With Devotion	:50⅗bg
		Wild Land	:49⅕b

5 FURLONGS—:57⅕

Horse	Time	Horse	Time
Alfie G.	1:01⅖hg	Fleetferd	1:04⅖b
Bold Review	1:04⅕b	First Slice	:59⅖b
Bussento	1:01⅖hg	High Steel	1:00
Cornish Castle	1:01 bg	Halo	1:01⅗b
Crystal Gaze	1:04⅕b	Idle Answer	:59⅗b
Corrugation	1:02 h	Imperator	1:01⅕b
Earlville	1:02⅖b	Left End	1:02⅕b
		Lefty	1:02⅕b
		Marry In Haste	1:02⅕b
		Paradise Lost	1:01⅖b
		Permanent	1:04⅕b
		Riverbank	1:01⅖b
		Rain Again	1:03⅕b
		Spunky Princess	1:01⅗b
		Tropical Sea	1:01⅗b
		Trainer Mickey	1:01 h

6 FURLONGS—1:08⅗

Horse	Time
Majority Ruler	1:14 h
Piaster	1:14 h

1 MILE—1:33⅗

Horse	Time
Certain Vote	1:42 h
NORTH BR'DWAY	1:39⅗h
True Knight	1:41⅗b

PROD (3 furlongs) had good speed. PRINCE DANTAN (4 furlongs) continues to train well. HIGH STEEL (5 furlongs) acts sharp. NORTH BROADWAY (1 mile) had jockey Wallis up.

California the clockers tend to be honest as well as competent. And their footnotes to the daily workout listings make valuable reading (see above). Positive comments like "Prod had good speed" and "High Steel acts sharp" are worth remembering.

I keep a complete set of the daily workout listings so I can get more information about a horse's training than the past performances provide. This is especially helpful for evaluating first-time starters. While the past performances list only a horse's last three workouts, a first-time starter may work fifteen or twenty times before he makes his debut in actual competition. By checking these workouts, a studious handicapper can get a complete picture of the horse's preparation, and perhaps locate swift workouts that give a better indication of his capabilities than the ones listed in the *Form*.

OTHER PAST PERFORMANCE SYMBOLS

ham X				**126**	**B. c (1970)** by Pretense—Sequoia, by Princequillo.										
					Breeder, Claiborne Farm (Ky.).			1973.. 6 4 1 0 $140,528							
ner, S Sommer. Trainer, F Martin.										1972.. 4 1 2 1 $9,2__					
r21-7 7Aqu	1 1-8 1:49⅘ft	2½	126	2¹	2¹½ 2¹½ 2ʰ	Vel'q' J2	ScwS 87	Angle Light 126	Sham	Secretariat 8					
r31-7 SA	1 1-8 1:47 ft	9	120	3³	2¹½ 1²	12¼	Pin'yLJr²	SpwS 97	Sham 120	Linda'sChief	Out of theEast				
r17-738SA	1 1/16 1:41⅘ft	6-5	123	6⁶	64¼ 6⁵	47¾	Pin'yLJr³	HcpS 85	Lind'sCh'f126	Anc'tTitle	O't of theE'st 9				
12-738SA	1 1/16 1:45 m	1-10	▲118	3²	5² 3²	12½	Pin'yLJr³	SpwS 77	Sham 118	Out of the East	Scanting 5				
2-738SA	1 1/16 1:41⅖ft	1-3	▲118	4⁵	3³ 1½	1⁶	PincayLJr²	Alw 95	Sham 118	Table Run	Untangle 6				
n 1-736SA	1 1/16 1:42 ft	1-2	▲118	5⁵	4¹ 1⁸	1¹⁵	PincayLJr⁷	Alw 92	Sham118	D'bleVar'ty	QuantumJump 7				
c 9-72²Aqu	1 1:37 m	9-5	▲121	1⁴	1³ 1⁴	1⁶	Vel'quezJ⁶	Mdn 82	Sham 121	Water Wheel	Radnor 13				
23-723Bel	1 1:37⅘ft	2¾	118	5²	1½ 1¹	2ʰ	GustinesH⁵	Mdn 83	Dicks Boots 118	Sham	Drollery 8				
13-723Bel	7 f 1:24 ft	9-5	▲120	2ʰ	1½ 2ʰ	22½	GustinesH¹	Mdn 84	BroadwayPlayboy120	Sham	D'ksBoots 13				
28-723Bel	6 f 1:11 ft	28	120	9¹³	9¹⁵ 5¹⁰	37¾	Gust'esH⁴	Mdn 81	AngleLight120	TimelessM'ment	Sham 11				
April 30 CD 6f ft 1:11⅛h					April 17 Bel 5f ft :58h				April 12 Bel 1m ft 1:37⅖h						

"7 Aqu" indicates that Sham ran in the seventh race at Aqueduct. A complete list of track abbreviations appears in most issues of the *Racing Form*.

"2½" reveals that Sham's odds were approximately 2½ to 1. The symbol *e* in this column means he was part of a stable entry; the symbol ▲ indicates he was the favorite.

"2," the number next to his jockey's name, was Sham's post position.

"8," in the right-hand column of the past performances, was the number of horses in his last race.

"B. c (1970)" in the breeding line indicate Sham's color, sex, and year of birth. The colors of thoroughbreds are bay (B.), black (Bl.), brown (Br.), chestnut (Ch.), roan (Ro.), and gray (Gr.).

READING CHARTS

Thorough handicappers should keep a set of result charts, which describe the running of individual races and contain more information about them than the past performances.

EIGHTH RACE

Aqu

Dec'mb'r 26, 1973

1½ MILES. (1:47). ALLOWANCES. Purse $11,000. 3-year-olds and upward which h
not won a race other than maiden, claiming or starter. 3-year-olds, 119 lbs.; ol
122 lbs. Non-winners of $6,000 at a mile or over since Nov. 10 allowed 3 lbs.; maid
5 lbs. 3-year-olds which have never won at a mile or over allowed 3 lbs.; older, 5
(Winners preferred.)

Value to winner $6,600; second, $2,420; third, $1,320; fourth, $660. Mutuel Pool, $240,079.
Off-track betting, $60,026.

Last Raced		Horse	EqtAWt	PP	St	¼	½	¾	Str	Fin	Jockeys	Owners	Odds to
12- 8-73[7]	Aqu[4]	Bold Play	b3 119	6	5	3h	31	24	24	12½	PAnderson	Willwynne Stable	
12-20-73[8]	Aqu[5]	Bold Merit	b3 113	2	1	12½	13½	12	1h	2¾	EMaple	S Lehrman	
12-15-73[8]	Aqu	Dream With Me	b3 108	4	4	6	6	42½	410	31	DMontoya[5]	C Rosen	
12- 8-73[7]	Aqu[3]	Sacred Soul	b3 114	1	2	4h	2h	3h	3h	412	RTurcotte	Shinrone Farm	
12-12-73[5]	Aqu[2]	Sentimentalist	b3 119	3	6	55	52	5h	6	54½	JVelasquez	G R Gardiner	
12-17-73[2]	Aqu[1]	Scrooge Kelley	3 114	5	3	2h	4h	6	5½	6	JCruguet	Mrs J L Cotter	1

Time, :24⅖, :48⅖, 1:13⅖, 1:40, 1:53⅖ (no wind in backstretch). Track sloppy.

$2 Mutuel Prices:

6-BOLD PLAY	10.00	6.20	3.80
2-BOLD MERIT		8.80	4.80
4-DREAM WITH ME			5.00

B. c, by Chieftain—Thimbleful, by Needles. Trainer, W. C. Stephens. Bred by Mr. and Mrs. J. W. St
(Fla.).

IN GATE—3:23. OFF AT 3:23 EASTERN STANDARD TIME. Start good. Won driving.
BOLD PLAY, prominent while forced to stay wide around the clubhouse turn, moved nearest the p
leaving the backstretch, responded outside BOLD MERIT when set down in the drive, got the lead leaving
eighth-pole and drew off. BOLD MERIT bore out slightly immediately after the start, remained well away fr
the rail throughout and could not resist the winner while tiring in the final furlong. DREAM WITH
checked on BOLD MERIT's heels soon after the start, rallied on the rail leaving the backstretch and finish
with good courage. SACRED SOUL had no apparent excuse. SENTIMENTALIST also checked behind BO
MERIT after the start, had brief early speed, but did not appear to handle the going very well.
Overweight—Sacred Soul, 1 pound; Scrooge Kelley, 1; Bold Play, 3.

Most of the symbols in the charts are self-explanatory.
The one significant difference between them and the past
performances is in the running line. Instead of showing the
number of lengths by which a horse was trailing the leader
at each stage of a race, the charts show how far he was
ahead of the horse behind him. In the race above, Bold Play
finished first, 2½ lengths ahead of Bold Merit, who was
three-quarters of a length ahead of Dream with Me, who
was one length ahead of Sacred Soul, who was 12 lengths in
front of Sentimentalist. A chart reader has to add these
numbers to learn that Sentimentalist lost by 16¼ lengths.

Charts are especially useful because they indicate the
conditions of the race. A handicapper who encountered
Bold Play in a subsequent start would know from the past
performances only that he had won an allowance race. The

chart would reveal that he had won an event for "3-year-olds and upward which have not won a race other than maiden or claiming" — the lowest form of allowance race.

The footnotes in charts provide a detailed description of the way the race was run. A handicapper who reads them would know he could disregard Sentimentalist's bad defeat: "Sentimentalist checked behind Bold Merit after the start, had brief early speed but did not appear to handle the going very well."

There are many other valuable uses for the result charts, involving more sophisticated handicapping techniques, and they will be discussed in later chapters.

3

Larceny and Betting Coups

IT WAS IN a Miami telephone booth, of all places, that a young man named Mark experienced something every horseplayer dreams about. He stumbled onto a bit of genuine inside information about a betting coup.

Mark was an undergraduate at Georgetown University, majoring in equine studies. He spent much of his time gambling at Laurel, Bowie, Pimlico, and Charles Town, though he should have known better. The son of a bookmaker, he was having his education financed by the unsuccessful investments of his father's clientele. But Mark was a manic horseplayer anyway, and one winter he decided to take a break from the rigors of academe and fly to Hialeah for a week. It was a disaster. Mark went broke, borrowed money, and went broke again. Because of his father's professional standing he was able to get enough credit to go $3000 in debt to one bookie, $1500 to another.

After a climactic catastrophe at Hialeah, Mark went to a phone booth a couple blocks from the track to stall off his creditors and raise more capital. It was a double phone booth, and a man on the other side of the glass partition was on the phone. Mark heard him place a call to a famous movie star. Mark knew the actor was an enthusiastic horseplayer, and he strained to listen. "He's ready," the caller said. "Tomorrow's the day."

There was no mention of any horse's name, but Mark was not going to let this opportunity pass. He fixed in his mind the face of the man in the phone booth, and at six the next morning he was in the Hialeah stable area, tromping from barn to barn under the pretext of looking for a job as a groom. When Mark finally spotted his man, he noted the name of the stable where he was working, learned in the *Racing Form* that the stable had a horse entered in the third race, and went to a phone to bet as much as he could. The credo of bookmakers, of course, is to give their customers enough rope with which to hang themselves. Mark was able to place more than $1000 in bets and went to the track feeling serenely confident. His horse won at odds of 20 to 1. Mark collected nearly $25,000 from his bookmakers the next day, and returned to Washington with all the clichéd trappings of success: He was sporting a new wardrobe, driving a gold Cadillac, and displaying a decorative blonde on his arm.

All horseplayers envision a stroke of fortune like this, and many come to believe it is the only way they can beat the races. After a man has learned the rudiments of handicapping, he will inevitably be frustrated when he cannot immediately convert his new knowledge into consistent winnings at the track. He may think that the fault lies not within himself but in the nature of the game. Many crucial elements of horse racing do not appear in black and white in the pages of the *Daily Racing Form*. A horse's condition and capabilities may change drastically from one race to the next — and only insiders will know. A trainer may be manipulating his horse's form with drugs; a jockey may be losing deliberately with a horse — and only insiders will know. Perhaps the only ways to beat the game are either to become an owner or trainer, or to discover what the insiders are doing.

I was leaning toward this point of view during my frustrating fledgling years as a horseplayer. My inclinations were turned into convictions on a train ride from Boston to Narragansett Park one summer night in 1963. I could not have guessed, from his outward appearance, that the man sitting next to me would exert more of an influence on my mind than would any of my professors at Harvard. Wearing a rumpled suit and an ancient straw hat, he looked like a typical racetrack bum. But when I caught a glimpse of the *Racing Form* he was studying so intensely, I got a different impression of the man. The paper was completely covered with esoteric symbols and notations, utterly incomprehensible to me, that suggested the man was a very serious student of the game.

I asked the stranger his opinion of the horse I liked in the second race that night; he had finished second by a nose in his most recent start and looked like a solid favorite. The man glanced at the horse's record and said, in a faintly foreign accent, "I wouldn't touch him." He pointed toward the upper right-hand corner of the past performances, where it was noted that the horse had raced ten times during the year with one victory, three seconds, and three thirds. "The stable is always trying to win with this horse," he said, "and he doesn't get the job done. Whenever a horse runs second or third, I consider it a black mark against him. It means he was trying to win and couldn't. The crazy public loves to lose its money on horses like this. Not me."

I asked the man whom he preferred in the second race. He pointed to the name of a horse that had raced twice in his career, losing both starts by 20 lengths. He was a maiden running against winners — a type of horse that every handicapping book says can be automatically eliminated. By what logic did he pick such a hopeless animal?

"The logic of illogic," the man said, and did not elaborate. He was obviously not prepared to share all his wisdom with a stranger. I was not sure if my companion was a genius or a madman, but I was fascinated and I stayed with him as we got off the train. My faith was slightly shaken when his maiden in the second race was beaten by 20 lengths again; the horse I had liked finished second, as usual. After eight races neither of us had cashed a ticket, but the man was confident and enthusiastic about an animal named Carbreuse in the ninth race.

I couldn't imagine what virtues he saw in a horse who had managed to win only once in his last forty attempts, and that had lost each of his last eight races by ten lengths or more. The man pointed out that Carbreuse had been racing in $3000 company for most of the year. He was dropped to $1500 and was beaten badly at 8 to 1. In his next race for $1500, he was beaten badly at 21 to 1. "They weren't trying in those races," the man said. "They've been waiting until the price is right. And I think tonight is the night." He told me to study Carbreuse's running line in his most recent race, which looked like this:

$$6^9 \quad 8^{12} \quad 9^{16} \quad 7^{12}$$

This, the man explained, was what he called the *Z* pattern. Carbreuse had dropped back steadily throughout most of the race but had come on at the end, gaining four lengths in the stretch. It was the jockey and trainer's way of testing him. They had let him run only during the stretch, giving him a workout-within-a-race. Carbreuse had responded, and now the stable was ready to cash a bet.

I bet my last $5 and watched in ecstasy as Carbreuse went to the front, led all the way, and held on to win by a neck. He paid $119.60 to win. My hands were trembling as I collected more money than I had ever won in my life. I knew that I had had the remarkable fortune to encounter a genius who marched to the sound of a different drummer.

On the train ride home, the man introduced himself as Mr. D. He said he had come to Boston to serve as the consul for a South American country, and occupied the dull hours in his office by studying the *Racing Form*. When the government of his native country was overthrown by a left-wing coup, Mr. D. was out of a job and started betting the horses full-time.

A horseplayer's temperament will often influence his betting. Mr. D.'s political views — his convictions about the treachery and duplicity of the Communists — helped shape his philosophy of handicapping. He believed in the conspiracy theory of horse racing. Only naive bettors looked for the best horse in a race; Mr. D. wanted to know who was trying to win and who wasn't. He viewed all horses as tools that were manipulated by their trainers. The trainers were ruthless, calculating, omnipotent. Their mission in life was to deceive the public, to orchestrate a horse's form until they could cash a bet at the proper odds. Horse racing was a larcenous game, and to be a successful bettor a man had to be able to detect the larceny. To a struggling handicapper who had been baffled by the intricacies of the sport, Mr. D.'s philosophy was very seductive. I became his protégé.

Mr. D. taught me that the cornerstone of his handicapping method was consistency. He wanted horses who had a high winning percentage and, even more important, had a "clean record" — a minimal number of second- and third-place finishes. If a horse had ten races, three wins, no seconds, and no thirds, Mr. D. would conclude that he was a perfect betting tool. The trainer had tried to win three times, and had succeeded three times.

To discover when a horse would be trying to win, Mr. D. looked for various signs in the way he had run his most recent race, and invented his own private language to describe them — "the *Z* pattern," "middle flashes," "convats." One of his discoveries, the change of pace, brought me my triumph on Sun in Action years later. It is the most brilliant single tool I have ever seen for detecting horses who are ready to wake up, seemingly out of the blue, and win at long odds.

A horse who dramatically changes his usual running style — for example, a confirmed stretch runner who inexplicably shows early speed and tires — will often improve mysteriously the next time he runs. After Mr. D. taught me about the change of pace, I encountered a classic embodiment of the pattern in the past performances of a horse named Parma Town at Thistledown Race Track on June 16, 1965. His recent running lines looked like this:

$$3^{2\frac{1}{2}} \qquad 6^{8} \qquad 5^{5} \qquad 4^{2\frac{1}{4}}$$
$$1^{h} \qquad 3^{3} \qquad 7^{5\frac{1}{2}} \qquad 8^{11}$$
$$1^{\frac{1}{2}} \qquad 3^{2} \qquad 4^{4\frac{1}{2}} \qquad 10^{7\frac{1}{4}}$$
$$4^{2} \qquad 3^{3\frac{1}{2}} \qquad 3^{4\frac{1}{2}} \qquad 4^{6\frac{1}{4}}$$

Parma Town had displayed a consistent running style throughout his career: he would always show early speed and tire. In his next to last race, he had taken the early lead and faded to finish far out of the money. In his most recent race he had started to drop back as usual. After a half mile he was running sixth by eight lengths. Then, uncharacteristically, he rallied to finish fourth, 2¼ lengths behind the winner. Regardless of the time of the race or the quality of his competition, Parma Town had managed to do something he had never done before, and it was a meaningful sign. He won and paid $57.20.

I cashed one of my most memorable $2 bets on a change of pace in 1967 in Toronto, where I had been dispatched to cover a soccer game. I had left Washington a day early so I could make a detour through Chester, West Virginia, where Waterford Park was offering a nineteen-race double-header. After losing disastrously, I arrived in Canada without enough money for my plane fare back home, so I naturally made an excursion to Woodbine Race Track in an effort to recoup. A horse named M.J.'s Boy was entered in the first race with these past performances:

J.'s Boy	110	B. g (1964), by Royal Visitor—Jenny, by Firethorn.

M.J.'s Boy had broken fourth and tired badly in his racing debut. The next time he ran he broke fourteenth and managed to finish tenth. This was, technically, a change of pace, and I felt obliged to bet $2. M.J.'s Boy paid $298.50, the second-biggest win price in North America that year.

In addition to his various wake-up signs, Mr. D. talked a lot about "the logic of illogic." He explained it simply:

"When a horse is entered in a race where he obviously doesn't belong, watch out!" If a chronically unsuccessful $5000 horse were one day entered in a $10,000 claiming race, most handicappers would dismiss him summarily, but Mr. D. would ask, "What is he doing here?" He would suspect that the horse had been entered in a seemingly impossible spot to deceive the public and let the trainer execute a massive betting coup. Sometimes the logic of illogic would point toward horses so absurd that even Mr. D.'s most devoted disciple couldn't take them seriously.

We were at Lincoln Downs one night, handicapping a cheap claiming race at a mile and one-sixteenth. One of the entrants, Tiki of Maori, was a hopeless bum. In his last four starts, all at seven-eighths of a mile, he had shown brief speed and tired to lose by at least 20 lengths each time. I eliminated him at first glance. Mr. D. asked, "What is he doing here? This horse has been showing speed and tiring. It would make sense for the trainer to enter him at a shorter distance. Why a longer distance? This may be a betting coup." It was always necessary for the disciple to treat the master with reverence, so I said, "Mr. D., you know I have the greatest respect for you and your methods. But I think this horse is just a little far-fetched." We argued about the horse's merits or lack thereof until post time, when it was too late for Mr. D. to get a bet down. Tiki of Maori won by six lengths and paid $89. Mr. D. didn't let me forget about that race for years; he was less distressed about the $89 than he was about the apostasy of his pupil.

The logic of illogic is a very dangerous technique for an inexperienced handicapper to use because it requires him to bet horses who are clearly bad ones. Sometimes a horse will be entered in an inappropriate spot because he is merely out for the exercise or because his trainer is stupid. More often a horse will be put in the wrong kind of race because the racing secretary has put pressure on the trainer to enter him so that the race will have a field of adequate size. But occasionally a bettor will encounter a horse entered under such suspicious circumstances that he deserves a second look.

A very implausible horse named Parted Seas was entered in a race at Saratoga in 1970. The animal had run only once in his career, in a $3000 maiden-claiming event at Lincoln Downs. At this rock-bottom level, he had gone off at 50-to-1 odds and finished sixth. A week later he was running against winners in a $3500 claiming race at Saratoga. Why had the trainer gone to the trouble and expense of shipping a horse from Rhode Island for a race in which he presumably didn't stand a chance? Maybe he was crazy. Maybe he wanted to take the waters at the spa. Or maybe he wanted to cash a bet. The answer came on the tote board two minutes before post time, when a flood of money poured onto Parted Seas and drove his odds down to 7 to 1. He won in a gallop.

Mr. D. believed that betting action is very important, that the tote board has the same significance in horse racing that the ticker tape does in the stock market. There is a school of thought on Wall Street that holds that it doesn't matter whether a company makes a profit or, indeed, whether it makes anything at all. The ticker tape tells everything. If a stock is being actively traded and its price fluctuates in certain ways, shares are probably being accumulated by knowledgeable insiders and the company is probably a good investment. Similarly, the tote board can often indicate where the smart money is going on a horse race.

An inexperienced horseplayer will frequently be misled by the tote board, because some of the most obvious types of betting action are the least meaningful. Sometimes an unlikely looking horse will be heavily bet in the first few minutes of wagering and open as an odds-on favorite. When this happens, it isn't the stable betting. The money probably comes from a bookmaker who has been overloaded with action on a particular horse and wants to reduce his liability in case the horse wins.

Another form of betting action can trigger an outburst of mass hysteria at the racetrack. A horse is a legitimate 20-1 shot in the early wagering but his odds begin to drop steadily. He goes to 15-1, 10-1, 8-1, 5-1, 7-2, 5-2, as more money pours in with each flash of the tote board. Everybody at the track observes the betting action, and as post time approaches bettors are rushing frantically to the windows, knocking over little old ladies in their paths, to cash in on the hot horse. Nobody knows how these stampedes begin, but they are seldom caused by genuine stable betting. And these obvious hot horses do not win with great frequency. When insiders are really betting on a horse whose virtues are well concealed, they will do so as subtly as possible so that the masses will not jump on the bandwagon.

A sharp trainer may do all his betting in the last minute or two before post time. When a horse plummets from 15-1 to 10-1 in the last flash of the tote board, that betting action is usually significant. More often, though, there will be no eye-catching fluctuations in the price of a horse who is being bet by knowledgeable insiders. He will receive steady support throughout the betting and go to the post at odds much lower than his record would seem to warrant. There is no easy or systematic way to detect this subtle betting action. A horseplayer must have the experience to know the sort of horses that the public does and doesn't bet.

A handicapper who wants a quick (and probably costly) education in betting action and racetrack larceny ought to visit Churchill Downs during the week of the Kentucky Derby. The Kentucky tracks seem to have more sharpies to the square inch than any other area of the country, and they all save their best tricks for Derby Week, when the out of town suckers come to Louisville to be fleeced. The 163,628 people who attended the centennial Derby in 1974 also got to witness a betting coup of classic proportions. These were the past performances for the third race that day:

d Churchill Downs

7 FURLONGS (chute). (1:21⅖). CLAIMING. Purse $6,500. 4-year-olds and upward. Weight, 122 lbs. Non-winners of two races since March 15 allowed 3 lbs.; a race, 6 lbs.; in 1974, 10 lbs. Claiming price, $16,000; 2 lbs. for each $1,000 to $14,000.

ild Joker 110   Ch. g (1970), by Jester—Ultimate Weapon, by Bold Ruler.
Breeder, R. L. Carter (Ky.).   1974   5   0   1   0 $800
er, R. N. Hardin. Trainer, G. Hild.   **$15,000**   1973   17   1   3   2 $10,280

25-743Kee	6½ f 1:18 ft	9½	116	2³	2³	2³	2⁵	Pat'nG¹	c10000 82	R'sh aBet116 MildJ'ker MamasH'eN'w	9
9-742Kee	6 f 1:10⅖ft	15f	113	5⁴	7⁸	7⁸¾	8⁹	Cam'lRJ⁷	14000 81	Et'rn'lL'k116 L'ngD'cis'n J.Finxpilter	12
9-742Kee	7 f 1:24⅕ft	25	112	1h	1h	4¹½	6¹¹	Pat'sonG⁵	13000 74	Aerodrome116 D'b'n'reHost Ind'nSp'd	10
23-746Hia	6 f 1:10⅖ft	48	108‡	43½	10¹¹	10¹⁷	11¹⁴	Sag'iaR⁷	15000 77	IrishSweep'r117 ChiefTamao Cliff'rdR.	12
7-746GP	6 f 1:09⅖ft	61	112	9⁹¾	12¹²	12¹⁹	12¹⁶	Gallit'oG²	18000 76	P'tEverg's116 Br'ssC'n G.Ham'nOwen	12
15-736Atl	6 f 1:12 ft	2¾	116	2¹	4⁶	5⁵½	5⁷½	Sol'neM²	18000 74	SundaySupper116 StillFlying AlsoJoe	8
29-737Atl	6 f 1:11 ft	7¼	115	5²¾	7⁹¼	7⁷¼	7⁹¾	Solom'eM³	Alw 78	MovingTarget116 Buck a'dWing Kilt'g	7
22-735Atl	6 f 1:11 ft	6¾	115	2½	2h	3nk	3nk	Solo'neM⁷	Alw 87	Myst'ryR'l'r113 M'v'gT'r'g't MildJ'k"r	7
1-737Atl	6 f 1:10⅖ft	3e	115	4¹	4¾	2h	3¹	Solom'eM⁸	Alw 89	HomeJerome116 OurTown MildJoker	8
21-737Mth	6 f 1:10⅖ft	6½	114	2¹½	3¹½	3²½	1nk	Solom'eM⁷	Alw 90	MildJoker114 BestJiminto Still'Flying	7

April 17 Kee 4f ft :50b   **April 14 Kee 3f ft :36b**   **April 7 Kee 3f ft :36⅗b**

ush a Bet 119   Dk. b. or br. g (1969), by Nar...Jhua—Besbet. by Ballydonnell.
Breeder, J. W. Mecom (Tex.).   1974   7   2   2   0 $7,200
er, Audley Farm Stable. Trainer, D. Smith.   **$16,000**   1973   15   1   4   1 $10,049

25-743Kee	6½ f 1:18 ft	6-5 ▲116	1³	1³	1³	1⁵		Br'f'ldD²	10000 87	R'sh aBet116 MildJ'ker MamasH'eN'w	9
13-743Kee	6 f 1:11⅗ft	5	116	1²	1²	1¹½	2½	Val'zanF¹	10000 83	Chief Intent 120 Rush a Bet HastyBay	10
17-748FG	1-40 1:41 ft	3¾	116	2½	9¹⁵	9¹⁵	Eas.	And'nJR⁵	13000	Sea ofF'rt'ne116 S'ndyR'j'ct FluteBoy	9
26-745FG	6 f 1:11⅕ft	3	114	8⁴½	8¹³	8⁵½	7¹²	Copl'gD⁸	15000 80	JohnJet113 ModestMorn SatinLark	8
16-743FG	6 f 1:11 gd	15	114	5²¾	5⁵	3²	2¹½	CoplingD²	15000 91	R'll a'dT'ss120 R'sh aB't B'ck t'eS't'm	6
28-746FG	1-40 1:41⅗ft	14	113	3nk	8¹⁹	8¹⁹	8²²	Rub'coP⁸	14000 63	TommyG.118 PunkinTime Ch'm'gT'rry	8
5-746FG	1¹⁄₁₆ 1:45⅗gd	2¾	116	1²	12	1¹½	13½	An'nJR²	c10000 87	Rush A Bet116 SpeakOut FairFlight	7
29-735FG	6 f 1:12⅘ssy	3½	111	2½	2¹½	2³	5²¾	BreenR¹	12500 81	UncleZip116 SatinLark K'nt'ckyFlip'r	8
24-735Atl	6 f 1:11⅗ft	6½	115	1h	3²½	3²	34	UsseryR⁸	12500 80	IrishHighball 119 Dillprince Rush aBet	8
13-742Atl	6 f 1:11⅕ft	7½	115	74	3²½	3³	2³	Sol'neM¹⁰	11000 80	IrishHighb'll 115 R'sh aB't B'nitaBl'e	10
6-735Atl	1¹⁄₁₆ 1:45⅕ft	7½	116	3³	11½	1²	2¾	UsseryR¹⁰	10000 80	Fall Rush 108· Rush aBet He'sSolid	12

May 2 CD 4f sy :49b

(cont'd on next page)

Daring Baby 111
Dk. b. or br. f (1970), by Daring Knight—Plea's Baby, by Gallahad
Breeder, R. E. Rapp (Cal.).   1974 7 0 0 3 $4
Owner, H. E. Sutton. Trainer, C. E. Welch. $16,000   1973 21 2 3 5 $2:

Apr20-74⁷Kee	6½ f 1:17⅕ft	25	112	11¹³10¹²	9¹¹	7¾	FiresE²	20000 83	FavoriteRoad116 Aerodr'me JodiPe
Mar24-74²SA	6½ f 1:17⅕ft	3½	117	6⁴ 6⁵	56½	57¼	Cam'sR⁵	c16000 80	Ⓕ Kamadora 112 Celary RubySata
Mar15-74⁵SA	6 f 1:10⅗ft	10	118	6⁵ 54½	5³	3¾	Camp'sR⁵	20000 87	Morn'sBest112 LastMinute DaringB
Feb28-74⁶SA	1¹⁄₁₆ 1:44⅖gd	9½	114	77½ 63½	54½	5⁸	CampasR³	Alw 70	Ⓕ Reputat'n117 St'telyG'me DearInt
Feb17-74²SA	6 f 1:11⅖ft	37	117	11¹¹ 7⁹½	9⁵½	33½	CampasR⁶	20000 80	Ⓕ K'lb'sF'ly118 Maur'n'sB't D'r'gB't
Feb 8-74⁵SA	Ⓣ 1½ 1:49⅖fm	20	114	63¼ 63½	99½	9¹⁶	ValdezS²	Alw 64	Ⓕ Grasp'g115 Sultan'sB'ty JollyAng
Jan18-74⁹SA	1¹⁄₁₆ 1:46⅖sl	20	114	2² 21½	21½	33½	ValdezS³	Alw 66	Ⓕ Wistfully115 Met'poMiss Dar'gBal

April 7 SA 5f ft :59⅖h   April 5 SA 4f ft :48h

Not So Well 112
B. g (1970), by He Jr.—Dottisan, by Dotted Swiss.
Breeder E. Lowrance (Okla.).   1974 7 0 0 2 $3
Owner, E. Lowrance. Trainer, J. Eckrosh. $16,000   1973. 13 0 2 4 $8

Apr20-74⁷Kee	6½ f 1:17⅕ft	31f	116	8⁷½ 88¾10¹⁵10²⁰	C'b'llRJ⁹	20000 72	FavoriteRoad116 Aerodr'me JodiPe
Apr 5-74⁷OP	6 f 1:12½ft	14	123	11¹¹110⁹ 8⁶ 5⁴¾	Campb'lRJ⁸	Alw 79	MaryDugan112 GayG'her Bo's andOh
Mar27-74⁸OP	1-70 1:42⅜ft	50	113	4⁶ 3³ 3⁵ 36¾	SpindlerL³	Alw 76	OfficeK'g113 D'mondH'shoe N'tSoW
Mar20-74⁷OP	1-70 1:44⅕ft	26	118	11¹⁹11¹²10¹⁵10¹⁶	UsseryR⁹	Alw 59	BoldDave113 FragileFolly S't'n'sS'tr
Mar 6-74⁷OP	6 f 1:12⅖ft	6½	123	76½ 6⁵ 74½ 74½	UsseryR¹¹	Alw 78	CountryTradition113 Peeber BoldDa
Feb27-74⁷OP	5½ f 1:06⅖ft	12	117	8¹² 7¹¹ 5³ 3nk	UsseryR⁶	Alw 87	Delin't'n124 F'rnl'ghC't'ge NotSoW'
Feb18-74⁷OP	6 f 1:13 sy	5¼	123	7¹⁶ 7¹¹ 69½ 49½	Patt'sonA¹	Alw 70	DanielB'ne123 Peeber CountryTr'dit'
May25-73⁸CD	6 f 1:26 sy 2-3	▲113		46½ 42¼ 3⁴ 2⁴	B'rqueK²	17500 73	Juni⁶ F. 112 Not So Well Podac

April 29 CD 5f ft 1:03⅖b   April 16 Kee 4f ft :51⅕b   Mar 17 OP 4f ft :48⅖b

Lover's Flight ✲ 112
B. g (1967), by Certain Flight—Hallie Dear, by Aera.
Breeder, Far Cry Farm, Inc. (Ky.).   1974 6 0 2 2 $7
Owner, J. E. O'Bryant. Trainer, J. E. O'Bryant. $16,000   1973 10 2 3 3 $16

Apr 6-74⁵OP	1¹⁄₁₆ 1:45⅖ft	9½	115	46½ 33½ 2h 2h	LivelyJ²	17500 79	SolidMist118 Lover'sFlight WrightD
Mar23-74⁷OP	1-70 1:43⅖ft	3	113	65½ 4² 5¾ 54½	LivelyJ²	17500 72	RedTamao114 StevieW'vie BruteForc
Mar16-74¹⁰OP	1-70 1:44 ft	4½	115	45 4³ 2⁴ 22½	LivelyJ⁴	17500 73	BruteForce119 L'v'r'sFl't Pr'cePres
Mar 2-74¹⁰OP	1-70 1:43⅕ft	3¾	115	75 75½ 45½ 3⁵	LivelyJ²	17500 79	NobleKingd'm116 RedT'm'o Lov'sFl
Feb20-74⁸OP	1-70 1:42⅖ft	5½	115	5⁶ 84½ 79½ 79½	Wh'dDE⁷	20000 75	OurT'deW'ds111 P'l'zEnc're R'dT'ma
Feb15-74⁷OP	6 f 1:12⅖sy	4½	115	88½ 9¹⁴ 55½ 33½	UsseryR⁵	15000 78	ToolinAr'nd110 Pr'mR'ss L'v'r'sFlig
Aug21-73⁶Lib	1-70 1:44⅖ft	4-5	▲120	6⁴ 5⁶ 4⁶ 4¹⁰	BlackAS⁶	14000 66	Petrous113 Sport'gly YouPickedAb'
Jly 26-73⁷Lib	1 1:39⅖ft	2½	122	43½ 43½ 4³ 3³	UsseryR⁵	25000 73	GunWadding116 S'cessR'd Lover'sF
Jly 17-73⁸Lib	1-70 1:42⅖ft	9-5	▲118	1½ 1² 1⁴ 1½	UsseryR⁵	22500 86	Lover'sFli't118 Trop'lSuns't Intrav'n

May 1 CD 5f ft 1:02⅖b   April 25 CD 3f ft 1:03b   March 22 OP 4f ft :50b

Hasty Departure 115
B. g (1970), by Wallet Lifter—Opium Den, by Indian Hemp.
Breeder, Loma Rica Ranch (Cal.).   1974. 4 1 2 9 $4
Owner, Mr. & Mrs. W. Hicks. Trainer, L. Niles. $14,000

Apr27-74⁵CD	6 f 1:12⅖ft	13	113	63½ 89½ 43½ 12¾	TauzinL⁸	7000 84	H'tyD'p't're113 R'nd'IsB'sin H'pyCl'w
Mar12-74⁴OP	6 f 1:13⅖ft	5¾	116	6⁹ 4⁶ 5²½ 21½	UsseryR⁵	6250 77	BigK'g116 HastyDep't'e H'mb'g'rP't'
Feb27-74³OP	6 f 1:13⅖ft	3½	115	4⁴ 4³ 1h 2no	ZakoorW²	c4500 81	Sunburn117 H'tyDep't're Pr'ceH'bee
Feb11-74²OP	5½ f 1:06⅖ft	12	117	10⁸ 96½ 9⁷¹¹16½	ZakoorW¹¹	5000 79	B's'nsF'lc'n117 How-Tum Kr'ks InS'
Nov17-73⁴CD	6 f 1:12⅖ft	5	114	54½ 41½ 2h 2h	ZakoorW⁶	4750 82	B'd ofTh'ria119 H'styD'p't'e F'rB'g
Nov 2-73⁵CD	6 f 1:13⅖ft	5	119	4½ 1½ 2h 1½	ZakoorW⁶	3750 79	H'styD'p'r't'e119 St'mpyJ'e P'goT'r'
Sep24-73⁴Det	6 f 1:12⅖ft	6-5	▲118	3nk 1h 1½ 1³	EngleJ⁸	3200 77	HastyDep't're118 Haw'iBoy D'naL R
Sep 7-73²Det	6 f 1:14 ft	3-2	▲116	65¼ 3¹ 1½ 1½	EngleJ⁸	2500 70	HastyDeparture116 MiniSk'ny Sw'sT

April 26 CD 3f ft :37b   April 20 CD 5f ft 1:03b   Mar 11 OP 3f sy :37b

Red Hot Tamale ✲ 116
Ch. rig (1968), by Tamao—Miss Tahiti, by Tahitian King.
Breeder, W. B. Robinson (Ky.).   1974 12 2 1 2 $11
Owner, S. Jones & J. Stebbins. Trainer, C. E. Picou. $16,000   1973..13 3 4 2 $24

Apr20-74⁷Kee	6½ f 1:17⅕ft	38	118	53¼ 43½ 56½ 68½	M'lloM¹⁰	20000 84	FavoriteRoad116 Aerodr'me JodiPe
Apr10-74⁷Kee	6 f 1:09⅖ft	22	116	2¹ 5⁸ 5⁸ 7¹³	S'l'monG⁵	25000 82	Str'ngSide122 C'lMeJ'die G'ld'nGree
Mar30-74⁶Lat	6 f 1:07 sy	12	119	44½ 45 47½ 4¹¹	Mang'loM⁴	Alw 72	Pop'l'rD'm'nd115 CariC'ty B'teR'axt'
Mar16-74⁸Lat	1¹⁄₁₆ 1:47⅗sm	44	115	33½ 3⁸ 3⁶ 4¹³	FriarJW²	HcpS 59	B'tleg'r'sPet116 L't'r'sJ't'r B'b't'sl'g
Mar 9-74⁸Lat	6 f 1:15 ft	9½	122	52½ 5⁴ 4⁵ 37½	SolomonG⁷	Alw 62	FleetTudor119 LuckAh'd R'dH'tT'm'
Mar 2-74⁸Lat	1 1:45 sy	3½	119	2¹ 1⁶ 1⁸ 1½	SolomonG⁴	Alw 54	R'dH'tT'male119 Mr.Ch'mp L'tt's'ns
Feb23-74⁸Lat	1 1:41⅖sm	7½	119	3¹ 21½ 2⁴ 4⁹	SolomonG⁵	Alw 64	BigSpade122 Bab'gton'sIm'e Mr.Ch'

May 1 CD 4f ft :49b   April 19 Kee 3f ft :36h   April 16 Kee 5f ft 1:01h

lative Shoes 116 Ch. g (1969), by Native Charger—Silver Shoes, by Goya II.
Breeder, L. Savage (Fla.).

ner, R. E. Harris. Trainer, R. E. Harris.

1974 9 2 3 1 $9,172
$16,000   1973.. 5 0 0 1 $1,105

r17-746Kee	6½ f 1:16⅗ft	50	114	9¹⁴	9¹⁴	7¹⁰	7¹⁰	WhitedDE⁹	Alw 86 StrongSide121 Br'stigert P'rlezEnc're	9
r 1-748Lat	1 1:42⅗sy	13	122	6¹⁷	6¹⁷	6¹¹	5¹¹	McKn'htJ⁴	Alw 55 BigSpade122 Lester'sJester Voyage	7
r11-748Lat	1 1:43⅖sy	3-2	▲115*	8³³	5²²	5¹⁵	2²	MorganM¹	Alw 60 AngelMissy 115 NativeShoes Voyage	8
b21-748Lat	1₁¹⁶ 1:49⅘sy	7	119	6²⁸	6⁹½	3½	1ⁿᵒ	SmithsonG¹	Alw 61 NativeShoes119 BigParty Once Irish	7
r 7-748Lat	1 1:43 ft	2½	117*	6⁸	4⁶	3⁷	34½	MorganM⁴	Alw 59 Mr.Champ115 AngelMissy NativeSh'es	6
n31-748Lat	6½ f 1:20⅗gd	6¾	117*	6²½	2⁴	2⁷	22½†MorganM⁶	Alw 79 RedH'tTam'le115 Mr.Ch'p N've Shoes	7

†Dead heat.

| n19-748Lat | 1 1:47 m | 3½ | ▲114* | Fog. | | 2⁵ | | MorganM² | Alw 39 SnowFacePat117 NativeSh's Nadarko | 8 |
| n12-747Lat | 6 f 1:11⅘ft | 8½ | 109* | 7⁸½ | 5⁵½ | 3¹½ | 1ʰ | MorganM⁶ | Alw 89 NativeSh's109 T'sBigGem Exemplary | 8 |

April 30 CD 4f ft :50⅖b   April 24 CD 5f ft 1:04⅖b   March 23 Lat 6f ft 1:19⅗b

ederal Ruler ✱ 115 Ch. h (1969), by Irish Ruler—Vala, by Cosmic Bomb.
Breeder, Farnsworth Farm (Fla.).

ner, R. Cotb. Trainer, A. Montano.

1974. 10 2 1 0 $6,870
$14.000   1973. 18 2 3 1 $11,156

r22-749Aqu	7 f 1:24⅖ft	3½	114	9⁵½	8⁸	9⁸	9⁵	Cor'roAJr⁷ 7750 74 Pembles112 MoreL'dings Old'stMich'l	12
r11-749Aqu	1 1:37⅗ft	2¾	▲118	7⁹½	3⁴½	2³	1½	Velasq'zJ¹ 5000 79 F'd'r'lR'l'r119 Old'st Mich'l RioT'n'y'n	9
r 4-749Aqu	6 f 1:10⅗sy	5	116	7⁸	7⁹¾	8¹¹·8¹⁴	Cas'daM³ 10000 76 JollyD'cer116 J'hnDegr't E'rlyJ'd'm't	8
r27-745Aqu	6 f 1:11⅘ft	10	116	5³¼	3¹½	2½	2ⁿᵏ	C'roAJr¹² 10500 87 Corporat'n116 F'd'lRuler WitnessSt'd	12
r19-742Aqu	1 1-8 1:52 ft	2⅜e	118	4¹	¹1ʰ	3¹½	6⁵½	Vel'quezJ¹ 8500 69 PatrolPrince116 Penetrante Pr'ceB'lo	7
r 6-746PR	1₁⁷₁₆ 1:49⅕ft	3½	115	5⁵½	6⁹½	5⁷	6⁴½	VelezH⁵ Alw IncaWarrior114 Catbette Alurnchorus	7
b24-748PR	1₁⁷₁₆ 1:49⅗ft	3	115	3¹½	1ʰ	1ʰ	1¹¼	VelezH⁹ 10000 FederalRul'r115 Sense ofD'ty Classico	9

March 23 Bel trt 3f ft :35⅕h

The public figured to concentrate its betting on two horses in this field. Lover's Flight had lost his most recent race by only a head, and now was dropping slightly in class. Rush a Bet had beaten cheaper horses very convincingly, leading all the way to win by five lengths. But neither of these horses was favored. Daring Baby — who was a filly running against males, who was winless in seven starts during the year, who had been badly beaten at 25 to 1 in her last race — was bet steadily and heavily, and went off at 9 to 5. The untutored Derby Day crowd could not possibly have made her the favorite; the smart money was responsible. Just a few days before, the same stable had won a race with a horse named Gaelic Coffee who came from California to Kentucky, ran one dismal race, dropped slightly in class, went off as an inexplicable 9-to-5 favorite, and won by seven lengths. Now Daring Baby showed the identical pattern. An outsider could not know what the stable was doing with the horse and why it was so confident, but any perceptive conspiracy theorist had to bet Daring Baby out of sheer, blind faith. Blocked for a quarter mile, she came four horses wide entering the stretch and won going away.

Sometimes the most meaningful betting action is of a negative variety: a horse who has obvious handicapping virtues, who is sure to be heavily supported by the public, will go off at a suspiciously high price that suggests the smart money is avoiding him completely. A handicapper usually should not be frightened because he is getting generous odds on a horse he likes. But when the odds are too generous, he should be wary.

Even an untutored handicapper could have spotted a standout in the ninth race at Saratoga on July 30, 1974. Monetary Principle, a maiden, had run impressively against allowance horses in his last start, losing by a nose. Since that race he had worked six furlongs in a phenomenal 1:10⅗. He looked like a potential stakes horse. And now he was entered in a maiden race.

Because his credentials were so obvious, Monetary Principle figured to be an odds-on favorite. He wasn't. His odds hovered around 5 to 2 until a few minutes before post time. Then the public, thinking it was being offered a bargain, drove his price down to 7 to 5. The lukewarm support that Monetary Principle had received through most of the betting, and his suspiciously high final odds, suggested that something was wrong with him. And something was. He was trounced by 15 lengths.

A week later Monetary Principle was entered in the same sort of race. Despite his bad loss he received strong betting action and went off the favorite. This time he won by 11 lengths.

Any observant horseplayer can cash good bets periodically by trying to divine the intentions of trainers and detect betting coups. For a long time, while I was operating at the larcenous New England tracks under Mr. D.'s influence, I thought this was the only way to beat the races. But when I started covering horse racing for a newspaper and learned more about the sport and the people in it, I recognized the fallacy of this approach to handicapping. When a horse-player is betting on the basis of thievery, coups, and inside information, he is betting on the trainer's judgment. He must assume that the insiders are all-knowing and all-pow-erful; when they bet, their horse is going to win.

As I became acquainted with many trainers, owners, and jockeys, I learned that this notion conflicts head-on with reality. The insiders are just as fallible as any horseplayer. The mysteries of handicapping are mysterious to them, too.

Very often, when a longshot wins and conspiracy-minded horseplayers assume his victory was the product of a well-planned betting coup, the owner and trainer will be utterly surprised by their horse's performance. When I bet Sun in Action, I took it for granted that trainer Ron Bateman had been manipulating the horse's form and was now ready to gamble on him. After Sun in Action won, I asked jockey Martin Fromin if he thought the trainer had cleaned up on the race. "No," Fromin said. "He'd probably laugh at you if you asked him. Normally trainers will tell you if they're betting their money. They'll lay a story on you about why his last races were bad. But Bateman just said he didn't know much about the horse and told me to ride the way I wanted."

A good trainer will usually know his own horse and know when he is ready to run his best race. But even when the trainer has laid the groundwork for what he thinks will be a winning performance, he still has to beat a field of other horses, many of whose trainers have done the same thing. Because they are so committed to their own horses, trainers and owners can seldom handicap a race with objectivity and frequently misjudge their opposition drastically. Every day I go to the track I hear tips and tidbits of information from insiders who are genuinely convinced their horses will win. The insiders' batting average is no better than that of average horseplayers who rely on the *Racing Form* for all their information.

As skeptical as I am about tips, I sometimes find them irresistible. No rational man could have resisted trying to capitalize on the piece of inside information I heard at Saratoga in the summer of 1973. The source of it happened to be the best trainer in America.

One Sunday afternoon I was visiting the stable of Allen Jerkens, where a friendly touch football game was being played. After the game, Jerkens strolled around his barn talking about his horses. He came to one stall and said, "This horse is so good now that I get scared every morning when I come to look at him." The animal's name was Triangular. An old stakes-class grass horse, he had been out of competition for six months. But he was training beautifully under the master's tutelage, and Jerkens was contemplating a gamble. He could, of course, enter Triangular in an allowance race where he would be facing tough competition. But Jerkens was thinking about putting him in a high-priced claiming race, where he would surely outclass his opposition. I waited anxiously for the big day. And finally, on the next to last day of the Saratoga meeting, Triangular was entered in a $45,000 claiming race. I bet with confidence.

Triangular broke last, made one ineffectual move on the last turn, and faded to finish last. On the same afternoon, Jerkens also saddled a horse named Prove Out, that he had bought just a week earlier. He didn't know much about the horse yet. Prove Out won by six lengths, shattered the track record, and paid $11.80. Jerkens was as stunned by his victory as by Triangular's defeat. If the best horseman in America can be so wrong, the typical trainer who tries to concoct betting coups is certainly apt to be wrong much of the time.

A horseplayer who pays too much attention to larceny and inside information is likely to lose, not only because betting coups often fail, but because this preoccupation will wreck the rest of his handicapping. There was one season in Maryland when I became totally paranoid about jockeys, suspecting that most of them were holding horses — that is, deliberately losing races — with great frequency. As a result, I couldn't evaluate a horse's previous races with any confidence; I always wondered if the jockey had been trying to win. If I did find a horse who looked like an excellent bet, I feared that the jockey might be holding him today. When I lost a bet on a horse I liked, I would ascribe the defeat to the rider's moral turpitude. At every stage of the handicapping process, my judgment had been undermined. I didn't handicap properly; I didn't bet my solid selections with confidence; I didn't analyze races after they had been run and try to learn from them.

I finally decided that my mental attitude was so self-defeating that the only way to function properly was to assume that the game is honest and that the results of races are true. By viewing the sport logically instead of conspiratorially, I found that the outcome of most races did seem to be the product of logical factors rather than conspiracies.

I consider the possibility of larceny in a race only when I am confronted by powerful evidence of it — such as unmistakable betting action, the suspicious presence of a horse in a race in which he shouldn't be entered, or a pattern of thievery in a horse's past performances that his trainer has employed with success before. But even under these circumstances, I still handicap the race. There are many times when I will conclude that the stable is trying to execute a betting coup, but I will still not bet the horse because I think he is not good enough and the trainer's judgment is faulty. Betting primarily on the basis of a trainer's intentions, or on inside information, is for people who don't have the knowledge to handicap properly. When I put my money on a race, I don't want to bet on anybody's judgment but my own.

4

Track Biases

BEFORE I MET Steve Davidowitz, I had spent some fifteen years looking for the elusive Secret of Beating the Races. I knew that it would not be easy to find but I knew it existed: the great principle that underlies the science of handicapping, that would work any time, anywhere.

I found the answer by pure chance when I sat on a bench near the paddock at Saratoga Race Track. A young man sitting a few feet away struck up a conversation with me and we compared notes on the day's races. It didn't take me long to sense that Steve Davidowitz was the most brilliant student of handicapping I had ever met. As we conversed, we saw that our lives as horseplayers had developed along parallel lines. We had both become addicted to racing in college, had both suffered through a lot of losers, and had both experienced one great betting triumph that had changed our lives. But I still had not found the Secret, and Steve had.

Steve's obsession as a youth had not been horses, but baseball. He was a high-school hotshot in New Jersey, pitching one no-hitter after another. He was offered a $30,000 bonus by the Milwaukee Braves but turned it down so he could go to college. In his freshman year at Rutgers University he wrecked his arm in a pick-up basketball game and saw his hopes for a major league baseball career shattered. At the time of this personal disaster, Steve was enrolled in a statistics class for which the teacher had assigned him a term project: Analyze the effect of post positions on races at Garden State Park. The sport fascinated him immediately, and it also provided him with an outlet for some of the self-destructive urges he was feeling after his injury. He started going to Garden State every day, and losing every day. He borrowed money from friends. He bet on credit with bookmakers. And he soon found himself $1500 in debt with no way to extricate himself.

Steve drove the 100 miles from school to his father's business, sat in front of his desk, and broke into tears as he related the whole story. His father listened impassively and then reached for his checkbook. "I'll give you the money you need," he said. "But I want you to promise that you'll never gamble again."

Steve promised. But gambling was already too much in his blood and not long afterward he found himself back at Garden State Park. He walked to the daily-double window but stood there unable to speak, unable to violate his pledge and place a bet. He sat through nine races and still couldn't bring himself to bet. Yet he couldn't abandon his interest in racing, and so he plunged into a chaste, academic study of the sport. He pored over the *Morning Telegraph* every day, learning all he could about handicapping. He became especially interested in workouts as indications of horses' conditions, and he studied the workout listings in the *Telegraph* diligently. As he did, he noticed a name that kept reappearing: Flying Mercury. This old horse had been such a fast sprinter that he had once outbroken Intentionally, who had then been considered the fastest horse in America. Flying Mercury had been idle for a long time, but his steady workouts at Garden State suggested that he was returning to top condition. Finally, his name appeared in the entries — in a mile-and-a-quarter handicap. This was an obviously inappropriate spot for a horse whose specialty was running three-quarters of a mile. But Steve was so intrigued that he went to see the race. Flying Mercury broke alertly but his jockey eased him back, and the horse finished 40 lengths behind the winner.

A few days later Flying Mercury was entered in a six-furlong race at Aqueduct, and Steve knew that this was the race for which he was being prepared. Steve drove to New York for that one race and bet $20 to win, $20 to place. Flying Mercury flew out of the gate, opened a five-length lead, and won with ease at odds of 38 to 1. Steve collected $1200 and drove directly to his father's office. He handed him the money and said, "I won this betting a horse." His father understood. And Steve understood, almost immediately, that Flying Mercury had changed his life.

"It made me know, for an absolute certainty, that there was logic behind this game and that it could be beaten," Steve said. "I never had really believed that you could know how a horse was going to run unless you walked up to his trainer before the race and asked him. But I was convinced by that one victory that I could know — that I could go up to a trainer before the race and tell him what his horse was likely to do."

The triumph of Flying Mercury did not immediately transform Steve into a winning horseplayer. Just as he had done during his disastrous losing streak, he would often bet on horses he thought had solid credentials and then watch them lose badly. This happens to every horseplayer, of course, but most of them chalk up the defeat to the inscrutability of the game. It confirms their deep-seated belief that nobody can beat the races. But Steve now believed that he could and would beat them, and whenever a seemingly outstanding horse was beaten he tried to comprehend what had happened. He didn't find the explanation in any one dramatic flash of insight. The answer crept into his consciousness slowly.

During his ill-fated betting binge at Garden State Steve had noticed, without recognizing the implications, that horses with inside post positions won an unusually high percentage of the races and that the best jockeys at the track tried to steer their horses toward the rail whenever they could. When he started going to Saratoga every August he witnessed an opposite phenomenon: Most of the winners were horses who broke from outside post positions and rallied in the middle of the track. As he handicapped at Saratoga he found himself thinking along these lines: "Here's a horse with early speed and an inside post position. He doesn't have much of a chance. But if they were running this race at Garden State, this horse would be a strong contender."

In order to pursue his interest in horses full-time, Steve went to work as a handicapper for the *Racing Form*, where his duties called for him to make selections in all the races at six or seven tracks a day. Here he confirmed his impressions about the diversity of the sport. When he was handicapping a race at Garden State, he preferred horses who had early speed, an inside post position, and a recent race over the track. When he was studying the Fair Grounds in New Orleans, he observed that horses trained by the brilliant Jack Van Berg would win countless races even though they defied all conventional handicapping wisdom. When he doped out races in New England, he saw that horses recently acquired by trainer Richard L. Barnett won a high percentage of the time. When he was dealing with a mile-and-one-eighth race at Aqueduct, he knew that horses with inside post positions would win most of the time.

Here it was, the Secret of Beating the Races: There was no one secret! The horseplayers like me who searched for the great underlying truth of handicapping were as misdirected as the alchemists who spent their lives trying to find the philosophers' stone. The game is diverse and it is perpetually changing. Methods that work beautifully at Bowie are almost useless sixty miles away at Shenandoah Downs. Handicapping rules that sounded axiomatic a year ago are obsolete today. The winning horseplayer is not the man who holds the proper set of dogmatic beliefs, but the one who can observe and adapt to the ever-changing conditions of the sport.

These conditions take many forms. I remember a season at Suffolk Downs when horses wearing mud caulks — cleated shoes that gave them better footing — would win practically every race on a sloppy track. Steve told me about a meeting at the Fair Grounds when he enjoyed great success simply by betting on the horse who was warmed up most vigorously before the race. These dominant factors appear and disappear for no apparent reason. But there are two types of changing conditions that a good horseplayer must be aware of constantly. One of them is the influence of trainers. Certain men, with methods uniquely their own, will consistently win races with horses who don't conform to any sort of established handicapping logic. (The importance of trainers will be discussed in the next chapter.) The other important variables are those caused by the racing surfaces over which horses run.

The profound influence of the track condition on the outcome of a race is a relatively recent phenomenon. Handicapping books of previous generations rarely mentioned it as an important factor. But horseplayers of the past lived when there was a defined racing season, conducted during the temperate months of the year. They never experienced the dubious pleasures of year-round racing, never had to cope with the effects of the weather on a racetrack in Rhode Island in the middle of January. I visited Narragansett Park on one day that made the traditional designations of track conditions — fast, good, sloppy, muddy, and heavy — laughably irrelevant. There had been a heavy snowfall and the moisture in the Narragansett track had seeped toward the rail, turning that part of the racing strip into a virtual bog. On the stretch turn snow that had been piled up in the adjacent parking lot had begun to melt, and the outside part of the track had been converted into a small lake. In between the bog and the lake there was a narrow strip of the track that was frozen. The horse who stayed on this hard path was an automatic winner.

Old-time horseplayers were also spared the experience of dealing with the mentality of the new breed of track superintendents who unabashedly manipulate their racing surfaces. Before the 1971 Preakness Stakes, for example, everyone was saying that the horses in the Triple Crown event were a very mediocre group. So Pimlico took action to insure that its big race wasn't mediocre. Tons of soil were scraped from the track, making it extraordinarily hard and fast. Cheap horses were running more swiftly than they ever had in their lives, and Canonero II won the fastest Preakness in history, giving management the spectacular race that it had wanted.

Though there are many possible causes for aberrant track conditions, their effects will take only a few basic forms:

1. The track favors front-running horses. This will happen on very hard tracks, like the one at Pimlico. Horses with early speed will tire less quickly than they would under normal conditions, for the same reason that human runners can go farther and faster on asphalt than they can on a sandy beach. Speed horses usually have an advantage on sloppy tracks, too, because come-from-behind horses are hampered by the mud that is kicked in their faces.

2. The inside part of the track is harder and faster than the outside. This usually helps front runners because they can outbreak their opponents and get to the good footing along the rail. A stretch runner, even if he starts from an inside post position, may have to move outside for running room.

3. The inside part of the track is deep and slow. Under these conditions, speed horses with inside post positions can rarely win. Horses breaking from outside posts have a distinct advantage, although stretch runners with inside posts can move off the rail and try to win by circling the field.

In theory, knowledgeable horseplayers should win a fortune whenever they encounter one of these types of track biases. When speed horses breaking from inside post positions are winning all the races, an observant gambler should be betting speed horses with inside post positions. But this is not as easy as it sounds. Even after meeting Steve Davidowitz, absorbing and intellectually accepting his ideas about adapting to the changing conditions of the sport, it took me years before I could capitalize properly on track biases.

To become successful horseplayers, most of us spend years studying and learning about class, condition, speed, and the other classic principles of handicapping. I have devoted a large part of my life to the creation and refinement of my speed figures, and I believe in them with an almost religious devotion. It is not easy for me to disregard the principles I believe in and the methods that have worked for me in order to bet a horse simply because he is breaking from post position one on a day when the inside part of the track is fast. I feel like an apostate turning his back on the faith in which he was raised.

It wasn't until the summer of 1973 that I was able to make money from a track bias, and I owe the breakthrough partly to my mother (who still can't quite grasp the difference between win, place, and show). I went to visit her in Erie, where a brand-new track, Commodore Downs, had opened just a few weeks before. The citizens of Erie were curious but uninformed about the new game in town, and numerous family friends had asked my mother to arrange an outing to Commodore, with me as their private tout. My mother, of course, was quite willing to show off her son the horse-player. But I knew I was going to look like a bumbling incompetent. Commodore Downs offers the rock-bottom level of races that are usually undecipherable even under optimum conditions. And since the track had been open for only a brief time, it would be impossible to do much worthwhile research into the handicapping methods that might work there.

When I visit an unfamiliar track I try to discover if any track biases exist. I calculate the percentage of front-running winners at each distance. I go through the *Racing Form* charts and list, in a separate column for each distance the track offers, the winning post position and the number of horses in the field. My compilation of the results of four-furlong races at Commodore Downs over a two-week period looked like this:

FOUR FURLONGS

Winning Post	Horses in Field
5	7
6	6
6	10
2	8
8	8
8	8
6	7
8	8
7	8
5	8
9	9
3	7
3	10
4	9
6	9
4	6

Then I added the number of winners and the number of starters from each post position and calculated the percentage of winners from each post. These were the results:

FOUR FURLONGS

Post	Winners	Starters	Percent
1	0	16	0
2	1	16	6
3	2	16	13
4	2	16	13
5	2	16	13
6	4	16	25
7	1	14	7
8	3	11	27
9	1	5	20
10	0	2	0

The results of my calculations for other distances were much the same, and they couldn't have been more fruitful. Horses breaking from outside post positions had an enormous advantage at Commodore Downs. Horses in posts one and two could be eliminated almost automatically, regardless of their credentials. It looked too good to be true, and so on my first night at the track I resolved to bet with restraint and concentrate on watching what was happening. Whenever a horseplayer suspects the existence of a track bias, he should study the early races on the card diligently, decide who is likely to show speed, who is likely to rally, who is likely to win, and then compare the actual running of the race with what he thinks should have happened.

The first race I saw at Commodore was, typically, a $1500 claiming event for horses that had not won a race in the last two years. There were only four horses in the field with records that suggested they might be bona fide members of the thoroughbred family. Brent's Tiger had early speed and post position one. Jocantry was dropping from the $2000 level and had post two. Roses of Mentor and Mr. Teal, breaking from posts four and five, had both run sharp races over the track against similar opposition. But none of these horses ever got into serious contention. Morie Pie, a 52-to-1 shot who had never been close to the lead in two years, broke from the No. 6 post and blew past all the contenders inside him on the turn. In the stretch, an equally unimposing-looking horse named Conscientious Lad, who had broken from post eight, circled the field and finished second. In the one minute five and two-fifths seconds that it had taken these plugs to negotiate five-eights of a mile, I had learned all I needed to know about handicapping at Commodore Downs. For the rest of the week I confidently disregarded any horse starting from the two inside post positions. I would have thrown out Secretariat if he had been on the rail in a $1500 claiming race. By concentrating on exactas and using horses in favorable post positions who had shown a glimmer of ability, I was hitting an average of five races a night.

An important lesson dawned on me during this winning streak. If I had known more about handicapping at Commodore Downs, if I were more aware of the methods of the trainers and the relative merits of the horses, I probably wouldn't have done nearly so well. I would have been bewildered whenever I encountered a horse with solid credentials who was breaking from an inside post position. But with no other tools to work with, I let the track bias dictate the horses I bet. I learned that whenever I see such a powerful bias — even at a track where I know all the angles — I should subordinate all my other handicapping ideas to it.

When I encounter a race in which the best horse — the

one with my top speed figure — is disadvantaged by the track bias, I will usually make a moderate bet against him. If his merits look so strong that I cannot resist, I will make a moderate bet on him, knowing that I probably shouldn't be doing it. But when I find a race where the best horse also has the track bias in his favor, I am inclined to bet all I can and then some. Such horses offer the best gambling opportunities in all of racing.

Unfortunately, these clear-cut situations don't arise often enough. But during my stay at Commodore Downs I hoped I would find at least one obviously superior animal who would be helped by the track bias. On my last day in Erie, I did. The opportunity came in an unlikely spot — a $2500 claiming race for maidens. Almost every how-to-beat-the-races book ever written has unconditionally advised its readers to avoid races for cheap horses who have displayed a chronic inability to win. Personally, I don't believe in any of these absolutist dicta about handicapping. While it is true that cheap maiden races are usually unbettable, the first race at Commodore Downs on June 22, 1973, was a classic exception. These were the past performances of the nine horses in the field (see pages 78–79).

Baldwin Twister was the favorite. She had sprinted to big early leads in six-and-a-half-furlong races at Jefferson Downs in Louisiana. She had collapsed every time, but now she was running only five-eighths of a mile, and the shorter distance would help her. If this race were being run on a typical half-mile track, where horses with inside post positions and early speed win with high frequency, Baldwin Twister probably would have been a standout. But this was Commodore Downs, and Baldwin Twister epitomized the type of horse that almost never could win at this track: a speedster breaking from the No. 1 post position.

Bullet Lady had run well to finish second in a four-furlong race at Commodore though she hadn't been able to gain in the stretch. She had weakened in her previous start at four and a half furlongs. Five furlongs seemed to be a bit too far for her. And even if she had shown ability to handle the distance, she would still have been a speed horse breaking from the No. 2 post, and thus a likely loser at Commodore.

Grand Lou Ann, No. 3, had never shown any ability and could be instantly eliminated. The same was true of Miss Bush Ahead, Gomesa's Baby, Lay Arms, and Milk Bottle.

Edwards Country, breaking from post position five, had run in a $2500 maiden race a week before. After starting from an advantageous outside post position, he made a move at the leaders on the turn, but weakened slightly in the stretch of a four-furlong race. In his previous attempts to go five furlongs or more, he had tired badly. Edwards Country figured to have an edge over Baldwin Twister and Bullet Lady simply because of their post positions, but his credentials were otherwise unimpressive.

Wembley Legend had raced only once, which in itself is a recommendation in a maiden race. The other horses in the field had established themselves as losers; Wembley Legend at least had not yet shown that she was a hopeless bum. Her racing debut on June 8, in which she broke ninth and rallied to finish fourth, was much better than it appears on the surface. The winner of that race, Lonesome Sailor, stepped up in class and won an allowance race by four lengths the next time he ran; he was obviously much better than the typical winner of a $2500 maiden race. Makemeadeal, who had finished a length in front of Wembley Legend, had also come back to win his next start, as we can see in the top line of Edwards Country's past performances. Makemeadeal had destroyed Edwards Country by eight

COMMODORE 5 FURLONGS

START / FINISH

5 FURLONGS. (.59⅗) MAIDEN CLAIMING. Purse $1,500. Weight, 3-year-olds, 120 lbs. Claiming Price $2,500.

Baldwin Twister
Own.—Noullet M

B. f. 3, by Metier—Kitty Sue, by George Gains
Br.—Rester M L (Ala)
Tr.—Delahoussaye J
$2,500

115

	St.	1st 2nd 3rd	Amt.
1973	3 M	0 0 1	$192
1972	2 M	0 0	$165

26May73-4JnD	fst 6f :23	:47½ 1:21%	3 ↑ Md 5000	5 4 1³ 1¹½ 2² 6¹² Terre J E Jr	b 107	19.00	67-15 Mr. Ideal 120⁶ Wailing Wind 113¹ Corporals Guard 115¹	Speed, tired 10
14May73-1JnD	fst 6½f :23	:48½ 1:23	3 ↑ Md 2500	3 4 1⁵ 1hd 1¹½ 4²½ Terre J E Jr⁵	b 110	7.70	67-20 Terriwin 120hd Jab MyBubble 1131½ GrandmammaSugar 115¹	Weakened 10
10May73-1JnD	fst 6½f :22%	:47% 1:22%	ⒸMd 1500	5 2 1⁴ 2² 4⁶¹ Terre J E Jr	b 110	19.90	66-18 Miss Jet Princess 1172½ Chart East 112² Graceful Grace 110³½	Weakened 10
3Nov72-4JnD	fst 6f :23½	:48 1:22%	Clm 4000	4 7 9¹⁵10⁴¹0⁹ — Tauzin L	114	14.70	— King Rocks 112¾ Trson Quemado 112² Ozone Queen 108nk	Eased 10
3Nov72-1JnD	fst 6f :23%	:48% 1:48%	Md Sp Wt	4 9 3³ 3³ 3²¾ Tauzin L	b 116	17.00	81-17 Zel's Gal 116¹½ Social Debutante 116¾ Baldwin Twister 116¹	Rallied 10

LATEST WORKOUTS   Jun 19 Com 3f gd :39 b

Bullet Lady
Own.—Maxwell A D

B. f. 3, by Abashed—Bullet Baby, by Paul H
Br.—Maxwell A (Okla)
Tr.—Maxwell A D
$2,500

110⁵

	St.	1st 2nd 3rd	Amt.
1973	3 M	1 0 0	$397
1972	0 M	0 0	

13Jun73-5Com	fst 4f	:23% :47%	3 ↑ Md 2000	3 4 2½ 3½ 2² Maxwell J	115	4.30	— Flag Flyer 120² Bullet Lady 115no Executrix 1172¼	Gamely 8
26May73-9Com	gd 4½f :24	:49% :55%	Md 2500	4 2 2³ 3½½ 4²½ Maxwell J	115	6.50	— Lonesome Sailor 120³ Bab's Flash 115²½ Makemeadeal 120¹	Speed, tired 6
10Apr73-2HP	sl 4f	:23% :48%	3 ↑ Md 3500	5 8 6⁶ 9¹² 9¹⁵ Snyder D	115	9.00	69-16 Swift Tune 120¹ Right Trail 120³½ Third Thrill 111²	No speed 10

Grand Lou Ann
Own.—Crenshaw M

Ch. f. 3, by Aber Roussel—Miss Grand, by Quick Reward
Br.—Spiroff G Jr (Mich)
Tr.—McNerney W D
$2,500

115

	St.	1st 2nd 3rd	Amt.
1973	5 M	0 0 0	$209
1972	4 M	0 0 0	$228

15Jun73-2Com	fst 4f	:23 :47%	Md 2500	1 7 5⁸ 6¹¹ 4¹³ McNerney T	b 115	15.70	— Makemeadeal 120¹⁵½ Swift Signal 1152½ EdwardsCountry 120²½	No mishap 7
8Jun73-9Com	fst 4½f :23%	:48% :54%	Md 2500	3 4 9¹¹ 8¹⁵ 7¹⁹ McNerney T	b 115	20.10	— Lonesome Sailor 120³ Bab's Flash 115²½ Makemeadeal 120¹	No factor 10
25May73-4Com	sl 4½f :23%	:49% :55%	3 ↑ Md 2500	7 2 4⁵½ 5⁸½ 6⁹½ McNerney T	b 114	5.20	— Prince Placid 115¾ Dr. Swafford 120⁴ Rival Mark 115½	Tired 7
4Apr73-3HP	gd 6f :24%	:50% 1:18%	3 ↑ Clm 3500	10 10 10¹⁵ 9¹⁷ 9²⁵ 9²⁶ Low S	b 105	183.40	— Error Not 106nk No Mustard 113½ Carters Match 110²	No factor 11
28Mar73-4HP	gd 4f	:23% :48	3 ↑ ⒸClm 2500	3 10 10¹³10¹⁷10¹⁸ Paugh C D	b 105	113.20	— Lucy Beatrice 111⁴ Teebee 110¹½ No Mustard 113¹½	Trailed 10
14Nov72-3Det	my 6f :25%	:51% 1:19%	ⒸMd 5000	5 4 2² 6¹¹ 9²³ 9²⁰ Bacon M	b 117	12.70	— Ronbar 120¹½ Twiddley De 117⁶ Small Fortune 1172¼	No speed 12
7Nov72-3Det	my 6f	:24 :49%	ⒾMd 5000	1 6 4¹² 4⁹ 7⁹ 5⁹½ Strauss R	b 117	8.90	— Loonsong 117nk Jean's Music 117² Whimsical Lass 117²	No threat 8
3Nov72-1Det	my 5½f :24%	:49% 1:10%	Md 3200	9 4 1hd 3⁴ 3⁸ 4¹⁰ Snyder D	b 112	*1.50	53-34 Flying Gal 110² Little Beth 112⁷ Miss Hiccups 117¹	Weakened 11

LATEST WORKOUTS   May 18 Com 5f fst 1:03% b   May 15 Com 3f fst :38⅗ b

Miss Bush Ahead
Own.—Molero V A

B. f. 3, by Bush Ahead—Admiral Louise, by Beauguerre
Br.—Rapp F (La)
Tr.—Molero V A
$2,500

108⁷

	St.	1st 2nd 3rd	Amt.
1973	3 M	0 0 0	$30
1972	5 M	0 0 1	$242

15Jun73-2Com	fst 4f	:23 :47%	Md 2500	3 8 8¹³ 5¹⁰ 5¹³ Jett J⁷	108	19.10	— Makemeadeal 120¹⁵½ Swift Signal 1152½ Edwards Country 120²½	No threat 8
21May73-5JnD	fst 5f :23	:48% 1:00%	Clm 3000	7 7 7⁷½ 8¹⁷ 8²⁰ 9³⁶ Young J F	112	121.30	56-16 Wayward Winner 112no Meisje 107² Bab's Hill 110nk	No factor 8
5May73-2JnD	fst 4f	:22% :47%	Clm 2500	9 9 8¹⁶ 9¹⁶ 9¹⁹ Keller E D	115	104.20	72-09 Jo's Bad Girl 109¹ Two Tonco 114⁸ Witch Of Benevinto 117²	No factor 9
27Dec72-4FG	fst 6f :22%	:47% 1:14%	ⒾMd Sp Wts	7 5 7⁵ 9⁸ 11²⁰ 11²¹ Young J F	115	32.70	55-20 Intaner B. 118⁴ Easy Pic 110¹ Raybum's Red 118¾	No speed 12
7Dec72-1FG	sl 6f :22%	:47% 1:14%	ⒾⒸMd 3500	2 11 1hd 3⁴ 5⁸½ 7¹² Young J F	119	33.10	62-23 NitNevergivesin 119½ Dode sRequest 119¹ MidofOsiris 119⁶	Sluggish start 12
14Nov72-1JnD	gd 4f	:23% :48%	Md Sp Wt	2 5 5⁴½ 6⁶½ 6⁹ Menard N	119	11.70	71-14 Honey Hook 119½ Little Jean Swaps 114⁵ Angie M. 114¹½	No threat 10
12Oct72-1JnD	gd 4f	:23 :48%	Md Sp Wt	9 10 7¹¹ 6¹³ 6¹³ Martinez J U	116	5.00	74-08 Greek Bay 116² Star Of Sunla 113⁴ Lea Joe 119²½	No mishap 10
29Sep72-3JnD	fst 4f	:23 :47%	Md Sp Wt	5 5 5⁷½ 3⁶ 3⁹ Martinez J G	116	6.20	70-10 Chester McDee 1106 Melrose Cat 116² Miss Bush Ahead 1161	Rallied 10

Edwards Country

Own.—Sider A
Tr.—Sider L

B. g. 3, by Relum S W—Anns Time, by Time Signal
$2,500

														St. 1st 2nd 3rd		Amt.

| | | | | | | | | | | | | 120 | | | | $555 |

15Jun73- 2Com	fst 4f	:23	:47⅖		Md 2500	7 4	6¹¹	3⁵	3⁸	Tanner D	b 120	*2.30				Evenly 8
19May73- 1Jnd	fst 6½f	:22	:47½	1:22	3 ♦ Md 5000	1 1	1hd	3¾½	6¹²	Young J F	b 112	8.70				No mishap 10
12May73- 7Jnd	fst 6½f	:23	:47⅕	1:20¾	⑤Clm 6000	2 6	7⁵	8¹²	8²¹	Keller E D	b 112	19.60				No speed 8
30Apr73- 5Jnd	fst 5f	:23	:47⅕	1:01	⑤Clm c-3500	3 4	2¹¾	6⁴½	8⁷½	Menard N	b 115	*1.20				Brief speed 8
19Apr73- 1Jnd	gd 4f	:22	:47⅕		3 ♦ Md 4000	3 4	3⁴½	2¹½	2nk	Domingue J⁵	b 107	*1.30				Bad start 10

LATEST WORKOUTS Jun 12 Com 3f fst :38⅗ h

Gomesa's Baby

Own.—Rhoton N L
Tr.—Clark R H (Va)

Ch. f. 3, by Laugh Aloud—Gomesa, by Nadir
$2,500

												115				Amt.

13Jun73- 5Com	fst 4f	:23⅖	:47⅖		3 ♦ Md 2000	6 6	7⁵½	4¹¹	5⁵¾	Mills B	110	30.00				Tired 8
2Jun73- 3Com	gd 6½f	:23⅕	:49	1:23⅕	Md 2500	5 5	2⅔	6⁸	6¹⁶	Montesano P	115	23.50				Early speed 6
26May73- 4Jnd	fst 4½f	:24	:49⅗	:55⅗	Md 2500	5 5	5⁵	6⁷¾	6⁶¾	Montesano P	115	9.70				No factor 6
5May73- 5Pen	fst 5f	:23⅗	1:02		Md 2500	8 6	11⁸	11¹⁷	11⁹¾	Sheppard D	118	19.90				No factor 11
1May73- 2Wat	fst 5½f	:23⅖	1:06⅖		3 ♦ Md Sp Wt	3 5	3⅔½	5⁵½	6⁶¾	Masters K	115	35.40				Fell back early 8
25Apr73- 1Shd	sly 3½f	:23¼			3 ♦ Md 2500	8 7	8⁷½	8⁵	9¹¹	Finnefrock B	115	5.40				No factor 10
6Apr73- 2Dov	fst 3½f	:23¾			3 ♦ Md 1500	5 2	2⅔	4⅔½	4⁴½	Whitemen P	109	4.55				Weakened 9
3Aug72- 3Poc	fst 5½f	:23⅗	1:07		Md Sp Wt	2 1	4²¾	4⁷	3¹⁰	Reynolds L	117	9.70				Fair try 6

LATEST WORKOUTS Apr 30 Wat 3f fst :38⅗ b

Lay Arms

Own.—Harris D
Tr.—Laffargue G J

B. f. 3, by Open Arms—Taylor, by Royal Clove
$2,500   Br.—Locke G E (Ark)

												105¹⁰				Amt.

| 15Jun73- 2Com | fst 4f | :23 | :47⅖ | | Md 2500 | 4 5 | 4³ | 4⁸ | 7²⁰ | Theall S | b 120 | 38.10 | | | | Tired 8 |
| 8Jun73- 9Com | fst 4½f | :23⅖ | :54⅖ | | Md 2500 | 7 5 | 6⁶½ | 7¹⁰ | 8¹⁹ | Theall S | b 120 | 30.20 | | | | No factor 10 |

LATEST WORKOUTS Jun 5 Com 2f fst :25 hg

Wembley Legend

Own.—Barnard C F
Tr.—Starkey J H

Ch. f. 3, by Jersey Legend—Miss Wembley, by Old Rockport
$2,500   Br.—Corkran Dr T R (Md)

												115				Amt.

| 8Jun73- 9Com | fst 4½f | :23⅖ | :54⅖ | | Md 2500 | 6 9 | 7⁸ | 5⁷ | 4⁵¾ | Heim K | b 115 | 13.80 | | | | Belated rally 10 |

LATEST WORKOUTS Jun 20 Com 3f fst :39 b   Jun 16 Com 5f fst 1:03⅗ b

---

Milk Bottle

Own.—Douglas J
Tr.—Cartimiglia L A (La)

B. g. 3, by Cyclotron—Mesmerizer, by Jet's Date
$2,500   Br.—Douglas J

												110¹⁰				Amt.

15Jun73- 2Com	fst 4f	:23	:47⅖		Md 2500	6 1	7¹²	8¹⁸	8³⁷	Baratinni D¹⁰	b 110	33.80				Far back 8
8Jun73- 9Com	fst 4½f	:23⅖	:54⅖		Md 2500	4 10	10¹⁵	10²¹	10²⁸	Dupre T	b 127	30.20				Trailed 10
23May73- 1Jnd	fst 4f	:23	:47⅕		3 ♦ ⑤Md 2500	1 9	9¹³	9¹⁵	9²³	Baratinni D⁵	b 107	37.60				Far back 9
5May73- 1Jnd	fst 6½f	:23¾	1:22⅕		3 ♦ Md 5000	9 9	9¹⁵	10²¹	— —	Derouen G	b 111	22.20				Outdistanced 10

LATEST WORKOUTS Jun 21 Com 3f fst :39⅗ b

(Edwards Country record)

	St.	1st	2nd	3rd
1973	5	M	1	0
1972	0	M	0	0

-- -- Makemeadeal 120⁵½ Swift Signal 115²½ Edwards Country 120⁴¼
51-15 I Can Dance 114hd Concentrate 107² ⑩Hurrican Harley 109½
62-18 Tracey Own 112² She's Tight 109½ Manchac Pass 112¾
84-14 Speedy P. D. 115¾ Spinella 110² Windburner 110¹
91-07 WitchOfBenevinto 107nk EdwardsCountry 107¾ Bib'sAngel 109¼½

(Gomesa's Baby record)

	St.	1st	2nd	3rd
1973	7	M	0	0
1972	3	M	0	1

-- -- Flag Flyer 120² Bullet Lady 115no Executrix 117²¾
-- -- Waygoer 120⁴¼ Elgin Kitty 115hd Hall's Hero 120⁵
-- -- Sweet Market 115² Hall's Hero 120hd Swift Signal 115nk
-- -- Rose Tal 115no Furiant 118¹ Help's Barry 113³
68-17 Dr. Jasper 122²¾ Jodi's Go Go 109⁶ Martin's Boy 116¹
74-14 Gin Money 114¹ Hy Way Joy 112⁵ Jeanie Kelly 109hd
84-09 Nautical Nymph 107²½ Eagle's Pilot 123²¼ Zozo Johnny 123no
83-11 Flaming Nail 113² Siempre's Melody 120⁵ Gomesa's Baby 117¹⁻³

(Lay Arms record)

	St.	1st	2nd	3rd
1973	2	M	0	0
1972	0	M	0	0

-- -- Makemeadeal 120⁵½ Swift Signal 115²½ Edwards Country 120⁴¼
-- -- Lonesome Sailor 120³ Bab's Flash 115¹¾ Makemeadeal 120¹

(Wembley Legend record)

	St.	1st	2nd	3rd
1973	1	M	0	0
1972	0	M	0	0

-- -- Lonesome Sailor 120³ Bab's Flash 115¹¾ Makemeadeal 120¹

May 30 Com 3f sly :39⅗ bg

(Milk Bottle record)

	St.	1st	2nd	3rd
1973	4	M	0	0
1972	0	M	0	0

-- -- Makemeadeal 120⁵½ Swift Signal 115²½ Edwards Country 120⁴¼
-- -- Lonesome Sailor 120³ Bab's Flash 115¹¾ Makemeadeal 120¹
65-11 Skeeter Jacobs 112²½ Steady Juror 107¹½ Spinella 112⁵
-- -- Miss Poker Chip 111¹½ I Can Dance 114¾ I'll Be OnTime 120¾

lengths — and Edwards Country looked like Wembley Legend's strongest opponent in today's race.

Wembley Legend was the best horse in the field. He would be helped by the No. 8 post position. Two of his chief rivals would probably be eliminated from contention by their inside post positions. Before the race I announced to my mother and our companions at Commodore Downs that Wembley Legend was a cinch. And she was. She ran away with the race, winning by five lengths and paying $9.40 to win. "Son, you may have chosen the right calling," my mother conceded as she headed toward the cashier's window.

If situations like the Wembley Legend race arose on a regular basis, I would have retired to a villa in Marrakesh long ago. But they don't. Whenever I am operating at a track with a powerful bias — say, speed on the rail — I can wait for days or weeks without finding a horse who has my top figure, early speed, and an inside post position. The gods who oversee horse racing do not intend that this game be too easy. But there is another application of track biases that does produce many winners, whose virtues are usually so subtle that they go off at excellent odds.

One of the most pronounced track biases I ever saw came at Bowie in mid-February, 1973. There had been several days of heavy rain in the Washington-Baltimore area. The Bowie racing strip was inundated, and because of its drainage system all the moisture seeped toward the rail. The rains were followed by a fast freeze, which trapped the moisture on the inside part of the track. The soil on the Bowie track is usually kept in a granular condition, but the water made these granules adhere to each other so that the inside part of the track was as hard as a superhighway. As a result, practically every winner was a horse that raced along this narrow path. There was a day when six of the nine races were captured by a horse breaking from post position one. Here are the *Racing Form* charts for the first three races at Bowie on one of the days during this extraordinary speed-on-the-rail period:

Official Racing Charts

Bowie Race Course

© Triangle Publications, Inc., 1973.

BOWIE, MD., SATURDAY, FEBRUARY 17, 1973—BOWIE RACE COURSE (1 mile)
Meeting scheduled for sixty days (January 2 to March 16). (Four dark days to be announced.)
...thern Maryland Agriculture Association. President, F. George Tucker. American Totalisator. United and ...ett Starting Gates. Teletimer, automatic timing. Film Patrol. Complete finish of each race confirmed by ...es Precision Photo Finish, Inc. Trackman, Dick Carroll.
Weather clear. Temperature 23 degrees.
Length of stretch from last turn to finish, 1,080.15 feet.

Steward representing Maryland State Racing Commission, J. Fred Colwill. Stewards, Merrall MacNeille ...d J. Melvin Mackin. Placing Judges, J. Heislen, F. G. Gabriel and Lawrence R. Lacey. Patrol Judges, ... Blind, P. O'Dell, P. Pitts, Jr. and T. J. Baker. Paddock Judge and Timer, E. T. McLean. Clerk of Scales, ... Young. Starter, Edward Blind. Identifier, J. W. Gogel Sr. Racing Secretary and Handicapper, Lawrence J. ...bundi. Assistant Racing Secretary, E. Litzenberger.

Racing starts at 1:00 p. m. Eastern Standard Time. Percentage of winning favorites corresponding meeting ...2, .29; current meeting, .35. Percentage of favorites in the money, .66. Daily Double wagering on first and ...cond races. Exacta, third, fifth, seventh and ninth races. No entries or field horses permitted in Daily ...uble or Exacta races. Mutuel take, 15 per cent (State, 5.34; track, 8.91; Improvement Fund, .50; Pension ...nd, .25).

The superior figure following the jockey's name indicates the number of pounds apprentice or rider allowance ...imed, s spurs, b blinkers. NOTE: All riders are equipped with whips unless otherwise designated in footnote ...low chart.

FIRST RACE
Bow
February 17, 1973

6 FURLONGS (chute). (1:08⅗). CLAIMING. Purse $3,500. 4-year-olds and upward. Weight, 122 lbs. Non-winners of two races since Jan. 6 allowed 3 lbs.; a race, 6 lbs.; a race since Dec. 30. 9 lbs. Claiming price, $3,000.
Value to winner $2,100; second, $770; third, $420; fourth, $210. Mutuel Pool, $64,392.

Last Raced		Horse	EqtAWt	PP	St	¼	½	Str	Fin	Jockeys	Owners	Odds to $1
-29-73²	Bow³	Brave Gem	4 113	1	8	1h	11½	13	1²	CCooke	R F Cicala	3.50
- 2-72¹	Lrl¹¹	Reaction	b6 113	10	2	8³	6³	5½	2¹	ORosado	C E McDonald	25.80
-31-73¹	Bow⁴	William de Great	b7 113	5	5	2h	4h	6⁴	3ⁿᵒ	JArellano	R E Dutrow	4.90
-12-72²	Bow¹¹	Apache Way	b6 113	8	1	3³	31	2h	4³	VBraccialeJr	Pacesetter Stable	4.80
-13-73¹	Bow²	Bard of Cornwall	b4 113	2	9	4½	2h	4h	5ⁿᵒ	ASBlack	R T Stokes	5.20
-10-73⁶	CT⁶	Right Risk	b6 113	11	4	6h	5½	3h	6¹	WJPassmore	D E Reckart	109.00
-30-72²	Bow¹	Bal K.	b5 119	6	6	5h	7	7²	7²	EWalsh	F D Vechery	3.10
-20-73¹	Bow⁸	Dawning Sun	b4 110	4	12	9h	9⁶	8⁷	8⁸	GMcCarron	C C Unglesbee	15.30
-30-73²	Bow⁹	War Parade	7 123	3	7	12	12	10⁴	9¹	TBarnes	J Costew	44.70
-20-73¹	Bow¹⁰	Brise de Mer	b6 113	9	11	7½	8½	9²	10³	JCanessa	Ida Geller	41.60
-27-73²	Bow¹²	Rated M.	4 113	12	3	11¹½	10¹	11h	11½	RStovall	W M Backer	101.50
- 6-73¹	Bow¹⁰	Mr. Judex	b10 113	7	10	10²	11h	12	12	DRWright	R E Vogelman Jr	16.90

Time, :23⅗, :45⅘, 1:11⅘. Track fast.

(cont'd on next page)

Official Program Numbers ↴

$2 Mutuel Prices:

1-BRAVE GEM	....	9.00	6.20	4.
10-REACTION	....		20.00	10.
5-WILLIAM DE GREAT	....			4.

Dk. b. or br. g, by Big Brave—Ginnygem, by Road House. Trainer, M. Angelastro. Bred by Hopki Smith (Md.).

IN GATE—1:00. OFF AT 1:00 EASTERN STANDARD TIME. Start good. Won driving.

BRAVE GEM had room inside to take the lead, then continued gamely through the stretch run to as the best. REACTION, never far back, rallied inside and between horses in the stretch and beat the in the late stages. WILLIAM DE GREAT vied for the early lead and, after being headed, kept going wil while saving ground. APACHE WAY, outside of horses, went gamely to the end. BARD OF CORNW hustled along early, began to weaken entering the final eighth. RIGHT RISKY, widest, hung after ge close to the lead. BAL K. could not keep a contending position after the midway mark. DAWNING went evenly. WAR PARADE and the rest were outrun.

Overweight—War Parade, 1 pound; Dawning Sun, 2.
Apache Way claimed by M. Miller, trainer H. E. Worcester III.
Scratched—Navy Coach, Bow Shannon, Gwanadier, Windward Passage, Kathy's Pet, Chariot Race.

SECOND RACE	1 ¹/₁₆ MILES. (1:41⅗). CLAIMING. Purse $4,000. 4-year-olds and upward. Weight,

Bow

February 17, 1973

lbs. Non-winners of two races since Jan. 6 allowed 3 lbs.; a race, 5 lbs.; a race Dec. 30, 8 lbs. Claiming price, $4,000; 1 lb. for each $250 to $3,500.
Value to winner $2,460; second, $880; third, $480; fourth, $240. Mutuel Pool, $102

Last Raced	Horse	EqtAWt	PP	St	¼	½	¾	Str	Fin	Jockeys	Owners	Odds
1-13-73² Bow⁴	Royal Choice	b4 114	1	2	1½	1h	1h	1¹	1¹¼	VBraccialeJr	A P Bovello	
2-10-73⁹ Bow⁶	Huapango	b8 117	6	11	6²	3¹	3³	3¹½	2nk	JKurtz	Margaret A Jacobs	
2-10-73⁹ Bow⁴	Better Bee Quick	5 114	7	10	8½	7½	4h	4⁴	3³½	CJimenez	Audley Farm Stable	
2- 3-73⁹ Bow⁶	Parenteral	4 114	12	12	12	11¹	8¹½	5²	4⅔	ASBlack	R Staszak	
2- 6-73³ Bow⁸	Mafufski	b4 114	2	4	2³	2³	2³	2¼	5³⅔	GMcCarron	C Unglesbee	
1-29-73⁹ Bow⁵	Flashmaster	5 113	9	4	9¹½	9²	9h	7²	6³½	CCooke	R Stephano	
2- 3-73² Bow⁸	Fields of Eton	b6 119	11	8	7¹	8²	7¹	6¹½	7½	EWalsh	E F Schoenborn	
2- 3-73⁹ Bow⁸	Colony Prince	4 114	10	9	10²	6²	6h	9⁴	8²⅓	BMFeliciano	Jean B Bradley	
2-12-73² Bow⁶	Dixie Doctor	4 114	5	5	5¼	4²	5²	8h	9¹	AAgnello	G Radford	
2- 5-73² Bow⁸	Super Amber	b4 114	8	7	11¹	12	11¹²11	10¹¼	10¹¼	AGomez	P Jacobson	
2- 5-73¹ Bow⁴	Adaptive	8 114	3	3	3h	5¹	10⁵	10²	11	JDavidson	C H Harding	
2-12-73⁵ Bow¹⁰	Star Bama	b5 113	4	6	4h	10¹	12	Eased.		WJPassmore	Helen Barabas	

Time, :25, :49⅕, 1:14, 1:40⅕, 1:46⅗. Track fast.

$2 Mutuel Prices:

1-ROYAL CHOICE	....	7.40	5.00	3.2
6-HUAPANGO	....		9.80	5.2
7-BETTER BEE QUICK	.....			4.4

Dk. b. or br. c, by Alternative—Heritage Cave, by Blue Heritage. Trainer, J. Tammaro. Bred by A Bovello (Md.).

IN GATE—1:28. OFF AT 1:28 EASTERN STANDARD TIME. Start good. Won driving.

ROYAL CHOICE raced inside, held MAF UFS KI off nicely to the last eighth, then was able to handle others with authority. HUAPANGO, well placed and never far back, tried hard but was no match for winner. BETTER BEE QUICK, smoothly ridden into a striking position, lacked a good rally thereafter continuing wide. PARENTERAL, without early speed, was able to get through inside in his rally. MAFUF had no excuse. FLASHMASTER went evenly. FIELDS OF ETON raced wide. COLONY PRINCE made his on the outside but faltered entering the stretch. DIXIE DOCTOR and ADAPTIVE could not keep pace. SU AMBER lacked speed. STAR BAMA was eased while being badly outrun.

Overweight—Star Bama, 1 pound.
Adaptive claimed by C. I. Frock, trainer C. I. Frock.
Claiming Prices (in order of finish)—$4000, 4000, 4000, 4000, 4000, 3750, 4000, 4000, 4000, 4000, 4000, 3
Scratched—Arctic Pole, Prince Joker, Drink Up, Mayhem, I Ching, Last Ripple.

Daily Double (1-1) Paid $42.60; Double Pool, $152,048.

THIRD RACE	1 ¹/₁₆ MILES. (1:41⅗). CLAIMING. Purse $5,000. 4-year-olds and upward. Weight,

Bow

February 17, 1973

lbs. Non-winners of two races at one mile or over since Jan. 6 allowed 3 lbs.; one race, 5 lbs.; such a race since Dec. 30, 8 lbs. Claiming price, $6,500; 1 lb. for each to $6,000. (Races where entered for $5,000 or less not considered.)
Value to winner $3,000; second, $1,100; third, $600; fourth, $300. Mutuel Pool, $83,201.

Last Raced	Horse	EqtAWt	PP	St	1/4	1/2	3/4	Str	Fin	Jockeys	Owners	Odds to $1
8-73⁴ Bow¹	T. Fred	b5 114	6	4	1³	1³	1²	1³	1³½	JDavidson	Row Farm	2.00
3-73⁵ Bow¹¹	Dasha Bitters	b5 113	4	11	10¹½	8¹½	3²	2ʰ	2⁴	GMcCarron	E A Roller	40.30
10-73⁷ Bow⁷	Seven Sails	5 114	1	2	5¹	5ʰ	2ʰ	3⁵	3²¼	AAgnello	L F Wilcox	50.70
8-73⁵ Bow⁸	Lord Luvus	b6 114	3	3	7²	11	9³	6³	4½	CJimenez	Starlight Farm	10.80
2-73⁵ Bow⁷	Plucky Star	4 110	7	7	9¹½	7ʰ	6½	4¹	5¹	BMFeliciano	M Martin	26.30
6-73³ Bow⁴	Shy Moment	6 115	5	6	11	9ʰ	7¹½	5¹	6⁵	RPlatts	J D Cochrane	6.00
22-73⁵ Bow³	Powder Peddler	5 114	8	10	8ʰ	6½	5²	7ʰ	7ʰ	GCusimano	N E Rinaldi	4.70
10-73⁶ Pen¹	Royal 'n Nimble	4 119	2	1	2ʰ	2½	4ʰ	8¹	8¹	AGomez	Double B Stable	10.40
6-73³ Bow²	Angle Right	b7 119	9	5	4¹½	3¹	8ʰ	9⁸	9⁹	RHoward	J J Kaminski	4.00
6-73³ Bow⁶	Wolf It Down	4 109	11	8	3ʰ	4²	10⁴	10½	10³	SNeff⁵	Audley Farm Stable	55.80
22-73⁷ Bow⁵	Doux Go	b4 114	10	9	6ʰ	10½	11	11	11	JKurtz	R Mascuilli	13.10

Time, :24⅖, :48⅗, 1:13⅕, 1:38⅗, 1:45⅖. Track fast.

$2 Mutuel Prices:
6-T. FRED	6.00	4.40	3.80
4-DASHA BITTERS		22.00	14.60
1-SEVEN SAILS			14.80

Dk. b. or br. h, by Rip 'n Skip—Spent Money, by Auditing. Trainer, R. E. Dutrow. Bred by R. J. Turcotte Y.).

IN GATE—2:01. OFF AT 2:01 EASTERN STANDARD TIME. Start good. Won handily.

T. FRED sprinted to a good lead early, made the pace on his own courage, stopped bid approaching the etch, then was in command again. DASHA BITTERS, unhurried early, was able to slip through inside once lying and, although no match for the winner, easily beat the rest. SEVEN SAILS saved ground, held well il inside the last eighth, then weakened. LORD LUVUS had a mild rally to pass beaten horses. PLUCKY AR went wide to pull within striking distance, then leveled off. SHY MOMENT lagged back half the e, moved on the outside thereafter, but could not get close. POWDER PEDDLER made a brief rally, n stopped. ROYAL 'N NIMBLE had no excuse. ANGLE RIGHT raced forwardly to the far turn, then gave y. WOLF IT DOWN and DOUX GO were outrun.

Overweight—Shy Moment, 1 pound; Plucky Star, 1.

Claiming Prices (in order of finish)—$6500, 6250, 6500, 6500, 6500, 6500, 6500, 6500, 6500, 6500, 6500.

Scratched—Swapping Doctor, Quill Pen, Sing Man Sing, Shining Royal, Chinihue, Scotch Broth.

Exacta (6-4) Paid $187.00; Exacta Pool, $119,285.

A serious handicapper should scrutinize the charts of each day's races at the track he follows, especially when a bias exists. Even if he had not been at Bowie on February 17, a reader of these charts would have been able to comprehend what the track was like. The first winner, Brave Gem, broke from post position one and, according to the footnotes, "had room inside to take the lead, continued gamely through the stretch to win as much the best." In the second race, Royal Choice broke from the inside post position and led all the way. In the third race, the first three finishers all raced on the inside. T. Fred opened an early three-length advantage and led all the way; although the footnotes do not specify it, we can assume he was on the rail. The second-place finisher, Dasha Bitters, "was able to slip through inside once rallying." The third horse, Seven Sails, "saved ground."

These charts, and the other ones for the same day, indicate clearly that horses who possessed early speed and could get to the rail had a tremendous advantage. When these horses run again, we must remember that their good performances on February 17 were more the result of the aberrant track condition than of their own ability. Even if a horse wins by a huge margin and earns a speed figure like Citation's, we should discount his performance. But the betting public doesn't do this. When Royal Choice ran a week later over a normal track, the Bowie patrons were impressed by his wire-to-wire victory and made him the 6-to-5 favorite. With no track bias to help him, he finished fifth. When T. Fred ran again, the bettors saw his 3½-length victory on February 17 and made him the 8-to-5 favorite. He was beaten. Brave Gem was a 5-to-1 shot in his next start and was trounced by 23 lengths. In my early experiences handicapping with speed figures, I lost a lot of money on horses like Brave Gem, T. Fred, and Royal Choice. I was hypnotized by the impressive times in which they had won, and was oblivious of the conditions under which they had earned their big figures. Now when I evaluate a horse who ran well with the track bias in his favor, I discount that performance almost completely and handicap the animal off his prior races on a normal track.

Just as horses that have benefited from the track bias should be viewed with skepticism when they run again, the chances of horses who were disadvantaged by the bias should be upgraded. We must watch races carefully, or at least study the charts meticulously, and make a list of horses that showed some sign of life but couldn't run their best race because of the bias. In the first three races on February 17, there were many horses that gave strong indications of being able to win over a normal track. Better Bee Quick was one of the favorites in the second race, going off at 9-to-2 odds. But he was a stretch runner breaking from the No. 7 post position; an observant handicapper at the track that day would have eliminated him without a moment's hesitation. But Better Bee Quick ran well under the circumstances and finished third. The footnotes say, "Better Bee Quick, smoothly ridden into a striking position, lacked a good rally thereafter while continuing wide." The reason he lacked a good rally was that he was running on the part of the track where no horses could accelerate. In his next start, over a normal racetrack, Better Bee Quick was entered against similar opposition and won by 3½ lengths, paying $7.40.

Angle Right had come into the third race on February 17 with two excellent efforts behind him and was second choice in the betting at 4 to 1. He showed early speed from the No. 9 post, but two horses from inner post positions outbroke Angle Right and prevented him from getting to the rail. After a half mile, Angle Right gave up. He retreated to finish ninth, 17 lengths behind the winner. A week later Angle Right was entered in a weak $6500 claiming race. He figured to be an easy winner if he ran his good race, but he went off at 7-to-2 odds because of that dismal 17-length defeat. Handicappers who knew that they could discount that loss because of the track bias collected a $9.80 payoff.

Of all the horses who raced during the speed-favoring period at Bowie, there was one who had by far the most intriguing dope. His name was Right Risk, and the chart of the first race on February 17 tells the whole story. Right Risk had been running at Charles Town, where his record had been atrocious. He was justifiably a 109-to-1 shot at Bowie. His already remote chances of winning were rendered nonexistent by his No. 11 post position. Right Risk was running sixth after a quarter mile, fifth after a half mile, third entering the stretch, and finally finished sixth by six lengths. The footnotes of the chart said, "Right Risk, widest, hung after getting close to the lead." It was easy to visualize what had happened. Right Risk was trying hard to win; he made a big move on the outside, the sort of move that usually wins races. But he was virtually running on a treadmill in the middle of the track and couldn't overcome the disadvantage. Almost all the horses who finished in front of him had either broken from favorable post positions or had made their moves along the rail.

When I spot a horse like Right Risk, who ran well against a track bias, I don't go wild with enthusiasm until I evaluate the time of the race. Maybe he got into contention only because his rivals were so slow. But the Teletimer indicated that Right Risk had been pitted against exceptionally good $3000 horses. His race was run in 1:11 ⅘. The only other six-furlong event that day was an allowance race that served as a prep for Bowie's biggest race of the year, the $100,000 John B. Campbell Handicap. The classy horses in that allowance race had run in 1:11 flat — a mere four-fifths of a second faster than the $3000 claiming race.

Right Risk was the sort of horse I have fantasies about but never encounter in real life. He had run a remarkable race, trying to overcome insurmountable obstacles in an exceptionally fast race. But the next time he ran, his past performances would suggest that he was a terrible horse who had finished an indifferent sixth in his most recent effort. I waited anxiously for his name to reappear in the Bowie entries.

Seven days later, Right Risk was entered in the first at Bowie. He had drawn the inside post position. His opposition was negligible. The *Racing Form*'s morning line listed him at 30 to 1. I went to the track that day with unshakable confidence that I was going to win a small fortune. I didn't. Right Risk had been scratched. I couldn't imagine why. Perhaps the horse had been hurt. Or perhaps the trainer was looking for an easier race. I didn't know where he could find one, though one remote possibility did cross my mind. Dover Downs, a little track in Delaware that was a two-hour drive from Bowie, offered a cheaper brand of racing than the Maryland tracks. Trainers based in Maryland, New Jersey, and Pennsylvania would often ship their horses to Dover on Saturday or Sunday in search of easy pickings. These superior out of town horses would almost always win. Steve Davidowitz had observed this phenomenon, and we had spent the two previous weekends at Dover betting almost exclusively on these horses, who had a clear class advantage over the locals.

Steve was out of town on the weekend that Right Risk had been scratched at Bowie, and I planned to forgo the long trip. But I did wake up early Sunday morning to check the Dover entries and see if Right Risk, or any other horses I recognized, was entered that afternoon. The information was not in the edition of the *Racing Form* that was delivered to my front door. The *Racing Form* had recently started publishing a Special Sunday Edition that was the only place to find Dover entries. It was sold at one newsstand on the other side of Washington. So I went back to bed. This, it turned out, may have been a $35,297 mistake.

The next day I glanced at the Dover Sunday results in an afternoon newspaper and the name leaped out of the page at me: Right Risk had won the eighth race and paid $13.10 to win. The race had been an extremely weak field of six $2500 claimers, the sort of spot where I could have bet Right Risk

5

Trainers

LUCIEN LAURIN AND ELLIOTT BURCH traveled very different paths before they became archrivals in the upper echelon of the training profession. The son of a laborer in a Quebec paper mill, Laurin quit school at the age of sixteen to become a jockey. When he became too heavy to ride anymore, he turned to training. He got his first modest bankroll with a mare he had bought for $30, and he managed to live from hand to mouth by campaigning a stable of a few cheap horses on the leaky-roof circuit. It was a long struggle before he moved up into the big leagues of racing and finally earned national fame as the trainer of Secretariat and Riva Ridge.

Burch was born to be a successful horseman. His father

and grandfather had both earned niches in the Racing Hall of Fame for their accomplishments as trainers. After attending Lawrenceville, Yale, and the University of Kentucky, Burch worked for eight years as his father's assistant and took over his job with the Brookmeade Stable when he retired. Two years later he trained Sword Dancer to win the Horse of the Year title. Since becoming the trainer for Paul Mellon's Rokeby Stable in 1966, he has developed two more Horses of the Year, Arts and Letters and Fort Marcy. While Laurin can be alternatively cocky, sullen, and combative, Burch is always cool, rational, and articulate, the perfect patrician.

The paths of the two men began to cross regularly in 1972, when Laurin was training Riva Ridge and Burch was handling Key to the Mint. Riva Ridge had won the Kentucky Derby and had seemed destined to win the three-year-old championship until he suffered a stunning defeat in the Preakness. Laurin was shaken. He lashed out at his jockey, Ron Turcotte, irrationally blaming him for the loss. Many second-guessers thought that Laurin was so rattled by the Preakness that he wasn't going to be able to train his horse properly for the Belmont Stakes, the final leg of the Triple Crown. Burch, who may have shared this view, honed Key to the Mint into razor-sharp condition for the Belmont, working him six furlongs in 1:10 three days before the race. But Laurin confounded all his critics when he sent out a perfectly prepared Riva Ridge to win the Belmont by seven lengths, while Key to the Mint struggled home fourth.

After the race, Burch did something that is rare for members of his profession. He did not blame his jockey for Key to the Mint's defeat; he blamed himself. The fast workout just before the Belmont had been a horrible mistake. For a grueling mile-and-a-half race, a trainer must try to build up a horse's stamina, not sharpen his speed.

Burch had learned his lesson when Key to the Mint met Riva Ridge again in the fall, in Belmont's mile-and-a-half Woodward Stakes, a race that would determine the three-year-old championship. During the month leading up to the Woodward, Burch prepared his horse with workouts that were designed to build up his stamina. He sent Key to the Mint a mile and an eighth in competition with two stable-mates that were running at him in shifts. He followed that with a rare mile-and-a-half workout four days later. While Burch was concentrating all his energies on this project, Laurin may have been distracted. He had been upset to find himself in the midst of a controversy when Riva Ridge's owner, Penny Tweedy, made a baseless public charge that her horse had been drugged before a midsummer defeat at Monmouth Park. And Laurin was also becoming increasingly preoccupied with another horse in his barn, a two-year-old named Secretariat. Whatever the reason, Riva Ridge ran dismally in the Woodward, and Key to the Mint ran away with the race and the three-year-old championship.

Burch's training of Key to the Mint for the Woodward had been a masterpiece, but the heavens did not reward him for his expertise the next year. Instead it was Laurin who was blessed to be training Secretariat, the first Triple Crown winner in twenty-five years and one of the great horses of all time. After his sweep of the three-year-old classics, Laurin decided to give Secretariat his first test against older horses in the Whitney Stakes at Saratoga. His strongest possible rival looked like Key to the Mint, who was in excellent form at the time. But Burch didn't enter his horse in the Whitney. He did not want to lose a big one to Lucien Laurin. He made a bad calculation, for this was one of the few times in his career that Secretariat was vulnerable. The superhorse had been running a fever at Saratoga and he hadn't been acting right in his workouts. But Laurin made an even worse calculation. He entered Secretariat in the Whitney despite his below-par condition and was the victim of a stunning upset by an unknown named Onion.

Having blown a golden opportunity to beat Secretariat, Burch got his chance six weeks later in the ballyhooed $250,000 Marlboro Cup. Secretariat had not raced since his Saratoga debacle, and Laurin was trying to bring his horse back from an illness to face the greatest challenge of his career. Burch didn't think that he could do it. He said publicly, the day before the race, that he didn't even consider Secretariat to be Key to the Mint's most formidable rival.

But Laurin had demonstrated many times before that he thrives on adversity. When his horse's prospects look bleak, when he is being subjected to intense scrutiny and criticism, he does his best work. He had done it before the Belmont in 1972 and he did it in the Marlboro Cup. Secretariat won and set a world record for a mile and one-eighth. Key to the Mint finished last, demonstrating perhaps that when a trainer is too obsessed by another man's horse he cannot properly train his own.

Laurin and Burch had as much to do with the outcome of the big races of 1972 and 1973 as the horses they were training. They are two of the most astute members of their profession, but they are also flesh and blood beings who can have lapses as well as strokes of brilliance, who can experience self-doubt, overconfidence, jealousy, and self-deception. Every horse, whether he is a champion or a lowly claimer, may be affected by similar human influences. Horseplayers who want to understand the game and beat the races must recognize the enormous importance of trainers. It is not enough merely to evaluate the ability of horses; we must evaluate the men behind them as well.

Before trying to deal with the nuances of different trainers' methods, a handicapper should first know which horsemen in his area are generally competent and which are not. Their overall records usually provide a reasonable guideline. A trainer who wins with 20 percent of the horses he sends onto the track has to have some virtues.

During the 1973–74 Maryland season, I compiled statistics on most of the trainers in the state and found that the best winning percentage belonged to a small-time operator whose name I didn't even recognize: George J. Burns. His two-horse stable had compiled a 5-for-6 record. Claiborne Reed, a filly, had won all four of her races. Burns had handled her gingerly, running her only in appropriate spots when she was in peak condition. The other half of his stable, a cheap claimer named Potestas, was 1-for-2. Not long after discovering Burns's remarkable rate of success, I encountered Potestas in a $4000 claiming race at Bowie. The horse looked like a standout, except for one thing: he had not raced for twenty-six days and had had no workouts since his last start. Normally I would be very hesitant about betting a horse whose record gave no indication of his current condition. If he were trained by a man with a 1-for-40 record, I would be doubly skeptical. But even though I knew nothing else about the man, I knew that George J. Burns would not have entered Potestas in this race unless he were ready. I bet with confidence, and Potestas paid $7.20.

If a trainer wins with 20 percent of his starters during the course of a year, that does not mean that he will win at the same rate every week and every month. Like other types of competitors, trainers have hot streaks and cold spells. Sometimes these streaks will be caused by factors completely extraneous to racing — ill health or marital troubles, for instance — but usually they will fall into patterns that a handicapper can analyze and even predict. When the 1972 Maryland racing season began at Laurel, two of the men who were expected to dominate the trainer standings were John Tammaro and King Leatherbury. Their individual talent and the quality of their stables were comparable. Leatherbury had brought his horses from Delaware Park, where he had enjoyed a sensational meeting, running his horses often and winning often. By the time he reached Laurel, many of his horses were tired. Their form was starting to deteriorate. The higher-class horses in his barn had won so much that they were no longer eligible for allowance races with restrictive conditions, such as "non-winners of three races since February 15." Tammaro had brought his stable from Atlantic City, where during the last few weeks of the meeting he had not won many races. He had been making a conscious effort to prepare for Laurel. He rested and recycled some of his campaigners who had already had a hard season and had begun to decline. He claimed fresh new horses who would help him in Maryland. During the first month of the Laurel meeting, Leatherbury suffered through a terrible slump. His horses all seemed to run worse than the past performances suggested they should. Tammaro was red hot. Even his horses who showed dismal form at Atlantic City were coming to life. A horseplayer must not only recognize which trainers are generally successful. He must know which ones are winning *now*.

Many of the qualities that make a winning trainer are invisible to the public. A successful horseman will work hard. He will hire competent people to work for him and oversee them carefully. He will know each of his horses as individuals and will be able to sense the day to day changes in their conditions. He will understand horses' physiology, so he can detect problems and ailments just as they are developing instead of after they have become critical. Most of the virtues that a trainer displays in his behind the scenes activities will ultimately be reflected in the past performances of his horses. A handicapper can easily recognize certain signs of a trainer's competence.

A good trainer knows how to prepare a horse to win a specific race. Any second-rate horseman can put an animal onto the track, run him until he gets into shape, and win a purse or two. But it takes expertise to aim for a certain objective and find the optimum way to prepare a horse for it. Burch did it in the 1972 Woodward Stakes when he concluded that the best way to approach the race was to train Key to the Mint with a series of long, stamina-building workouts. A trainer with an unraced two-year-old of moderate ability might give his horse a couple of races for exercise against maiden-special-weight company, then drop him into a maiden-claiming race and equip him with blinkers. A trainer might prepare a sluggish router for a winning effort by entering him first in a sprint race that will sharpen his speed. The possibilities are endless. But whenever a handicapper sees an intelligent plan underlying a horse's past performances, he can usually conclude that the trainer knows what he is doing.

A good trainer will not race his horse when the animal's form is beginning to deteriorate. "When horses run hard five or six times in a row they'll generally tail off," says Allen Jerkens. "If a horse is a good eater and then stops eating as much, or if his coat starts looking duller, that's the key that tells you he's about to go off form. We are all tempted to go to the well once too often, but if you run them when they're tailing off it's much tougher to bring them back."

A good trainer will seldom run his horses in races where they don't belong — against competition that is too tough or at a distance beyond their capabilities. George Getz, a young Chicago-based horseman, says he has learned this lesson many times. Before he became a trainer, Getz had been a hotshot bowler. He carried a 200 average, but he couldn't resist head to head money matches with rivals who could always hit 210. Getz blew his paycheck every week. Instead of seeking weaker opponents, he became discouraged and depressed. His average dropped, and he finally gave up the sport completely. Years later Getz would realize that horses respond the same way when they face competition that they cannot handle. In 1971 Getz had a three-year-old colt named Royal Leverage who he thought was going to develop into a nice allowance-class runner. His owner wanted to run in the Kentucky Derby, and Getz complied with his wishes. Royal Leverage was soundly trounced, of course, and when he returned to Chicago he seemed totally discouraged by that defeat. The horse lost all his enthusiasm for training. He developed a phobia about the starting gate and wouldn't break from the gate without considerable prodding. "He finally broke down at the eighth pole at Sportsman's Park," Getz said. "I guess they burned him in the incinerator.

"This is no theory. It is a fact. If you run a horse way over his head, where he doesn't belong, he'll get discouraged or lose interest. And when you drop him back to his proper level, he won't run. I think this is what makes a good trainer. We all take care of our horses. We all call up the vet when they get sick. The thing that distinguishes the good ones from the bad ones is that they take time with their horses."

When a horseplayer has a realistic sense of what training is about, he should study every horse's past performances with the trainer in mind. Has he managed the horse intelligently? Is he preparing him for a specific race? By asking and answering these questions, a handicapper will begin to learn which trainers are competent and which are not. And he will often uncover good bets when he understands the trainer's intentions with a particular horse. A handicapper who scrutinized the past performances of the filly Poker Night in the Bed of Roses Handicap at Aqueduct on April 18, 1973, would have learned, even if he had never heard of the man before, that Allen Jerkens is a great trainer, and he would have found an excellent wager.

:er Night ✻	**110**	Lt. b. f (1970), by Poker—Vault, by On Trust.									
		Breeder, C. E. Mather II. (Ky.).						1973	6 5 1 0	$43,330	
r, Hobeau Farm. Trainer, H. A. Jerkens.								1972	7 2 1 1	$10,140	
-737Aqu	1 1:35⅖ft	3e 108	35½ 11½	13	11½	W'dh'eR⁴	HcpS 90	ⒻP'k'rNight108	Number'dAc'nt Ferly	6	
-737Aqu	6 f 1:09⅖gd	7-5 112	43½ 33½	2²	2¹	W'dh'seR⁵	Alw 95	ⒻW'dy'sD'ht'r118	P'k'rN't H'l'yH'n'h	6	
-737Aqu	6 f 1:10½gd	2-3 ▲110	3¹ 11½	13	1½	W'dh'seR³	Alw 92	ⒻPokerNight110	Krislin LuckyPayd'y	6	
-735Aqu	7 f 1:22⅗ft	1 ▲113	5² 2ʰ	1ʰ	1²	W'dh'seR⁵	Alw 88	ⒻP'kerNight113	G'dedMissile Sumba	6	
-736Aqu	6 f 1:10⅘gd	2½ ▲118	3nk 1¹	15	14½	W'dh'eR⁹	27500 89	ⒻPokerNight118	TikiTie D'c'nMind'd	10	
-738Hia	7 f 1:27 sl	4½ 114	77¾ 45	3²	'11½	W'dh'seR¹⁰	Alw 72	ⒻPokerNight114	SelfDefense TikiTie	11	
-726Aqu	1 1:37⅕ft	2¹ 116	65½ 57½	33½	2³	W'dh'seR¹	Alw 78	ⒻTr'pic'lH't116	Pok'rN'ht F'milyPr's	9	
-726Aqu	6 f 1:12⅕ft	18 116	10¹⁰ 88½	9¹⁰	96¼	W'dh'seR²	Alw 76	ⒻH'rl'yH'n'h120	F'm'neT'ch Tr'p'lH't	11	
-723Aqu	6 f 1:13 gd	3½e 116	6¹¹ 55½	2¹½	1¹¾	W'dh'eR⁵	17000 78	ⒻPokerNight116	Biscay'sBaby L'mp	7	
-722Aqu	6½ f 1:19⅕ft	6½ 120	84½ 83¾	2¹	1²	T'tteR¹	M16000 82	ⒻPokerN'ht120	Prop's'l StiffComp't'n	13	
-722Aqu	6 f 1:14⅘ft	7½ 120	115¼109¼	7⁹	3⁵	W'h'eR⁴	M13000 64	ⒻM'sNewb'ry118	Cobul'sC't P'k'rN'ht	14	

Jerkens had handled Poker Night rather cautiously and unambitiously throughout most of her career. Even after the filly had won two claiming races in 1972 and an allowance race at Hialeah in early 1973, Jerkens did not view her as anything special. On March 6 he had entered her in a claiming race and had been willing to lose her for $27,500. Four days later she won an allowance race in very fast time, and Jerkens evidently concluded here that the filly was going to be more than a run-of-the-mill sprinter. He took her out of competition from March 10 to April 3 and gave her a pair of mile workouts during this period, presumably to prepare her for distance races. After running Poker Night in two more sprints he entered her in the Bed of Roses, a mile stakes race. Usually, if a horseplayer encounters an allowance-class sprinter in a route states race, he must conclude that the trainer is being overly ambitious and that he is probably guessing about his horse's capabilities. But Jerkens had already demonstrated that he was realistic about Poker Night; he had never entered her in a race where she didn't belong. He obviously felt that she belonged in stakes company now. Nor was he guessing when he entered Poker Night at a mile. Jerkens had tested her in workouts at the distance. If he had not liked what he had seen, he could have found a six-furlong stakes race for his filly. Jerkens had managed Poker Night intelligently through all her races; now he was preparing her specifically for the Bed of Roses Handicap. She was a very logical bet and, as the past performances indicate, Poker Night won by 1½ lengths at 3-to-1 odds.

Quality horses are usually handled with more finesse than cheap ones, but sometimes a trainer will display comparable expertise in his management of a low-grade animal.

Mr. Janin ✲   **114** Dk. b. or br. h (1967), by Restless Native—Valerie J., by Great Ci
Breeder, C. W. Hancock (Md.).   1974   3 1 0 2
Owner, R. R. Brooks. Trainer, R. W. Dillon.   1973   2 1 1 0

Mar23-74⁹Pim	1₁₆ 1:46⅖ft	6	112	63¾	1¹	1½	1ⁿᵏ	Alb'rtsB⁴	H5000	73	Mr. Janin112 Mendelson River Aboa
Mar 6-74²Bow	6 f 1:12⅗ft	25	115	10¹⁰10⁷¾	7¾	34¼	Alb'rtsB¹¹	5000	75	Sir.Jig119 Hail'sSong Mr.Jar
Jan 1-74¹⁰Lrl	1 1:42⅛m	10	116	44½	2ʰ	21½	34	AlbertsB³	8000	58	GhostTrain 120 DaintyDick Mr.Jar
Dec 7-73⁹Lrl	1 1:40 ft	8½	116	63¼	1ʰ	1¹	1¹	AlbertsB¹¹	4000	73	Mr. Janin 116 Big Vin Potest
Nov20-73²Lrl	6 f 1:12⅖ft	27	115	43	3³	44¾	21½	AlbertsB⁶	3000	86	BoldUmber117 Mr.Janin ChargeRig
Oct 3-72¹Lrl	6 f 1:14 ft	8½	106¼	53½	35	43	68½	Mart'zJA⁹	3000	71	Priam B. 113 It Do V D

March 17 Pim 1m gd 1:41⅖h   Feb 27 Pim 7f ft 1:33b

Trainer R. W. Dillon had won a race with Mr. Janin in the

winter of 1973, and he would not forget how he had done it. The gelding had been idle for more than a year but Dillon brought him back to the races in fairly sharp condition. He finished second in a $3000 claiming event at six furlongs, and that was all the preparation Mr. Janin needed. In his next start he stepped up in class and won at a mile.

Dillon rested Mr. Janin for another two months and then repeated this pattern. He worked the horse seven furlongs — evidence that he was aiming to win a distance race again. He entered Mr. Janin in a six-furlong race as a prep and the horse ran creditably, closing strongly to finish third. He worked the horse a mile in 1:41⅗ — excellent time for a cheap claimer. Now he entered Mr. Janin at a mile and one-sixteenth. A handicapper who had analyzed the horse's record closely would have observed that Dillon had handled this animal very patiently, had found the way to set him up for a winning effort, and was now repeating the pattern.

Mr. Janin paid $13.80.

Scrutiny of a horse's record will often disclose that a trainer does not know what he is doing.

rotiri		115	Dk. b. or br. c (1971), by Tambourine—Originality, by Laugh Aloud.
			Breeder, Orme Wilson, Jr. (Va.). 1974.. 9 M 0 1 $1,260

er, J. L. Parrish.   Trainer, S. T. Payne.

6-745Del	1-70 1:44⅕ft	11	115	118¼ 99¾ 77¾ 66¾	McCar'nG2	Mdn 68	MarketKing115 BrightLust Sagetown 12
6-748Del	⊤ 1¹⁄₁₆ 1:47⅖sf	83	110	98⅓13151222 91⁶	McC'nCJ8	AlwS 50	SilverFl'rin122 Gr'dBr'ker ClydeWil'm 13
1-74²Del	6 f 1:12⅘ft	9¾	106.*12¹⁸12²¹10¹⁸91³	G'rgeDD10	Mdn 68	Forb'y'sRuler116 JaySq'red BrightL't 12
2-748Del	⊤ 1 1:40⅘sf	35f	108	12²²121³ 89 67¼	AgnelloA2	AlwS 63	Sp't'gH'd'he120 M'l'aB'y ClydeWill'm 12
3-745Pim	⊤1¹⁄₁₆ 1:46 fm	20	114	10¹² 94¼ 55½ 34½†AngelloA2	14500 76	C'zinsJimAndy109 ClydeWil'm Akr'tiri 10
†Dead heat.							
3-743Pim	1¹⁄₁₆ 1:46⅖ft	58	112	10¹51²¹¹ 8¹⁴ 89	AgnelloA10	Mdn 64	LateLateShow112 LatinHumor Jetstat 12
4-745Pim	1¹⁄₁₆ 1:47 sy	4¾	120	91³ 712 71³ 8¹⁴	Hart'ckW9	Mdn 56	Illegal Pass 115 Micaster Flashy Tee 9
7-743Pim	6 f 1:14⅘ft	9¼	114*	91³ 99¼ 74¾ 45	M'tinR8	M15500 69	Gilboa120 C'ntOnClem SusieCuc'mb'r 9
9-743Pim	6 f 1:11⅗ft	22	113*	8⁹¾ 8¹¹ 51⁰ 41³	M'tinR7	M14500 75	Wide Berth 108 Gilboa S. S. Houston 9
July 8 Del 5f ft 1:02b							

Akrotiri had run dismally in all his races over the main track, when trainer Shirley Payne decided to experiment and enter him on the grass. Akrotiri finished third in a $14,000 claiming race against winners — and his effort was much better than it appears on the surface. The winner of the race, Cuzzins Jim Andy, came back to win twice in allowance company on the grass. The second-place finisher, Clyde William, captured an allowance race and then finished third in a stake on the grass. Two other horses in the field, who had finished behind Akrotiri, also won subsequently on the turf. Payne had discovered his horse's proper milieu: Akrotiri figured to beat just about any field of maidens on the turf. But Payne did not enter him in a maiden race. He ran him instead in a stakes race at Delaware Park, where he was totally overmatched but still ran creditably. Then he ran him at six furlongs on the dirt, a type of race that Akrotiri had already demonstrated he could not win. And Payne continued to go out of his way to lose with a horse who was in sharp condition and was ready to win in an appropriate spot. I don't need much further evidence about his capabilities. When I encounter a horse trained by Shirley Payne in the future, I am going to view it with a great deal of skepticism. If the horse is entered in a difficult-looking spot, I certainly will not assume (as I would with Jerkens) that he is there because the trainer knows what he is doing.

Of course, no trainer is perfectly good or completely bad. Even the most successful men in the business have areas of strengths and weaknesses. A trainer who wins 20 percent of his races overall may win only 10 percent of the time with two-year-olds and 30 percent of his starts in grass races. Many of the factors in handicapping that horseplayers tend to view in absolute, dogmatic terms are actually variables that depend largely on the trainer.

Should a horseplayer bet on first-time starters? If the trainer is Frank Whiteley, he may. If the trainer is Elliott Burch, he shouldn't.

Should a horseplayer bet a sprinter who is going a distance for the first time? If the trainer is Allen Jerkens, he may. If the trainer is Laz Barrera, he shouldn't.

Should a horseplayer bet a claiming horse who is dropping precipitously in class? If the trainer is Frank Martin, he may. If the trainer is Dick Dutrow, he shouldn't.

A horseplayer will slowly acquire a knowledge of different trainers' talents and shortcomings in the course of his day to day handicapping. But sometimes he will have to undertake a hard, rigorous study to understand a man's method of operation.

During the 1972 meeting at Saratoga Steve Davidowitz and I were astounded and confounded by the training of Allen Jerkens. He won nineteen races during the twenty-four-day meeting, a performance that would have been good anywhere but was especially brilliant at a track that offers the most intense competition among top-class trainers. As much as Steve and I respected Jerkens, we could never seem to bet him at the right time. When his horses seemed to figure best, they often lost. When they figured second- or third-best, they would win. Before our excursion to Saratoga in 1973 I vowed that we wouldn't be fooled by Jerkens any more. I took all the *Racing Forms* from the previous season and tried to analyze his performance carefully. I listed all his winners and beaten favorites on a large chart and wrote down, next to their names, the class in which they were running, the distance they were running and the distance of their previous race, the number of days since their last race, their recent workouts, their odds. On the next page is the record of Jerkens' winners.

The statistics disclosed that Jerkens won mostly in allowance races. He was adept with fillies and with grass horses. He didn't win a single race with a two-year-old. He won

Name	Class	Last Distance	Today's Distance	Days	Works	Odds
Wakefield Miss	Alw (fillies)	6f	6f	4	none	5–1
Bill Boland	Allowance	7f	6f	13	3f 34⅘	1–1
Blessing Angelica	Alw (fillies)	1¹⁄₁₆	7f	8	3f 34⅘	8–5
Never Confuse	Clm 40,000	1¹⁄₁₆	6f	6	3f 36	7–2
Red Orange	Mdn 14,000	6f	7f	53	7f 1:27⅖	9–5
Blooper	Clm 35,000	6f	6f	65	3f 35⅕	7–1
Wakefield Miss	Alw (fillies)	6f	6½f	8	none	3–2
Lucky Pants	Allowance	6½f	7f	12	6f 1:12⅗	7–1
Onion	Allowance	1m	7f	15	5f 1:02⅖	3–1
Beaukins	Allowance (turf)	1m	1⅛	15	5f 59	5–2
Bill Boland	Allowance (turf)	6½f	1¹⁄₁₆	5	none	9–2
Wakefield Miss	Alw (fillies)	6½f	1⅛	8	none	3–1
Garland of Roses	Maiden (turf)	6½f	1⅛	6	none	7–1
Whale	Allowance	7f	6f	6	4f 50⅗	5–2
Blessing Angelica	Stake (fillies)	1¼	1⅛	8	3f 35⅗	4–5
Onion	Allowance	7f	7f	10	6f 1:12⅘	2–1
Blooper	Clm 25,000	6f	6f	4	none	7–2
Tunex	Allowance	7f	1⅛	9	5f 57⅗	3–5
Red Orange	Allowance (turf)	1¹⁄₁₆	1¹⁄₁₆	7	none	3–1

often with horses stretching out to a longer distance, and also won with horses going at a shorter distance. He won at all kinds of odds. But there was one pattern that fit eighteen out of his nineteen winners. Jerkens' winners either had raced within the last eight days, or else showed a recent workout so fast that it left no doubt about their current condition. Wakefield Miss, his first winner of the 1972 meeting, was coming back four days after her most recent start. Bill Boland had been away thirteen days but had worked three furlongs in a sizzling 34⅘ seconds since his last race. Blessing Angelica was coming back after eight days. And so on.

In 1973 at Saratoga Jerkens was the leading trainer of the meeting again and almost all his winners fit the pattern. But there was one glaring exception. His sprinter Onion had been laid off for more than two months, showed a succession of indifferent workouts — a half mile in 53 seconds, three furlongs in :38⅗, a mile in 1:47 — but won big, setting a track record. A few days after his victory I was interviewing Jerkens for a newspaper story and couldn't resist trying to learn why Onion had contradicted his pattern.

"I did a lot of homework on your training methods and thought I found a pattern that was pretty reliable," I said, "but Onion didn't fit it."

"I don't have any pattern," Jerkens answered, explaining that every horse is an individual, and a good horseman has to treat him as an individual instead of operating with some preconceived formula.

"I guess you're right," I conceded. "According to my research, Onion should have had a very fast workout before he ran."

Jerkens said, "He did. Two days before the race, on Sunday, he worked a half mile in forty-six flat on the training track. The clockers missed it."

Trainers may have patterns that they don't even recognize themselves. A horseplayer who learns their methods will have knowledge more valuable than any inside information he could receive from a stable. Trainers' opinions about their horses are usually very subjective and often wrong. But a handicapper can possess objective evidence that will tell him when a trainer is likely to be right or wrong.

Nowhere is an understanding of trainers' methods more important than in Maryland. During the 1973–74 season there was widespread suspicion that some trainers were using drugs illegally and indiscriminately on their horses, and that racing officials either weren't testing for these sophisticated medications or weren't enforcing the rules. As a result, the time-honored principles of handicapping seemed almost irrelevant.

Harvey Pack, a horseplayer friend of mine from New York, visited Bowie one Saturday and stopped by the press box to get a few pointers. "Is speed holding up here?" he asked. "Is the rail fast?" The Maryland regulars chuckled at his naiveté. At Bowie, we explained, we don't handicap horses. We look for horses trained by Dick Dutrow, King Leatherbury, John Tammaro, and Raymond Lawrence, Jr., and try to guess which ones will be waking up today.

In the second race Dutrow had entered a horse whom he had recently claimed. Redeem Battle had tired in the stretch of every one of his races, and had lost to $9500 rivals in his last start. Now he was facing $12,000 opposition. Harvey protested that no rational handicapper could bet this horse, but Redeem Battle closed strongly for the first time in his life and won at 5-to-2 odds.

Lawrence had a horse in the third race whom he had claimed nine days before. Flint Castle had been soundly beaten for $12,000 and now was stepping up to $17,000. "This one's impossible," Harvey said. "He'd have to improve seven or eight lengths to win here."

When Flint Castle won at 16 to 1, Harvey put his *Racing Form* aside. "Hey, it's Leatherbury's turn now," he said. "Does he have any horses in the next race?" Harvey had learned how to handicap, Maryland style.

Even though I understood the importance of trainers, I

was maddened and frustrated by what was happening in Maryland. Races were not being won by horses that had been trained in any definable, analyzable way. They were being won by horses who were improving overnight by five or ten lengths, mysteriously and unpredictably. It seemed that a rational sport had been turned into a guessing game. Without much hope of succeeding, I undertook detailed studies of all the leading trainers' records over a period of several months, trying to learn if there was any way to predict their horses' sudden form reversals. I found that even under these difficult conditions I could discover the hole card of most trainers.

Lawrence had unbelievable success winning with horses in their first start after he had claimed them or purchased them privately. He won with 50 percent of his new acquisitions, often under the most improbable circumstances. Bobpat had lost four races in a row by 20 lengths or more when Lawrence bought him. He promptly won at odds of 40 to 1, raising suspicions that his trainer may have been giving him something stronger than carrots. Whatever the reason for Lawrence's success, a handicapper could profit by betting automatically and blindly on the horses he had just claimed.

J. J. Lenzini had an uncanny ability to win distance races with faint-hearted sprinters. He would take a horse who had been tiring repeatedly at six furlongs and enter him at a mile and one-sixteenth, where the usual principles of handicapping would suggest that he had no chance. But these horses would win for Lenzini, and they made excellent bets at good prices.

The most remarkable pattern, perhaps the most reliable trainer pattern I have ever seen, belonged to King Leatherbury. It was not easy to detect because it had four components. Leatherbury would lay off a horse and drop him in class. The horse would show no workouts that would suggest he was in condition, but he would receive strong betting action and he would win. Leatherbury trained a filly named Moore Sassy who was a solid $7500 animal when she was in form. But she began to run poorly, descending the class ladder to $5000, where she was still unable to win. Leatherbury rested her for a month, corrected her problems, and entered her for $4000. Running a $7500 animal in a $4000 race is like shooting fish in a barrel, but most horseplayers could not deduce that she was ready on the basis of one nondescript three-furlong workout. Somebody knew, however. Moore Sassy was 8 to 1 in the morning line and was bet down to 5 to 2. She won impressively. The Leatherbury horses with a similar pattern win about 50 or 60 percent of the time. A horseplayer who recognizes them can bet them blindly.

As I wrote in an earlier chapter, I don't like to bet horses exclusively on the basis of a trainer's intentions and judgment. But, realistically, I know that the best horses I can select with my own handicapping are not going to win much more than 50 percent of the time. If I know that a trainer wins that often with horses who conform to a particular pattern, I will wager on them regardless of what I consider to be their handicapping merits and demerits. The ego gratification for a horseplayer may not be so great when he bets on the basis of a trainer's judgment rather than his own, but the money is just as green.

6

The Horses' Appearance

ON THE DAY BEFORE the Gulfstream Park Handicap in 1965, the track management staged a press breakfast at which newspapermen could direct questions to the trainers of horses in the race. As is customary at such affairs, the writers asked innocuous questions and the trainers responded with innocuous answers. They did, at least, until Clem Florio of the Miami *News* rose to interrogate Eddie Neloy, who trained Gun Bow, the fastest horse in America and the odds-on favorite for the Gulfstream race.

"Mr. Neloy," he asked, "what's wrong with Gun Bow?"

The room suddenly fell silent; then Neloy smiled and said, "Don't scare me like that. As far as I know, he's all right."

"When he worked six furlongs the other day," Clem said,

"he went all right for half a mile and then he started to waddle."

Clem had watched the workout, and as Gun Bow came through the stretch he thought he noticed that, instead of reaching forward with both his legs, the horse was reaching off slightly to the side with his right leg — a sign that something might be ailing him.

The other journalists in the room started hissing, booing, and yelling, "Sit down!" but Clem persisted: "You've always said that Gun Bow has beautiful action. Can you explain what that waddling is?"

"I never noticed that he did it," Neloy said. "I think I should know my own horse."

The next afternoon Clem watched intently through his binoculars as the horses came onto the track for the $100,000 race. Gun Bow looked good in the post parade; he wasn't sweating and he was striding smoothly. But as he warmed up Clem noticed that his head was turned down and sideways — another sure sign, he thought, that something was bothering the champion. He also observed that a long-shot named Ampose looked extraordinarily fit and energetic on the track. Clem bet Ampose and saw his judgment fully confirmed as Ampose rallied to win and pay $33.40, while Gun Bow struggled to finish third.

To the vast majority of horseplayers at the track, the outcome of the Gulfstream Park Handicap defied explanation. No handicapper could have studied the *Racing Form* and logically concluded that Ampose was going to defeat Gun Bow. But horse races are not run on paper. They are run by flesh and blood creatures who are susceptible to hundreds of ailments. There is probably no horseplayer in America who can match Clem Florio's astuteness at judging a horse's appearance. I have watched him for several years in the Maryland press boxes, where he now works as a handicapper for the Baltimore *News-American*, and I know that he is almost unfailingly right when he says a horse is sore or lame, when he says a horse is developing a physical problem that will bother him one or two races hence, when he says that a horse has been hopped up.

Clem's background prepared him uniquely to deal with the appearance and condition of racehorses. A former professional boxer, known somewhat hyperbolically as "the Ozone Park Assassin," he had a first-hand knowledge of physical conditioning. As a groom for the legendary trainer Sunny Jim Fitzsimmons, he acquired an understanding of horses and their ailments. As a serious handicapper, he could intelligently relate this understanding to horses' performances.

Clem grew up in the Ozone Park section of New York, just a few blocks from Aqueduct Race Track, where betting the horses was a way of life. Clem worked at Aqueduct during the summer when he was ten, learned the principles of handicapping from older men who hung out in the neighborhood coffee shops, and started betting with a bookmaker on 100th Street when he was thirteen. He quickly began thinking like all the other horseplayers in his neighborhood: When a horse figured to win but didn't, he would blame the defeat on the jockey, concluding that the thieving little rat had lost intentionally.

After Clem began attending the track regularly he sensed that there might be another way to explain the losses of horses who had figured to win. He noticed many times that a horse would look good on the track and win, then come back the next week, looking terrible, and lose. He couldn't understand why the condition of a horse would change so frequently, but he had observed a similar phenomenon in his own training as a fighter. He would often do his roadwork over the Aqueduct track. One day he might breeze through a mile in six minutes; the next day he would struggle to the finish line in seven minutes.

Clem finally began to comprehend the reasons for the changing condition of equine athletes when he went to work for Fitzsimmons. He saw that the strain of racing took a physical toll on horses — especially in their ankles and knees. When a horse's ankle started to swell, his performance on the track would deteriorate. Not only was the horse hurting, but his ailment had prevented him from being trained properly for his races. Clem noticed that horses with physical problems behaved in ways that were perceptibly different from the manner in which healthy horses acted. They showed many of the same characteristics that Clem, as a bettor, had already noticed were signs of a horse about to run a poor race.

When he learned to judge all aspects of a horse's appearance and to relate this appearance to the *Racing Form*, Clem found that he could understand the game and explain many of its apparent contradictions as he had never been able to do before. One spring when he was injured and out of work, he took a $46 compensation check to the track and launched a winning streak that lasted the entire year. Every day he would study the *Racing Form* in depth before he went to the track. Before each race he would go to the paddock, observe the horses, and make preliminary notes on his program. Then he would dash to the grandstand, where he could get a topside view of the animals as they warmed up and approached the starting gate. He would dash to the windows to make his bet, dash back to his seat and watch the race, looking for horses who got into trouble. One day toward the end of the season Clem's brother came to the track and watched him go through this grueling routine. He saw Clem peering through his binoculars at the horses, saying, "Come on, you son of a bitch, warm up . . . That's right . . . Now let me see what you're going to do . . . Now turn around so I can get a good look at you." Sensing that it was not altogether healthy for a grown man to be talking to animals, Clem's brother grabbed his arm, told him, "The referee is stopping this contest," and dragged him home.

Observing and judging the appearance of horses is perhaps the most demanding facet of handicapping. And, for me at least, it is the most difficult to learn and master. I don't have the knowledge or the instincts to sense when a horse is feeling good. I can barely distinguish a Secretariat from a battle-scarred $1500 claimer. To teach this backward pupil, Clem tried to break down the different components of a horse's appearance that he observes before a race.

Overall Appearance: "You look for a quiet horse — quiet, but with a controlled energy. If he has a stable pony with him, as most horses do, he looks like he wants to outrun the pony. He might try to thrust his head in front of the pony or over the pony's neck. You can tell there's power there. But when a horse is fractious — champing at the bit, tossing his head from side to side, stamping his feet — he's too nervous, and he's dissipating his energy before the race."

Wetness: "On a cold day, it's very negative when you see a horse wet, lathered up around the neck, loins, in behind his tail. He definitely won't run his best race. This isn't so important on a hot day, when you could expect anybody to sweat."

Fluidity of Motion: "When I ran and got tired my legs would get stiff; later I came to realize the explanation — that oxygen is not feeding into the muscles properly. When a horse is stiff-legged in a warm-up, if he's not striding out properly, if his movements are choppy, there's something wrong. What you look for is a fluidness of movement. You look for a horse's ankles and knees to curl — bend, if you will — the way a weight lifter's arms and legs curl when he lifts a weight."

Feet: "You want a horse who puts his feet down squarely, grabs the ground, and takes a full stride. When they pick their feet up real fast, with a short jerky motion, it's a sign something in the foot is stinging them."

Ears: "One of the worst signs a horse can show is when he has his ears pinned back as he's going to the post. Forget about him. When he gets to a point in a race where he puts a little pressure on himself, he'll stop. When a horse is feeling good he'll usually have his ears pricked, like he's trying to hear something. And when a horse has been drugged, you can usually tell it by the rigidity of the ears. He looks like a bird dog who's pointing when he's got a bird spotted. The ears won't flop, won't wiggle."

Tail: "A horse who swishes his tail going to the post, with a straight up-and-down swish, is telling you that he's feeling good."

Head: "You want a horse to go to the post with his head straight. When he turns his head to the side and down, and it stays that way, something's wrong. He's hurting. This is infallible."

Bandages: "I don't put too much emphasis on bandages, but if a horse has bandages on his front legs for the first time, it's probably negative. There's probably something wrong with his tendons."

Seeing the Gate: "When a horse gets to the starting gate a couple minutes before post time, you can see if he's willing. If he kind of challenges the gate, charges it, that's a real good sign — especially with older horses who have already shown you they're feeling good. This is one of the best indications I've ever seen that a horse is going to run well."

The Jiggle: "This is something that has to be seen. It's a very special look that you see maybe once or twice a year when a horse is going to the post. You get the feeling that if you got next to the horse you'd almost hear him screaming to run. The horse will give constant short starts; he's not fractious, but it's almost as if he's saying, 'Please turn me loose.'"

A handicapper may occasionally cash bets on the basis of appearance alone, but he should learn to relate this factor to the horse's form. It is not a good policy to bet on a slow chronic loser just because he looks healthy. Appearance is most important when it represents a change from the way a horse usually looks. When a horse habitually looks good — like Gun Bow — and one day comes onto the track displaying negative signs, he can be eliminated. Or at least his chances can be greatly downgraded. When a horse who usually looks bad comes onto the track exuding energy, it is one of the best betting situations in racing.

One of the most gifted horses of the sixties was the Wheatley Stable's Reviewer, a colt whose talent was matched by his physical problems. Reviewer always looked terrible in the post parade. He would be drenched in sweat and would be taking choppy strides. Because of his various ailments he could never be trained properly. Yet he consistently managed to run first or second against the best horses in the country.

Clem saw Reviewer win a race at Belmont Park one day and noticed that the colt looked slightly better than usual. A week later, he read in the *Racing Form* that Reviewer had worked a mile in 1:36 — a time that would be brilliant for any horse and was unbelievable for one that had never been able to withstand rigorous training. When Reviewer was entered in the Nassau County Handicap, Clem went to Belmont to see if the horse's seemingly improved condition was reflected in his appearance. He could barely believe what he saw. The horse was so full of energy that the jockey had trouble restraining him on the way to the post. This was a classic betting opportunity, and Clem took advantage of it. Reviewer not only won easily, but he also covered a mile and an eighth in a breathtaking 1:46⅖, shattering Belmont's track record.

Looking at horses on the track before a race is only one of the ways in which a handicapper's visual skills can help him. An observant student of the game will learn to watch the running of races — to follow all the horses in the field instead of just the one he has bet on — and try to spot horses that encounter bad racing luck. One September day Clem called me and told me to come to Timonium, where he had "an absolute cinch." When I arrived at the track and looked at the past performances of the cinch, I thought I had wasted a trip. Boogaloo Dancer was 0-for-15 for the year; in his last start, against similar opposition, he had rallied to finish an indifferent third. Clem explained that the horse had broken last, started to make a move, was blocked and knocked back to last again. He tried to make another move, and was knocked back again. He finally circled the field and finished third. Yet the *Racing Form* charts didn't mention a word about any trouble in the race. The chart-makers are only human and therefore fallible. Boogaloo Dancer came back to win by six lengths at 6-to-1 odds.

Sometimes a horseplayer with a keen eye will see and profit from things that he isn't even looking for. One day at Laurel Clem was watching the post parade before a cheap claiming race and exclaimed, "Hey! He just hit that horse with a joint!" — meaning a battery, an electrical device used to stimulate a horse illegally. Clem had seen a jockey jab a horse with the base of his whip, where batteries are often concealed, and the horse responded with a sudden lunge forward. I suggested to Clem that maybe he was a bit punchy after eighty-five middleweight fights. The horse won and paid $91.

Clem's visual perceptiveness paid off in another way during a summer when he was working as a clocker in Chicago. He would arrive at Arlington Park each morning at dawn, cut across the infield, and take his position to time the horses' workouts. One morning he was walking across the track and observed a fresh set of hoofprints in the dirt. Clem was intrigued, for trainers do not work their horses under the cloak of darkness unless they have larceny in their hearts.

Clem began reporting to the track before sunrise, waiting for a reappearance of the night rider. Five days after his initial discovery he was shivering in the early morning cold when he heard a sound that sent further chills down his back. The sound went clip-clop, clip-clop, and Clem saw a dark bay horse with a small patch of white at his heel running around the track — fast. He had never seen the horse before, so he stealthily followed him to the stable area and watched him being led to the barn of a trainer named Jones. Clem raced back to his files and looked up all of Jones's horses that had raced at the meeting. None of them was a dark bay with a patch of white over the heel.

A couple of weeks later Clem saw that Jones had entered a horse named John's Bouquet, who hadn't raced for two years, in the sixth at Arlington. He went to the paddock before the race and there was the mystery horse. John's

Bouquet looked fit and energetic, and Clem bet with enthusiasm. The horse ran like a thief in the night and won at 7 to 1.

"The next day," Clem recalled, "I had to go to the bank. I walk in and who's there but Jones. He's got a big manila envelope under his arm. It's sort of rounded and bulging. I went up to him and said, 'Hi, what you got there?' He said, 'Oh, just some papers.' We had a laugh, and then he disappeared into the vault."

7

Speed Handicapping: I

AMONG SERIOUS HANDICAPPERS there are two major schools of philosophy. In one intellectual camp are the empiricists, who view every race as a unique problem to be solved by intuition and analysis. They evaluate horses' records by weighing many factors and subtleties, and reject the notion that a horse's ability can be measured in any precise, concrete way. In the other camp are the rationalists, the speed handicappers, who believe that a horse can be measured by how fast he runs. Speed handicappers perform various arcane calculations to translate a horse's ability into a number. If an animal earns a figure of 99, he is superior to a rival who earns a 92. His age, sex, class, breeding, and even his name is irrelevant.

No area of handicapping inspires more passion or controversy. The advocates of speed figures share the view of Pat Lynch, an astute New York handicapper, who says, "Time is the one absolute truth in the game." The critics — who include the writers of most books on betting the races — view speed handicappers as madmen looking for certainty and easy answers in a game in which they don't exist. Author Tom Ainslie approvingly quotes a horseplayer who says, "Very few speed handicappers are lolling in loot. In fact, one of them we know is rarely let out of the attic, and steadfastly maintains he is Martin Van Buren."

For most of my career as a horseplayer, I shared this skepticism. But when I finally became acquainted with a few bettors who believed in speed handicapping, I was infected by their messianic fervor. I started making my own figures. I proceeded gingerly at first, with the caution of a bather dipping one toe in a cold lake. But soon I was completely immersed. Discovering figures was one of the momentous events of my life.

I became more enraptured by the technical process of computing figures than I was by the sport of racing itself. I relied on them religiously, disregarding almost everything else I knew about handicapping, and managed to win modestly. When I finally learned to put the figures in proper perspective and used them in conjunction with the other important principles of handicapping, I became confident, for the first time in my life, of my ability to win consistently at the track.

Speed figures clarified mysteries, subtleties, and apparent contradictions of the sport that I had always thought were beyond human understanding. I realized that all other handicapping tools, even the most sophisticated ones, fail to attack what should be the central question in any race: Who is better than whom? A horse may be perfectly prepared for a race by an outstanding trainer, but if he is inherently ten lengths inferior to his opposition, that preparation probably won't help him win. A horse may have a powerful track bias in his favor, but if he is a much slower animal than his rivals, the bias may not make him win. To handicap a race intelligently a horseplayer must know, above all else, which horse has superior ability. Time is the one way to measure this ability with precision. It is by far the most important factor in handicapping.

The most difficult part of speed handicapping is making the initial commitment to learn it. The virtues of other aspects of handicapping that have been discussed in this book — such as trainers' methods and track biases — are self-evident. A serious horseplayer should be able to perceive readily that these are subjects worthy of study and mastery. But an uninitiated horseplayer cannot know if speed handicapping is useful until he tries it. He will suspect that a lengthy study of speed figures may only lead him up a blind alley. When he confronts the inevitable initial difficulties and confusion, when he takes a look at all the charts and technical material on the ensuing pages, he will undoubtedly wonder if it is worth the effort.

So the reader must accept this on faith for the time being: Speed figures are the way, the truth, and the light. And my method of speed handicapping is, I believe, without equal. If a man truly wants to learn how to beat the races, the answer is contained in these next three chapters.

Speed handicapping would not be at all complex if horse races were conducted on artificial surfaces that never changed from day to day. Any bettor could look at horses' final times and correctly conclude that an animal who runs six furlongs in 1:11 is superior to one who runs the distance in 1:12. But the conditions of racetracks change constantly. Rain may make them deeper and slower. Sunny, windy weather may dry them out and make them faster. The movement of the tides may affect tracks located near an ocean, like Suffolk Downs and Gulfstream Park. Track superintendents may, at their whim, add or remove soil to make a racing surface slower or faster. So a horse who runs six furlongs in 1:11 one day may very well run in 1:13 the next. Times cannot be taken at face value.

To gauge the condition of a racetrack, a horseplayer could probably take daily samples of the soil and have them analyzed by a professional agronomist. But a more practical way to judge the speed of a track on a given day is to look at the times of the races that were run over it. If a $5000 claiming race was run in 1:15, and a stakes race was run in 1:12, the track was relatively slow. If $5000 claimers ran in 1:12 and stakes horses in 1:09, the track was obviously very fast.

To judge any horse's time, a speed handicapper views it in the context of the times that other horses ran on the same day. By doing this, even a novice could have found a superb bet in the sixth race at Bowie on January 19, 1973, a $13,000 claiming race in which there were only two strong contenders.

Prez's Son had run on January 8 in a $13,000 claiming race, finishing second by four lengths. The winner's time was 1:10 for six furlongs. According to the rule of thumb that says one length equals one-fifth of a second, then Prez's Son's time was 1:10⅘.

Sandlot had last run in a $10,000 claiming race on January 5, losing by a neck. His time was 1:12. At first glance, Prez's Son appeared to be 1⅕ seconds faster than Sandlot, but an analysis of the tracks over which they had run previously told a different story.

These were the times of the six-furlong races on January 8, the day Prez's Son ran:

$3000 claiming race for three-year-olds	1:11⅕
$7500 maiden-claiming race	1:12
Allowance race for three-year-olds	1:10
Low-grade allowance race	1:10⅗

Prez's Son had obviously raced over a lightning-fast track. His time of 1:10⅗ was not spectacular, considering that it was only one second faster than the time of a race for rock-bottom three-year-old claiming horses.

These were the six-furlong times on January 5, when Sandlot ran:

$5000 maiden-claiming race	1:16⅕
$3000 claiming race for three-year-olds	1:15⅗
$5000 maiden-claiming race	1:15⅗
Maiden-special-weight race	1:14
$16,000 claiming race	1:12⅗

This track was extremely slow. A $3000 claiming race for three-year-olds was run in 1:15⅗ — nearly four seconds slower than horses of the same class had run on January 8. Sandlot's race was by far the best of the day. Although he was running for a $10,000 claiming price, he had run three-fifths of a second faster than the winner of a $16,000 claiming race.

The majority of the fans at Bowie were impressed by the apparently fast time of Prez's Son and made him the 6-to-5 favorite. But speed handicappers, who evaluate horses' times by considering the track over which they ran, knew that Sandlot was the superior horse. They collected a $5.80 payoff after he beat Prez's Son by four lengths.

Horses like Sandlot are, unfortunately, all too rare. In most cases, a cursory examination of previous days' result charts will not disclose the winner of a race. It is not enough for a handicapper to know merely that certain days were very fast, others were very slow, and others were roughly average. He must be able to measure the condition of a racetrack with some precision. If a track was two-fifths of a second faster one day than the next, a speed handicapper has to know it.

A numerical measurement of the speed of a racing surface is called a track variant. The *Daily Racing Form*'s past performances include a variant for each of a horse's previous races. It is calculated by averaging the difference between the time of each winner on a day's program and the track record for the distance he ran. If the times on a particular day average $3\frac{1}{5}$ seconds — or sixteen-fifths of a second — slower than the track records, the variant is 16. A track with a variant of 16 would be four-fifths of a second faster than a track with a variant of 20. Theoretically.

The *Racing Form*'s track variants contain one fatal flaw that makes them practically useless for serious speed handicapping. They don't take into consideration the quality of the horses who were running on a given day. A typical racetrack may offer, on a Friday, a run-of-the-mill program with many cheap claiming races, and the winners will be covering six furlongs in 1:12 and 1:13. The racing strip could be identical the next day, but the higher class horses who are traditionally entered on Saturday programs will be running in 1:10 and 1:11. The *Racing Form* variant will therefore be much lower for Saturday than Friday, suggesting that the track was considerably faster, when in fact it only means that faster horses were running on Saturday.

If a handicapper knew the average times in which horses of different classes were to run, he could make a more accurate track variant. He could compare the time of a

$3000 claiming race with the average for $3000 claiming races, the time of a stakes race with the average for stakes races, instead of comparing them both with the same track record.

Average times for the various classes of horse races are not published anywhere, so a would-be speed handicapper must compile them himself. The procedure is the one phase of making figures that is excruciatingly boring. When I am tackling an unfamiliar track, I closet myself in my handicapping room with a minicalculator, a set of the charts of all the races run at the track during the previous year, several big sheets of poster paper, a few sharp pencils, a bottle of Jack Daniel's, and a belief that the ensuing hours of drudgery will eventually pay off. I mark on the poster paper columns for each class level offered at the track — all the prices of claiming races, all the prices of maiden-claiming races, maiden-special-weight races, stakes races, and allowance races. Since there are many species of allowance races, I divide them either according to their conditions or their purse value. I establish separate categories for races limited to two-year-olds or three-year-olds. After listing in the appropriate column the time of every race that was run over a fast track, I average the times in each class. These were my averages for older horses running six furlongs during one season in New York:

CLAIMING RACES

$3000	1:13
$4000	1:12⅘
$5000	1:12⅕
$6–7000	1:12
$8–10,000	1:11⅘
$11–14,000	1:11⅗
$15–20,000	1:11⅖

MAIDEN-CLAIMING RACES

$5000	1:13⅗
$6–7000	1:13⅕
$8–11,000	1:13
$12–15,000	1:12⅘

MAIDEN-SPECIAL-WEIGHT RACES

All ages	1:12

ALLOWANCE RACES

Nonwinners of one race other than maiden or claiming	1:11⅗
Nonwinners of two races other than maiden or claiming	1:11⅖
Nonwinners of three races other than maiden or claiming	1:11
$15,000 purses	1:10⅗
$20,000 purses	1:10⅖

STAKES RACES AND HANDICAPS	1:10

(Races limited to fillies and mares are, on the average, one-fifth of a second slower than the above times.)

When a horseplayer has compiled such a set of par times for the track at which he operates, he is equipped to analyze the results of a day's races and measure the condition of the racetrack with reasonable accuracy. On a hypothetical day at Belmont Park, a $7500 claiming race is run in 1:11⅖, a $15,000 claiming race in 1:11⅕, a maiden-special-weight event for fillies in 1:11⅕, an allowance race with a $15,000 purse in 1:10⅕, a stakes race in 1:10⅖. How fast is the track? A speed handicapper can analyze it systematically:

CLASS	PAR TIME	ACTUAL TIME	DIFFERENCE
$7500 claiming	1:12	1:11⅗	fast by ⅗
$15,000 claiming	1:11⅖	1:11⅕	fast by ⅕
Maiden (fillies)	1:12⅕	1:11⅘	fast by ⅗
$15,000 allowance	1:10⅗	1:10⅕	fast by ⅖
Stake	1:10⅕	1:10⅖	slow by ⅕

We average the figures in the right-hand column — the difference between the par times and the actual times of the races — and find that the average race on this day was run two-fifths of a second faster than it should have been. The track variant is + ⅖. When horses who raced on this day are entered again, we can adjust their times accordingly. A horse who ran six furlongs in 1:12 will be credited with an adjusted time of 1:12⅖. By performing these simple calculations every day, we can build up a set of track variants that will enable us to evaluate the speed of every horse we encounter in our handicapping.

Without expending an unreasonable amount of energy, a casual racing fan can use the par-time method to make usable track variants. But for a serious speed handicapper the par-time method is not precise enough; it is only the first step toward making a perfect variant. While a large sampling of $3000 claimers may run six furlongs in an average time of 1:13, some races in this class will draw strong horses who run in 1:12; others may contain a bunch of candidates for the glue factory who have trouble running in 1:14. To make his variants as accurate as possible, a speed handicapper must take into account the abilities of individual horses. He may be computing a variant for a day when the par times and actual times look like the table on page 126.

Most of the evidence suggests that the track was only

CLASS	PAR TIME	ACTUAL TIME	DIFFERENCE
$3000 claiming	1:13	1:12⅘	fast by ⅕
Maiden	1:12	1:11⅘	fast by ⅕
$4000 claiming	1:12⅖	1:12⅗	fast by ⅕
$10,000 claiming	1:11⅕	1:10	fast by ⅘

one-fifth of a second faster than normal, but a $10,000 claiming horse ran 1⅕ seconds faster than the par for his class. What happened?

To understand the race, we examine the records of the horses in the field, the times in which they have run recently (adjusted by a track variant), and the way they finished. We find that the first three finishers — Horses A, B, and C — had all run their recent races in 1:11⅗. Horse A won by seven lengths, with Horses B and C a nose apart for second.

It is possible that Horse A ran his normal race, in 1:11⅗, and that B and C went off form drastically. Or else Horses B and C may have run their usual races, with Horse A improving sharply to beat them by seven lengths. If we see signs in A's past performances that he was ready to improve — perhaps he had just been claimed by a top trainer; perhaps he had been running against a track bias in his most recent start — we may deduce that this is what happened. Horse A figured to run in 1:10⅕ to beat B and C by seven lengths while they were running their usual 1:11⅗. So instead of using the par time for $10,000 claimers of 1:11⅕, we use this projected time of 1:10⅕. Comparing it with the actual race time of 1:10, we see that the track was one-fifth of a second fast, as the other results on the same day had suggested.

When I started making track variants, I relied largely on par times and would project a time only when I encountered a race that glaringly contradicted the other results of the day. But now I use par times only for the first two weeks or so of a new racing season, when I have no prior results with which to project times. Then I start using the projection method for every race, and I believe that the track variants it produces are the best that man can devise.

To project the running times of races requires a good deal of practice and knowledge. There are no easy rules to simplify the process, because judging whether horses have improved, deteriorated, or stayed the same since their last race requires all of a man's handicapping skills.

We are trying to make a track variant for a day on which the following hypothetical race is being run. It is a six-furlong event for $12,000 claimers, and these are the leading contenders:

Horse A, who won his last race in 1:11. He has been laid off for a month, with no good workouts during that time.

Horse B, who ran his last race in 1:12. He is a paragon of consistency who almost always records the same time.

Horse C, who ran his last race in 1:12⅖. He is trained by the leading trainer at the track.

Horse A wins by a length over B, with Horse C another length behind. What should the time of the race be?

It is conceivable that Horse A ran in 1:11 again. But if he did, the horses behind him had to improve sharply and implausibly, with B running in 1:11⅕ and C in 1:11⅖. It is more likely that A ran slower because of his recent inactivity, allowing B and C to finish close to him.

If A ran in 1:11⅘, B would have run in 1:12, his usual performance. Horse C's time would have been 1:12⅕, a slight improvement that might be due to his trainer's competence.

So we project a time of 1:11⅘ for A's victory: it is the most logical way to explain the way the horses finished. Now we can compare the projection with the actual time of the race. If A were clocked in 1:12⅖, we would conclude from this piece of evidence that the track was three-fifths of a second slow. If his actual time was 1:11⅖, the track would be two-fifths of a second fast.

Occasionally, even the most astute practitioner of this method of making track variants will encounter a race or a day's program that doesn't make sense. For example:

RACE	PROJECTED TIME	ACTUAL TIME	DIFFERENCE
1	1:13	1:13⅗	slow by ⅗
2	1:12⅘	1:13	slow by ⅕
3	1:12⅘	1:13⅗	slow by ⅗
4	1:12	1:10⅖	fast by ⅘
5	1:12	1:12⅖	slow by ⅖

The fourth race is a bewildering mystery. All the other evidence seems to suggest that the track is somewhat slow, but this one race was run much faster than it should have been. Suspecting that my projection was an error, I would reanalyze the race, trying to interpret the horses' past performances in a way that would enable me to project a time of about 1:09⅖, which would jibe with the other results. But if the race still defied explanation, I would disregard it entirely for purposes of computing my track variant. And I would watch closely how the horses in this field perform when they run again. If one or two of them come back and run in the vicinity of 1:09⅖, I know the time of the race was legitimate. But if they subsequently run in 1:12, I disregard their extraordinarily fast time as a fluke, caused by freaky track conditions, atmospheric conditions, or perhaps a malfunctioning Teletimer. It happens sometimes.

Another problem that can arise in making a track variant might take a form like that shown on page 129. The condition of a racetrack will occasionally change suddenly during the middle of a day's program. It may happen because rain starts to fall during the afternoon. It may happen for no apparent reason at all. In the case above I would make a separate variant for the first four races (fast by ⅕ of a second) and another for the last five races (slow by

RACE	PROJECTED TIME	ACTUAL TIME	DIFFERENCE
1	1:12	1:11⅖	fast by ⅗
2	1:13	1:12⅕	fast by ⅘
3	1:12⅕	1:11⅕	fast by ⅕
4	1:11	1:10⅕	fast by ⅘
5	1:11⅗	1:12⅕	slow by ⅗
6	1:12	1:12⅕	slow by ⅕
7	1:10⅘	1:11⅗	slow by ⅘
8	1:11	1:11⅖	slow by ⅖
9	1:13	1:13⅕	slow by ⅕

⅖). There will be other perplexing days in which the track variant may be different at different distances; sprints may be fast but route races run around two turns will be slow.

If we lived in a kinder world, racetracks would card nine races a day at six furlongs, and the task of speed handicappers would be relatively easy. But every thoroughbred track offers at least two different distances. Belmont Park confounds speed handicappers with races at five, five-and-a-half, six, six-and-a-half, and seven furlongs, and one mile, 1¹⁄₁₆, 1⅛, 1¼, and 1½ miles. Rarely will a horseplayer be treated to an easy race in which all the entrants do all their running at the same distance. Most speed handicappers approach the problem by translating a horse's time, at whatever distance he runs, into a numerical rating, so that they can more easily compare horses' performances at different distances.

The *Racing Form* past performances include speed ratings for each of a horse's races, and they are as ill-conceived as the *Form*'s track variants. The *Form* equates the track record for each distance with a rating of 100, and deducts one point for every fifth of a second slower than the record that a horse runs. Suppose a horseplayer were trying to compare two thoroughbreds at Aqueduct, one of whom ran six furlongs in 1:10⅘, the other, seven furlongs in 1:23. The Aqueduct track record for six furlongs used to be 1:08⅘. A horse who ran in 1:10⅘ was two seconds (or ten-fifths) slower than the record. So he would earn a rating of 90 (100 minus 10). The Aqueduct record for seven furlongs was 1:21⅘. So the horse who raced in 1:23 would get a rating of 91. He is one length superior to the six-furlong horse.

The fallacy of this method was exposed when the great horse Dr. Fager won Aqueduct's Vosborgh Handicap in the sensational time of 1:20⅕ for seven furlongs, breaking the record by a full second. Now a horse who raced seven furlongs in 1:23 would earn a rating of 86. Overnight he had become, under the *Racing Form*'s speed ratings, four lengths inferior to a rival who had raced six furlongs in 1:10⅘ and earned a rating of 90. This is patently absurd. There has to be some kind of logical relationship between times and six and seven furlongs, but it is ridiculous to base this relationship on the performance of one exceptional horse who sets a track record.

When a speed handicapper has compiled a set of average times for various classes to help him make track variants, he has accumulated evidence that will enable him to compare horses' performances at different distances. In Maryland, the most common races are $3000 claiming events for older horses. They are run practically every day of the season, at every distance. The average time for $3000 claimers may be based on as many as fifty or a hundred individual races. This large sampling provides a much more substantial basis for comparing times at different distances than the track records. At Laurel, for example, the average times of $3000 claimers are:

Six furlongs	1:13
Seven furlongs	1:26⅕
1⅛ miles	1:54

The difference between the average times at six and seven furlongs is 13⅕ seconds. If we are handicapping a seven-furlong race in which one horse has run the distance in 1:26⅗, and is meeting a rival who ran six furlongs in 1:12⅘, we add 13⅕ seconds to the latter's time and find that his effort equals 1:26 at the longer distance. He is three lengths superior to his opponent.

There is no universal set of comparative times that will work at every racetrack. The relationship of times in sprint races doesn't vary much — six furlongs in 1:13 will equal seven furlongs in 1:26⅕ at virtually every track that is at least a mile in circumference — but route races are different everywhere. At Pimlico, the average $3000 claimer runs six furlongs in 1:13 and a mile and an eighth in 1:53. At Aqueduct, where the short run to the first turn in route races prevents horses from getting into high gear quickly, a six-furlong time of 1:13 is equivalent to a mile and an eighth in 1:54⅖. At Bowie, where the first turn is traditionally much deeper and slower than the rest of the track, six furlongs in 1:13 equals a mile and an eighth in 1:55⅕. At Belmont, where all races shorter than a mile and a half are run around only one turn, six furlongs in 1:13 equals a mile and one-eighth in 1:52⅗.

Purists will object that comparing the efforts of horses at different distances is an exercise in futility and further indication of the warped mentality of speed handicappers. Every thoroughbred, from the humblest claimer to Secretariat, has a distance that he likes the best. Many horses who are crackerjacks at six furlongs would be gasping for air if they attempted to run seven furlongs, let alone a mile and one-eighth. This is quite true, and speed handicappers should resist the temptation to think that, just because six furlongs in 1:13 equals seven furlongs in 1:26⅗, a horse will cooperate and run precisely as fast as he should. These comparative times do not magically predict a horse's performance at a new distance. They only measure the level of his performance in previous races. But these comparative times are still very useful if a horseplayer evaluates them intelligently. If we are handicapping a mile-and-one-eighth race at Laurel, which pits a sprinter who runs in 1:13 against a router who runs 1⅛ miles in 1:54, we know that the horses' times are equivalent and we will probably prefer the one who has proved himself at the long distance. If a 1:13 sprinter were facing a 1:55 router, the decision would not be so easy. We would know that the sprinter's performance had been superior, and we would have to decide if he could do as well at a mile and an eighth. If his record showed that in the past he had the ability to negotiate a route, he might be a good bet.

To help horseplayers compare times at different distances, almost every tract on speed handicapping contains what is known as a parallel-time chart. As the name implies, the times for different distances are listed in parallel vertical columns. The handicapper using the chart simply looks across a horizontal line to relate a time at one distance to another. The parallel-time chart usually also includes a numerical rating for each time. We can construct one easily enough for Laurel, where we know that six furlongs in 1:13, seven furlongs in 1:26⅗, and a mile and an eighth in 1:54 are equivalent. We arbitrarily assign each of these times a rating of 80, and the parallel-time chart looks like this:

RATING	SIX FURLONGS	SEVEN FURLONGS	1¼ MILES
95	1:10	1:23⅕	1:51
94	1:10⅕	1:23⅖	1:51⅕
93	1:10⅖	1:23⅗	1:51⅖
92	1:10⅗	1:23⅘	1:51⅗
91	1:10⅘	1:24	1:51⅘
90	1:11	1:24⅕	1:52
89	1:11⅕	1:24⅖	1:52⅕
88	1:11⅖	1:24⅗	1:52⅖
87	1:11⅗	1:24⅘	1:53⅗
86	1:11⅘	1:25	1:52⅘
85	1:12	1:25⅕	1:53
84	1:12⅕	1:25⅖	1:53⅕
83	1:12⅖	1:25⅗	1:53⅖
82	1:12⅗	1:25⅘	1:53⅗
81	1:12⅘	1:26	1:53⅘
80	1:13	1:26⅕	1:54
79	1:13⅕	1:26⅖	1:54⅕
78	1:13⅖	1:26⅗	1:54⅖
77	1:13⅗	1:26⅘	1:54⅗
76	1:13⅘	1:27	1:54⅘
75	1:14	1:27⅕	1:55
74	1:14⅕	1:27⅖	1:55⅕
73	1:14⅖	1:27⅗	1:55⅖
72	1:14⅗	1:27⅘	1:55⅗
71	1:14⅘	1:28	1:55⅘
70	1:15	1:28⅕	1:56

Many casual racing fans cannot devote a great deal of their time to handicapping but still want to be able to bet intelligently when they go to the track. For them, the speed-handicapping methods described in this chapter will be especially useful.

The only time-consuming part of the process is the compilation of a set of average times for all the classes that a track offers. With these averages, a horseplayer can construct a parallel-time chart so that he can compare, at a glance, the performances of horses who have been running at different distances. With the averages he can use the par-time method and make track variants in only a few minutes a day. He will be able to assess, more accurately than the vast majority of bettors, the real meaning of horses' times.

8

Speed Handicapping: II

SHELDON KOVITZ, my classmate at Harvard, became fascinated by horse racing while he was studying for his doctorate in mathematics. Not only did he calculate his own speed figures, but he tried to translate every facet of handicapping into mathematical terms.

If a horse appeared on the track with a bandage on his left foreleg that he had not previously worn, Sheldon had a figure with which to adjust his numerical rating. If a wind was blowing at Suffolk Downs, Sheldon would measure its velocity with his portable anemometer and adjust the horses' times with his wind figures, which he had devised with the aid of an IBM 360 Model 40 computer. His sophistication had certain drawbacks. "I get so busy tabulating all the various data and keeping up with the results," Sheldon complained once, "that I don't have time to handicap." He never became a winning horseplayer, and finally gave up the game to devote himself to academic pursuits.

Most of Sheldon's racetrack cronies dismissed him as a lunatic, an opinion that seemed to be confirmed by his chronic lack of success as a bettor. But I sensed that the way he calculated his speed figures was solidly grounded in logic, and urged him to teach me his method. After understanding the mathematics behind his approach, using it for a few years, and comparing it with the ways other horseplayers compute their figures, I belatedly recognized that Sheldon was a true genius as a handicapping theoretician.

Not long after undertaking his study of racing, Sheldon made a discovery that was as stunning to me as it was obvious to him. He recognized that all the conventional parallel-time charts, which are the backbone of practically all the systems of speed handicapping, contain the same flaw. The error is a serious one, and to correct it requires a speed handicapper to advance to a much higher plateau of sophistication — into the realm of figures.

According to my parallel-time chart in the previous chapter, it takes a horse who runs six furlongs in 1:13 another 13⅕ seconds to cover an additional furlong. Correct. But the chart also says that a much faster horse — one who can run six furlongs in 1:10 — will also require 13⅕ seconds to travel an extra furlong. And a very slow horse — one who runs six furlongs in a dawdling 1:15 — will also run another eighth of a mile in :13⅕. This is totally illogical, but the same fallacy appears in just about every piece of literature on speed handicapping. Tom Ainslie, in his generally astute *Complete Guide to Thoroughbred Racing*, publishes a parallel-time chart that says a horse who runs six furlongs in 1:10 will go seven furlongs in 1:22⅖, covering the extra furlong in a swift 12⅖ seconds, which a very fast horse can do. But the same chart says a miserable plodder who runs six furlongs in 1:16 will run seven furlongs in 1:28⅖, covering the last eighth of a mile in a miraculous 12⅖ seconds. No wonder Ainslie is skeptical about the usefulness of speed handicapping.

Sheldon found a way to resolve these inconsistencies. The starting point of his method was the same as for traditional parallel-time charts. We learn times at different distances that are equivalent and assign the same numerical rating to them. Six furlongs in 1:13 is an 80. Seven furlongs in 1:26⅕ is an 80. Now, if horses run one-fifth of a second faster than these times, how do their ratings compare? Parallel-time charts would say they are identical. But this is a fallacy, because a fifth of a second is proportionately more significant at a shorter distance.

To make this a bit clearer, let us imagine we were making speed figures for human runners. The world record for 100 yards is 9.0 seconds. The world record for one mile is 3:51.1. If a runner went one second slower than the 100-yard record, his time would be :10.0 and he would be no better than an average high-school sprinter. But if he ran one second slower than the mile mark, in 3:52.1, he would still be one of the great track stars of history. Obviously, a fraction of a second in a short race is more significant than a fraction of a second in a long race.

Sheldon performed a relatively simple calculation to assess the relative importance of a fifth of a second at the different distances in horse racing. If a horse runs six furlongs in 1:13, he has covered the distance in 73 seconds, or 365-fifths of a second. One-fifth of a second represents

1/365, or .28 percent of his entire race. When a horse runs seven furlongs in 1:26⅕, one-fifth of a second is 1/431, or .23 percent, of the whole race.

We now know how to weight a fifth of a second at six and seven furlongs. Moving the decimal point over one place to make the figures more manageable, we know that a fifth of a second should be worth 2.8 points at six furlongs, 2.3 points at seven furlongs. If we have assigned a rating of 80 to a six-furlong time of 1:13, a horse who runs in 1:12⅘ earns a rating of 82.8. A horse that runs seven furlongs in 1:26 earns a rating of 82.3. A portion of a parallel-time chart would now look like this:

SIX FURLONGS		SEVEN FURLONGS	
1:12	94.0	1:25⅕	91.5
1:12⅕	91.2	1:25⅖	89.2
1:12⅖	88.4	1:25⅗	86.9
1:12⅗	85.6	1:25⅘	84.6
1:12⅘	82.8	1:26	82.3
1:13	80.0	1:26⅕	80.0
1:13⅕	77.2	1:26⅖	77.7
1:13⅖	74.4	1:26⅗	75.4

Using this method, we can construct a speed-rating chart that assigns a numerical value for every time at every distance a track offers. These are the basic equivalent times for the various distances at Aqueduct and Belmont, and the value we assign to a fifth of a second at each distance (see chart on page 139).

5 furlongs	1:00	(one-fifth = 3.3 points)
5½ furlongs	1:06⅖	(one-fifth = 3.0 points)
6 furlongs	1:13	(one-fifth = 2.8 points)
6½ furlongs	1:19⅗	(one-fifth = 2.5 points)
7 furlongs	1:26⅕	(one-fifth = 2.3 points)
1 mile	1:39⅖	(one-fifth = 2.0 points)
1¹⁄₁₆ (Belmont)	1:46	(one-fifth = 1.9 points)
1⅛ (Belmont)	1:52⅗	(one-fifth = 1.8 points)
1⅛ (Aqueduct)	1:54⅖	(one-fifth = 1.8 points)
1½ (Belmont)	2:36	(one-fifth = 1.2 points)

We assign each of these times a rating of 80, and then construct the entire speed chart, removing the decimal points and rounding off the numbers.

FIVE FURLONGS		5½ FURLONGS		SIX FURLONGS	
57	130	1:03	132	1:09	136
57⅕	127	1:03⅕	129	1:09⅕	133
57⅖	123	1:03⅖	126	1:09⅖	130
57⅗	120	1:03⅗	123	1:09⅗	127
57⅘	117	1:03⅘	120	1:09⅘	124
58	113	1:04	117	1:10	122
58⅕	110	1:04⅕	114	1:10⅕	119
58⅖	107	1:04⅖	111	1:10⅖	116
58⅗	103	1:04⅗	108	1:10⅗	113
58⅘	100	1:04⅘	105	1:10⅘	110
59	97	1:05	102	1:11	108
59⅕	93	1:05⅕	99	1:11⅕	105
59⅖	90	1:05⅖	96	1:11⅖	102
59⅗	87	1:05⅗	93	1:11⅗	99
59⅘	83	1:05⅘	90	1:11⅘	97
1:00	80	1:06	87	1:12	94
1:00⅕	77	1:06⅕	84	1:12⅕	91
1:00⅖	73	1:06⅖	81	1:12⅖	88
1:00⅗	70	1:06⅗	78	1:12⅗	86

(cont'd on next page)

FIVE FURLONGS		5½ FURLONGS		SIX FURLONGS	
1:00⅘	67	1:06⅘	75	1:12⅘	83
1:01	63	1:07	72	1:13	80
1:01⅕	60	1:07⅕	69	1:13⅕	77
1:01⅖	57	1:07⅖	66	1:13⅖	75
1:01⅗	53	1:07⅗	63	1:13⅗	72
1:01⅘	50	1:07⅘	60	1:13⅘	69
1:02	47	1:08	57	1:14	66
1:02⅕	43	1:08⅕	54	1:14⅕	64
1:02⅖	40	1:08⅖	51	1:14⅖	61
1:02⅗	37	1:08⅗	48	1:14⅗	58
1:02⅘	33	1:08⅘	45	1:14⅘	55
1:03	30	1:09	42	1:15	53

6½ FURLONGS		SEVEN FURLONGS		ONE MILE	
1:15	138	1:21	140	1:34	134
1:15⅕	135	1:21⅕	138	1:34⅕	132
1:15⅖	133	1:21⅖	136	1:34⅖	130
1:15⅗	130	1:21⅗	133	1:34⅗	128
1:15⅘	128	1:21⅘	131	1:34⅘	126
1:16	125	1:22	128	1:35	124
1:16⅕	123	1:22⅕	126	1:35⅕	122
1:16⅖	120	1:22⅖	124	1:35⅖	120
1:16⅗	118	1:22⅗	121	1:35⅗	118
1:16⅘	115	1:22⅘	119	1:35⅘	116
1:17	113	1:23	117	1:36	114
1:17⅕	110	1:23⅕	115	1:36⅕	112
1:17⅖	108	1:23⅖	112	1:36⅖	110
1:17⅗	105	1:23⅗	110	1:36⅗	108
1:17⅘	103	1:23⅘	108	1:36⅘	106
1:18	100	1:24	105	1:37	104
1:18⅕	98	1:24⅕	103	1:37⅕	102
1:18⅖	95	1:24⅖	101	1:37⅖	100

6½ FURLONGS		SEVEN FURLONGS		ONE MILE	
1:18⅗	93	1:24⅗	98	1:37⅗	98
1:18⅘	90	1:24⅘	96	1:37⅘	96
1:19	88	1:25	94	1:38	94
1:19⅕	85	1:25⅕	92	1:38⅕	92
1:19⅖	83	1:25⅖	89	1:38⅖	90
1:19⅗	80	1:25⅗	87	1:38⅗	88
1:19⅘	77	1:25⅘	85	1:38⅘	86
1:20	75	1:26	82	1:39	84
1:20⅕	72	1:26⅕	80	1:39⅕	82
1:20⅖	70	1:26⅖	78	1:39⅖	80
1:20⅗	67	1:26⅗	75	1:39⅗	78
1:20⅘	65	1:26⅘	73	1:39⅘	76
1:21	62	1:27	71	1:40	74
1:21⅕	60	1:27⅕	69	1:40⅕	72
1:21⅖	57	1:27⅖	66	1:40⅖	70
1:21⅗	55	1:27⅗	64	1:40⅗	68
1:21⅘	52	1:27⅘	62	1:40⅘	66
1:22	50	1:28	59	1:41	64

		BELMONT		AQUEDUCT	
1¹⁄₁₆ MILES		1⅛ MILES		1⅛ MILES	
1:41	128	1:48	121	1:49	128
1:41⅕	126	1:48⅕	119	1:49⅕	126
1:41⅖	124	1:48⅖	117	1:49⅖	124
1:41⅗	122	1:48⅗	115	1:49⅗	122
1:41⅘	120	1:48⅘	114	1:49⅘	121
1:42	118	1:49	112	1:50	119
1:42⅕	116	1:49⅕	110	1:50⅕	117
1:42⅖	114	1:49⅖	108	1:50⅖	115
1:42⅗	112	1:49⅗	106	1:50⅗	113

(cont'd on next page)

		BELMONT		AQUEDUCT	
1¹⁄₁₆ MILES		1⅛ MILES		1⅛ MILES	
1:42⅘	110	1:49⅘	105	1:50⅘	112
1:43	109	1:50	103	1:51	110
1:43⅕	107	1:50⅕	101	1:51⅕	108
1:43⅖	105	1:50⅖	99	1:51⅖	106
1:43⅗	103	1:50⅗	98	1:51⅗	105
1:43⅘	101	1:50⅘	96	1:51⅘	103
1:44	99	1:51	94	1:52	101
1:44⅕	97	1:51⅕	92	1:52⅕	99
1:44⅖	95	1:51⅖	91	1:52⅖	98
1:44⅗	93	1:51⅗	89	1:52⅗	96
1:44⅘	91	1:51⅘	87	1:52⅘	94
1:45	90	1:52	85	1:53	92
1:45⅕	88	1:52⅕	84	1:53⅕	91
1:45⅖	86	1:52⅖	82	1:53⅖	89
1:45⅗	84	1:52⅗	80	1:53⅗	87
1:45⅘	82	1:52⅘	78	1:53⅘	85
1:46	80	1:53	77	1:54	84
1:46⅕	78	1:53⅕	75	1:54⅕	82
1:46⅖	76	1:53⅖	73	1:54⅖	80
1:46⅗	74	1:53⅗	71	1:54⅗	78
1:46⅘	72	1:53⅘	70	1:54⅘	77
1:47	71	1:54	68	1:55	75
1:47⅕	69	1:54⅕	66	1:55⅕	73
1:47⅖	67	1:54⅖	64	1:55⅖	71
1:47⅗	65	1:54⅗	62	1:55⅗	69
1:47⅘	63	1:54⅘	61	1:55⅘	68
1:48	61	1:55	59	1:56	66

BELMONT 1½ MILES		BELMONT 1½ MILES	
2:29	125	2:29⅗	121
2:29⅕	124	2:29⅘	120

BELMONT 1½ MILES		BELMONT 1½ MILES	
2:29⅖	122	2:30	119
2:30⅕	117	2:33⅕	98
2:30⅖	116	2:33⅖	96
2:30⅗	115	2:33⅗	95
2:30⅘	113	2:33⅘	94
2:31	112	2:34	93
2:31⅕	111	2:34⅕	91
2:31⅖	109	2:34⅖	90
2:31⅗	108	2:34⅗	89
2:31⅘	107	2:34⅘	87
2:32	106	2:35	86
2:32⅕	104	2:35⅕	85
2:32⅖	103	2:35⅖	83
2:32⅗	102	2:35⅗	82
2:32⅘	100	2:35⅘	81
2:33	99	2:36	80

This chart resolves the problem of comparing times at different distances. When a horse runs six furlongs in 1:13, he should run seven furlongs in 1:26⅕, requiring 13⅕ seconds to travel the additional eighth of a mile. A fast horse who runs six furlongs in 1:09⅗ (a rating of 124) should cover seven furlongs in 1:22⅖ (also a rating of 124), running the extra furlong in 12⅗ seconds. A plodder who runs six furlongs in 1:14⅕ (a rating of 64) should go seven-eights in 1:27⅗ (also a 64), covering the last eighth in 13⅖ seconds.

Since we are now dealing with figures instead of actual times, we translate the other elements of speed handicapping — par times, track variants, and beaten lengths — into figures as well. They are much less cumbersome to use. We don't have to say, "This horse ran six furlongs in 1:12⅗ over a track that was three-fifths of a second slow, making his adjusted time 1:12, and today is running at seven furlongs, so his time for that distance translates to 1:25." Instead we can say, "This horse is a 94," which neatly summarizes his capabilities.

The chart of New York par times that appeared in the previous chapter would now look like this:

CLAIMING RACES

$3000	80
$4000	84
$5000	91
$6000	93
$7000	94
$8000	96
$9–10,000	97
$11,000	98
$12–13,000	99
$14,000	100
$15–16,000	101
$17–18,000	102
$19–20,000	103

MAIDEN-CLAIMING RACES

$4000	69
$5000	75
$6–7000	77
$8–11,000	80

MAIDEN-SPECIAL-WEIGHT RACES

All ages	93

ALLOWANCE RACES

Nonwinners of one race other than maiden or claiming	99
Nonwinners of two races other than maiden or claiming	103
Nonwinners of three races other than maiden or claiming	109
$15,000 purses	113
$20,000 purses	116
STAKES RACES	119

(*For races limited to fillies and mares, deduct three points.*)

These par figures can be applied to any distance. To make a track variant with the par-time method, we compare these figures with the actual figures for the races, as on the following hypothetical day at Aqueduct.

CLASS	DISTANCE	PAR	TIME	ACTUAL FIGURE	DIFFERENCE
$10,000 claiming	1 mile	97	1:37⅖	100	fast by 3
Maiden (fillies)	6 furlongs	90	1:11⅕	97	fast by 7
$15,000 allowance	7 furlongs	113	1:23⅗	112	slow by 1
Stakes	1¼ miles	119	1:49⅗	122	fast by 3
$17,000 claiming	6½ furlongs	102	1:17⅗	105	fast by 3

Averaging the difference between the par figures and the horses' actual figures, we find that the track was fast by three points. So the track variant for this day was −3. When any horse who raced on this day runs again, we subtract three points from his figure. If the track is slower than normal, say by eight points, the track variant will be

+8, and this should be added to the figure of every horse who races on that day.

When we use the projection method, the procedure is much the same. In a seven-furlong race, Horses A, B, and C have each run a figure of 94 in their most recent starts. Horse A, whose past performances indicate that he is ready to improve, wins by three lengths, with B and C second and third, a nose apart. Three lengths equal roughly three-fifths of a second, and three-fifths of a second at seven furlongs equals about seven points. So we project A's winning figure as 101. If he actually ran in 1:25⅕ — a figure of 92 — the evidence suggests that the track was nine points slow, and the variant should be +9.

The equation of one length with one-fifth of a second is used almost universally, but it is not quite accurate. A fast horse running in a sprint will obviously cover a length more quickly than a plodder going a mile and a half. The discrepancies are minor, and a reader whose head is reeling from all the figures on the previous pages may ignore the following chart for converting beaten lengths into figures at varying distances.

BEATEN-LENGTHS ADJUSTMENT CHART

Margin	5 Fur.	6 Fur.	7 Fur.	Mile	1¹⁄₁₆	1⅛	1½
neck	1	1	1	0	0	0	0
½	1	1	1	1	1	1	1
¾	2	2	2	1	1	1	1
1	3	2	2	2	2	2	1
1¼	4	3	3	2	2	2	1
1½	4	4	3	3	3	2	2
1¾	5	4	4	3	3	3	2
2	6	5	4	4	3	3	2
2¼	7	6	5	4	4	4	3

Margin	5 Fur.	6 Fur.	7 Fur.	Mile	1¹⁄₁₆	1⅛	1½
2½	7	6	5	4	4	4	3
2¾	8	7	6	5	5	5	3
3	9	7	6	5	5	5	3
3¼	9	8	7	6	5	5	4
3½	10	9	7	6	6	6	4
3¾	11	9	8	7	6	6	4
4	12	10	8	7	7	6	5
4¼	12	10	9	8	7	7	5
4½	13	11	9	8	8	7	5
4¾	14	11	10	9	8	8	5
5	15	12	10	9	8	8	6
5½	16	13	11	10	9	9	6
6	18	15	12	11	10	9	7
6½	19	16	13	12	11	10	8
7	20	17	14	13	12	11	8
7½	22	18	15	13	13	12	9
8	23	20	17	14	13	13	10
8½	25	21	18	15	14	13	10
9	26	22	19	16	15	14	11
9½	28	23	19	17	16	16	11
10	29	24	20	18	17	17	12
11	32	27	23	20	18	18	13
12	35	29	25	21	20	20	14
13	38	32	27	23	22	22	15
14	41	34	29	25	23	23	16
15	44	37	31	27	25	25	17

I won't go into the mathematics behind it, but the chart is more precise than the standard rule of thumb. If the winning figure for a six-furlong race is 102, and a horse is beaten by three lengths, what is his figure? The user of the chart looks down the left-hand column and finds three lengths, then moves his eye across to the column for six furlongs and finds the figure 7. He subtracts 7 from the winner's figure of 102, and finds that the horse's figure is 95.

9

Speed Handicapping: III

WHEN A HORSEPLAYER has learned how to make figures, he
will inevitably start to believe that he is omniscient. He will
suddenly be able to answer with ease the sort of questions
that befuddle most handicappers: Can a three-year-old beat
older horses? Can a sharp $3000 claimer step up to $5000
and win? He will be able to measure the capabilities of
horses more accurately than their trainers can. He will win
many bets almost effortlessly by wagering blindly on horses
who earn his top figures. And, without realizing it, he will
be falling into a trap.

It happened to me, as it happens to most newly converted
speed handicappers. I became so entranced by my figures
that I ignored the fundamentals of the game. I viewed the

figures as gospel, as certain indicators of what horses were going to do today rather than as measurements of what they had done in the past. Instead of using them as a tool, I let them dictate my decisions.

Speed figures are neither magic nor infallible. A handicapper who played every race by betting the horse with the highest figure for his last start might cash 30 percent of his wagers and eke out a modest profit. He could improve his percentage by winnowing out horses who do not meet basic handicapping requirements. And he could improve it even further by developing the ability to recognize when superior figures may be misleading.

After some expensive lessons, I now know to distrust figures that horses achieve under certain conditions.

I discount figures that a horse has earned with the assistance of a strong track bias.

I discount figures that a horse has earned on a muddy track, especially if he is running on a fast track today.

I downgrade figures that a horse has earned when he opened a big early lead and maintained it from wire to wire. Many horses can run like champions when they don't get competition, but wilt when they are subjected to pressure.

Even if a horse has run a big figure in his last start under seemingly normal conditions, I will hesitate to bet him on the basis of just one exceptional performance. A $3000 claimer consistently runs in the same range — 70, 75, 69, 73 — and then improves sharply to earn a figure of 90. Most speed handicappers would bet him enthusiastically; I wouldn't, unless I can find a reason to explain his improvement. If, for example, he had been claimed by an outstanding trainer, I might credit the man for transforming his new acquisition into a horse who would now run regularly in the 90s. But if the horse had improved for no apparent reason, I would expect him to revert to his usual level of performance — in the 70s — rather than to duplicate his last race.

The figure for a horse's last race is, of course, the most important one in his past performances. But the best bets uncovered by speed handicapping are not horses who have run one recent extraordinary race. They are, instead, horses who consistently run at the same level, whose normal figures are good enough to beat the opposition they will be facing today.

When a horse runs 70, 90, 72, 71, 92, I don't know quite what to expect of him. But when a horse runs 86, 87, 90, 87, 85, I know he should win a race in which none of his rivals ever does better than an 84.

Here is a race in which a speed handicapper could make a bet with unshakable confidence:

'th Bowie Race Course

1 1-16 MILES BOWIE

START ◆ ◆ FINISH

1 $\frac{1}{16}$ MILES. (1:41⅗). THE CROFTON HANDICAP. STARTER HANDICAP. Purse $6,500. 3-year-olds and upward which have started for a claiming price of $5,000 or less since June 30.

ailor's Ace   **107**   B. g (1970), by Great Jimminy—Polly's Ace, by Ace Admiral. Breeder, Rentie Hamilton (Tex.).   1973 18 3 2 2 $5,940

wner, J. S. Zinman.   Trainer, A. J. Delloso.

```
ec29-739Lrl    7 f 1:29  sl  31  112  42½ 54  711 714 Vasq'zG4  10000 52 Gray Idol 114  Hurtado  Tourforsure 8
ec11-732Lrl    1 1:40⅗gd  25  112  97⅔ 84½ 74½ 64½ HowardR1  7500 66 Tight  W'bbed113 MH P. NorthetP'k 12
ov27-737Lrl  ⑰ 1 1:37¾fm  39  112  816 78¾ 76½ 45  Hinoj'saH5  7500 78 Drum  I o. over  AtAGlance 9
ov20-737Lrl    1 1:39⅖ft  20  116  1112 97¾1215 88½ HowardR5  8000 66 AtaGlance115 Sh' D'sh Beau o'S's'it 12
```

54 69

Aint Copy   **110**   Dk. b. or br. f (1970), by Bunty's Flight—Shakney, by Jabneh. Breeder, Mr. & Mrs. J. Wilson (Can.).   1973 20 4 0 3 $12,290   1972 4 1 0 0 $2,015

wner, J. M. Hardy.   Trainer, J. M. Hardy.

```
ec26-739Lrl    1 1:44⅖ssy  5¼  115  46  43  23  1no McH'eDG2  7500 52 ⑤MintCopy115 EmaPo'chie DatsYou 6
ec15-737Lrl  1 1-8 1:52⅖ft  17  112  49½ 511 53½ 54  McH'eDG2H3500 82 Ghost in 115 O'bl'n Translator 7
ov30-736Grd    1 1:40  m   12  111  77½ 511 615 618 Dittf'hH6  Hcp0 62 ⑤Em...d'g1.. reAng'l R'y'lM's 7
ov21-736Grd    7 f 1:27⅘ssy  2¾  112  58½ 56½ 12  16½ HawleyS2   Alw 78 MintCopy112 AlitreShaid Lily'sPoint 6
```

76 82

Delta's Pia   **116**   Dk. b. or br. g (1970), by Pia Star—Delta Queen, by Bull Lea. Breeder, Danada Farms (Ky.).   1973 11 2 2 1 $7,818

wner, T. LaMarcra, Jr.   Trainer, W. J. Lewis.

```
ec19-739Lrl  1 1-8 1:53⅖gd  37  112  616 64  43  1no McC'ronG9  7000 80 Delta'sPia112 SilentJet ShootN'Dash 9
ov20-739Atl  1 1/16 1:46⅖ft  10  112* 59½ 212 28  26  TritsosP6  6500 67 Rigel 119  Delta'sPia  Larkel 7
ov13-739Atl  1 1/16 1:46⅖ft  21  117  89  710 59½ 59½ BarreraC9  6500 63 Rigel 115 Sneakin'Deacon Malvinas 10
ov 6-739Atl  1 1-8 1:52⅖gd  34  117  68½ 510 34  38  BarreraC4  6500 68 Ph'nt'Leader119 Ca'nbert D'lta'sPia 8
:t22-733Atl  1 1/16 1:48  ft  9-5 ▲117  3nk 1h  13  1no T'teRL5 cM5000 67 D'lta... 117  Haw'nFlight FairC'nty 8
ep20-731Atl    6 f 1:12⅖ft  33  117  72½ 55¾ 35½ 24  Gr'mPl11   M5000 74 Travel...an117  Delta'sPia Hebbtide 11
ep 6-731Atl    6 f 1:13⅘ft  21  117  83  78  67  66½ B'leVJr7   M5000 67 TamiamiTr'l 117 C'perB'ch Tr'v'linM'n 10
ug30-731Atl    6 f 1:12¾ft   5¼  117  75½ 510 69½ 611 HoleM5    M5000 68 DigThisDish117  HiN'Fast TravelinMan 7
```

72

(cont'd on next page)

Son Diver
122 Ch. h (1969), by Swoon's Son—Deep Blue Sea, by Nasrullah.
Breeder, T. Gentry (Ky.).
Owner, H. V. Howley. Trainer, J. A. Licausi.

| | | | | | | | | | | 1973 | 19 | 4 | 2 | 1 | $24,8 |
| | | | | | | | | | | 1972 | 3 | 1 | 0 | 2 | $3.7 |

Dec28-73⁹Aqu	1 1-8 1:53⅕ft	2½	▲120	13½ 12½ 1²	1²	C'roAJr¹⁰	c5000 69	SonDiver120	NavyNo MightlyBully
Dec 4-73⁷Aqu	1 1-8 1:50⅕ft	6-5	▲114	1h 1h 4¹	5⁷	Vel'q'zJ²	11000 78	Bold Wit 113	Spread the Word Sig
Nov22-73⁷Aqu	1 1-8 1:51⅗ft	8-5	▲118	2h 11½ 1³	13½	Vel'q'zJ²	c8500 80	SonDiver118	DoubleyRoyal Privado
Nov19-73⁹Aqu	1 1-8 1:50⅗ft	14	113	1h 11½ 12½	1⁶	Vel'q'zJ⁵	10500 83	Son Diver 113	Never Or Now Chili II.
Nov13-73²Aqu	6 f 1:11⅕ft	5½	116	7½½ 5³½ 3³½	24½	G'tinesH⁷	c6500 83	HolmesSmarty116	SonDiver BeR'stl'ss
Oct31-73¹Aqu	6 f 1:11⅖sy	23f	112	10⅞ 8⁸ 7⁷½	7⁶½	Gusti'sH¹⁰	9000 81	Steal aDance115	StansStory Chili II.
Oct22-73⁹Aqu	6 f 1:10⅘ft	19	116	12⅞107 8⁹½	8⁶½	GustinesH⁴	9000 82	HeadTable116	Messmate IrishMate
Oct11-73¹Bel	6 f 1:10⅗ft	35	114	5¹½ 1h 1h	2ⁿᵏ	GustniesH⁹	7500 90	SatansStory112	SonDiver NavyNo
Sep28-73⁵Atl	1 1/16 1:45⅜ft	5½	115	2h 1¹ 5⁶½	6¹⁷	Arist'neM⁶	8000 62	FallRush110	Enoc-A-Nee PlumGood

Shoot n' Dash
117 Ch. g (1970), by Shoot Luke—Dash n' Splash, by Condiment.
Breeder, Mrs. J. M. Branham (Tenn.).
Owner, W. Watts. Trainer, R. L. Maffay.

| | | | | | | | | | 1973 | 30 | 4 | 4 | 5 | $20,9 |
| | | | | | | | | | | | | | | $7,4 |

Dec31-73⁵Lrl	1 1:42⅖sl	3⅜	120	7¹³ 4⁶	3²½	2ⁿᵒ	Jimin'zC³	8500 61	At aGlance110 Shot n'Dash St'rtLittle
Dec19-73⁹Lrl	1 1-8 1:53⅖gd	3	120	8¹⁸ 7⁴½	3¹½	3¹	JimenezC⁸	8000 79	Delta IIₐ Silenₙₐ ShootN'Dash
Nov27-73⁷Lrl	Ⓣ 1 1:37⅘fm	6	120	7¹⁵ 8¹¹	8⁸¾	8⁶¼	Jim'nezC⁴	8500 76	Drumₜₚ Exꟾₒ AtAGlance
Nov20-73⁷Lrl	1 1:39⅘ft	10	122	9¹⁰ 7⁴¾	2¹½	2⅜	StovallR⁹	8000 73	AtaGlance115 Sh'tn'D'sh Beau o'S's'it
Dec 30 Bow 3f my :40b									

78 70

Cut the Deck *
111 Gr. g (1967), by Sure Welcome—Last Slam, by Slam Bang.
Breeder, M. Polinger (Md.).
Owner, Barbara Vranas. Trainer, M. Kuhn.

| | | | | | | | | | 1973 | 29 | 8 | 6 | 4 | $19,7 |
| | | | | | | | | | | 1972 | 17 | 5 | 2 | 2 | $6,0 |

Dec 8-73⁹Lrl	1 1:39⅘ft	8¾	113	2¹ 3¹ 4⁴	4⁷¾	Stov'llR²	H3500 68	Hardbₒₒₜ₂₂ Flirtin'H'rt Bag ofMist
Dec 1-73⁶Pen	1 1-8 1:52⅕ft	5	117	13 11½ 11	3²	StovallR¹	H3000 90	Wh't aₕ²₁₄109 C't theD'k H'lyH'me
Nov24-73⁷Pen	1 1/16 1:46⅗sy	3	120	1¹ 1h 2h	3¹	StovallR³	H3000 83	Cr'yB¹¹₁₁ Wh't aWh'k'r C't theDeck
Nov17-73³Lrl	1 1:37⅘ft	7	113	5³½ 6¹½ 4⁴	4⁷	St'vallR¹	H4000 77	Hardboot122 HappyTank ArloMan
Jan 1 Bow 6f my 1:21b									

72

Silly Buck
114 Ch. c (1970), by Absurd—Sassy Deer, by Once A Year.
Breeder, T. D. Bond, Jr. (Va.).
Owner, T. D. Bond, Jr. Trainer, H. E. Johnson.

| | | | | | | | | | 1973 | 12 | 2 | 1 | 3 | $5,18 |

Dec26-73⁵Lrl	6 f 1:15 sy	6½	116	6⁴½ 4⁶½ 3⁴½	3⁵½	LeeT³	14000 66	Time ofₚₗᵢₜᵧ₁₀₉ Revitalize SillyBuck
Dec13-73⁵Lrl	7 f 1:25⅘ft	4¹	116	11 1² 11	3³½	Kot'koR²	10000 81	StrongLᵢₙₑ₁₂₂ Bunnₐ Chₗₐ SillyBuck 1
Dec 6-73⁴Pen	6 f 1:13⅗gd	3	111	11½ 14 15	1⁹	KotenkoR⁴	5000 78	SillyBuckₐ₁ N'v'rLₐₛₑ omp'sAdmir'l
Nov20-73⁷ShD	6 f 1:17⅖ft	3¾	117	5³½ 3² 5³	4³½	Espin'saV¹⁰	Alw 63	Dayhoₜₜ120 Mac'sKnight HillCrown 1
Jan 2 Bow 4f gd :50⅖b									

78 72

Rapid Treat ⊗
115 Ch. ₙ (1968), by Flaneur II.—Step Daughter, by Air Hero.
Breeder, Mrs. H. Y. Haffner (Md.).
Owner, Double B Stable. Trainer, R. D. Ferris.

| | | | | | | | | | 1973 | 11 | 2 | 2 | 2 | $8,93 |
| | | | | | | | | | | 1972 | 27 | 3 | 5 | 2 | $21,2 |

Dec27-73⁹Lrl	1 1:44 m	2½	119	4³ 2½ 11	1⁴	BlackAS³	c5000 53	RapidTreat119 Don'tKnockMe BigViₙ
Dec20-73⁹Lrl	1 1-8 1:54⅖sl	2½	▲116	2⁴ 1½ 11½	12½	KurtzJ⁷	c4000 75	Rapidₜₑ₁16 Maₛₑₐ ContₑₑdCₒₗ
Dec12-73⁹Lrl	1 1:38⅕ft	4½	113	7³¾ 5⁸½ 4¹¹	4¹¹	KurtzJ⁷	5000 71	Amₕₑₓₐ₁₃ ItsNₐₜₐₗₐ D'bₒⱼ₁
Nov28-73³Lrl	7 f 1:26⅜ft	8¼	116	8⁶¾ 8⁶ 4²½	2ⁿᵏ	BarnesT¹	4000 78	BugleBuster120 RapidTreat KnockCⱼd 1

81 80 62

Dark Stone
119 Dk. b. or br. g (1969), by Rablero—Nasmo, by Nasco.
Breeder, L. & B. McDowell (Ky.).
Owner, The Cross Road Stable. Trainer, J. Tammaro.

| | | | | | | | | | 1973 | 15 | 3 | 2 | 2 | $12,23 |
| | | | | | | | | | | 1972 | 24 | 7 | 3 | 2 | $23,53 |

Dec26-73³Lrl	1 1:42⅖sy	12	116	10¹¹ 7⁴½ 5⁵½	3³½	†Br'eVJr¹⁰	12500 56	PictureFrame114 Octet DarkStone 1
†Disqualified and placed fifth.									
Dec10-73⁵Lrl	1 1:38⅜m	5	109*	9⁸½ 4⁸ 3⁷	3⁴½	MartinR⁷	9500 76	Thayₐₑ A₁₁ ₑₑₗ₁₁₆ Myₜₕ
Dec 3-73²Lrl	1 1:38⅗ft	10	115*	5⁵½ 2h 2h	2ⁿᵏ	MartinR¹⁰	8000 81	Husₕₜₚₚᵢₑ116 D'kStone Swₑₒ Samm 1
Nov17-73⁹Lrl	1 1-8 1:51⅖ft	7¾	111*	4⁴ 4⁶ 3²	1½	MartinR⁷	6500 90	D'kStone111 JoySmoke Vanderb'tAve.

84 86 83

The figures for each horse's last three starts are written on his past performances; none is given for races run on the turf, in the previous year, or on a different racing circuit. Sailor's Ace, for example, earned a 54 in his most recent start on December 29, and a 69 for the race before that. His third race back was a turf event, and no figure is listed for it.

Dark Stone's figures were, by a narrow margin, the best in this field. He had earned an 84 in his most recent race and was only about a length superior to Rapid Treat, who had run an 81. But Dark Stone had run in the mid-80s in every one of his recent races. He could certainly be expected to run a figure around 84 again. If so, who could beat him? Rapid Treat had never run better than an 81. Cut the Deck's best was an 81. Mint Copy had run an 82 in his next to last start. Shoot n' Dash's absolute best was a 78. The invader from New York, Son Diver, looked, on the surface, formidable, but his time of 1:53⅕ was very slow, by Aqueduct standards, on a track that was fairly fast. For Dark Stone to lose this race, he would have to run his worst race in months, or else one of his rivals would have to run his best race in months. At 8-to-5 odds he was an excellent bet, and the results of the race conformed to the figures. Dark Stone won by 1¾ lengths. Mint Copy ran back to his next to last race, his 82 figure, and edged out Rapid Treat for second place.

Speed figures help a handicapper evaluate the most troublesome and baffling sorts of horses — ones who are moving up or down in class. If a horse has been losing badly against $10,000 company and is now entered for $5000, will the class drop enable him to win? If a horse has been running very well for $5000 and is elevated to the $10,000 level, can he handle the rise in class? Speed figures provide an unambiguous answer. In the case of horses who are moving up in class, figures can often disclose lucrative betting opportunities because the vast majority of horse-players shy away from animals stepping up to meet supposedly better opposition. This is what happened in the ninth race at Saratoga on August 10, 1974.

9th Saratoga

6½ FURLONGS (chute). (1:15). ALLOWANCES. Purse $9,500. 3-year-olds and upwa which have not won a race other than maiden, claiming or starter. 3-year-old 119 lbs.; older, 124 lbs. Non-winners of $5,700 since July 15 allowed 3 lbs.; maiden 5 lbs. (Winners preferred.)

Dark Encounter   116   Dk. b. or br. c (1971), by Cornish Prince—Karate Skill, by Cohoes.
Breeder, Tricorn Farms, Inc. (Ky.).   1974 4 1 0 1 $7,3
Owner, F. G. Allen. Trainer, S. Watters, Jr.   1973 2 M 0 0

Jly 4-747Aqu 6 f 1:10½ft 3¾ 117 5³ 52¾ 65¼ 87¾ HoleM⁶   Alw 84 Nile Delta 114 Big Moses Bitache
Jun22-74²Bel 6 f 1:11¾ft 2½ ▲115 57¼ 4² 11¼ HoleM⁶   Mdn 85 D'kEnc't'r115 J't'oN'wOrl'ns Net
Apr30-74⁵Aqu 6 f 1:10½ft 2¼ ▲113 3¹¼ 42¼ 44¾ 47¼ VasquezJ⁷   Mdn 83 H⁵⁵a⁴ Sar⁵atch Ne⁵ativ⁵
Apr22-74³Aqu 6 f 1:10⅗ft 5¾ 108* 78¼ 43¼ 4⁴ 32¾ MoonL⁹   Mdn 87 F'tive113 angst'r'D⁵s⁵
Dec14-73⁴Aqu 6½ f 1:17⅕sm 3 ▲115⅜ 87¾ 714 713 MoonL⁹   Mdn 77 WhoaBoy122 RedStre⁵k Destiny Ben⁵ve
Dec 8-73²Aqu 6 f 1:10⅖ft 2e▲¹15¾ 9¹¹ 96¼ 5³¼ 43¾ MoonL⁸   Mdn 85 Erwin Boy 122 Mr. Beck Surf Catcher
Aug 4 Sar 5f ft 1:00⅗h   **Aug 2 Sar 3f ft :35h**   **July 29 Sar 5f ft 1:03b**

Pokers Brush   116   B. c (1971), by Poker—Brushwork II., by Botticelli.
Breeder, Mrs. Marcia W. Schott (Fla.).   1974 .12 1 1 2 $16,0
Owner, Marcia W. Schott. Trainer, J. E. Picou.   1973 .5 1 0 0 $3,8

Jly 29-74³Sar 1 1-8 1:49⅘ft 4¾ 102* 3¹¼ 32¼ 33¼ 2¾ LongJS⁴   Alw 91 Peleus 113 Pokers Brush War Reason
Jly 23-74⁵Aqu ⊤1 ¹⁄₁₆ 1:43 fm 9-5 ▲114 3⁶ 44½ 2¾ 37½ Riv'aMA³   Alw 91 F'k'rsBr'sh M'l'tsB'y
Jly 9-74⁵Aqu ⊤1 ¹⁄₁₆ 1:41⅘hd 20 114 56¼ 46 35 35¾ RiveraMA³   Alw 94 Wildland115 Camelford PokersBrush
Jly 4-74²Aqu 6 f 1:10½ft 7½ 117 76¼ 76¼ 75¼ 66¼ W'dh'seR⁵   Alw 86 Mag'll'nes 114 Big Moses Bitache
Jun24-74³Aqu 6 f 1:10⅕ft 18 116 44¾ 3¹¼ 2¼ 11 Vasq'zJ¹   27500 93 P'krBr'sh116 Mag'll'nes Pilot'sSon
Jun11-74⁴Bel 6 f 1:11¾ft 21 115 5¹² 58 46 36¾ RiveraMA¹   Alw 80 F'mlyPhysic'n115 R'dStr'k F'k'rsSB'n
May 3-74⁹Aqu 1 1:37¾ft 2¼ ▲113 5⁴ 67¼ 68½ 66¾ Turc'teR⁶   25000 72 Flashing Sword 113 Dicey Dreidel
Apr20-74⁴Aqu 1 1:35½ft 13 118 45¼ 53 46 47 Cord'oAJr¹   Alw 81 Bold a'dF'cy121 Turn toBo E'st'nP'g't
Aug 6 Sar 4f ft :46⅕h   **July 17 Bel 4f ft :49b**   **June 3 Bel 3f ft :35⅕h**

Toy King   116   B. c (1971), by Prince John—Justakiss, by Irish Lancer.
Breeder, Mereworth Farm (Ky.).   1974 6 1 1 1 $9,9
Owner, Poverty Hollow Farm. Trainer, V. J. Nickerson.

Jly 20-74⁷Aqu 6 f 1:10⅗ft 7¾ 114 7⁵ 65¼ 57 44¼ MapleE⁹   Alw 86 H'ppyDeleg'te117 RisingCr'st Aquin's 1
Jly 9-74⁵Aqu ⊤1 ¹⁄₁₆ 8 112 14 11¼ 2¾ 37¼ MapleE¹   Alw 91 Langton 113 Haraka Toy King
Jun29-74⁶Aqu 1 1:34⅖ft 5¼ 111 1¼ 3¼ 3³ 49¾ RuaneJ⁵   Alw 85 GulfsW'd117 S'y'sgtoN'chona
Jun 1-74⁴Bel 7 f 1:23⅘sy 4¼ 115 3² 3¼ 1½ 11 MapleE⁵   Mdn 83 ToyKing 115 Tuxedo Bushell 1
May15-74²Bel 6 f 1:11 ft 2¼ ▲113 78 66¼ 59¼ 610 MapleE⁶   Mdn 78 Debroumard113 Aquinas HatchetM'n 1
Apr30-74²Aqu 6 f 1:11⅗ft 2 113 2h 2h 1½ 2½ MapleE¹   Mdn 83 BobbyM'rcer113 ToyKing Gr'ndgyTw'p
Aug 7 Sar 4f ft :49h   **Aug 2 Sar 3f ft :38b**   **July 17 Aqu 4f ft :47¾h**

King's Day ✳   116   Blk. c (1971), by King of the Tudors—Day Line, by Day Court.
Breeder, Elmendorf Farm (Ky.).   1974 .4 0 0 0   (—
Owner, Elmendorf. Trainer, J. P. Campo.   1973 7 1 0 0 $5,9

Aug 3-74²Sar 6 f 1:11½ft 18 119 8¹⁰ 7¹² 99 84¼ SantiagoA⁵   Alw 80 Lothario 119 Aquinas Hudsonian
May 4-74⁹Aqu 1 1:37⅘ft 28 111 85¼ 9¹¹ 9²⁰ 9²⁹ VeneziaM⁸   Alw 51 SportsEditor111 ForeignAffair PiaKid
Apr24-74⁷Aqu 6½ f 1:18⅕ft 18 113 11⁹ 10⁷¼10¹¹ 8¹³ SantiagoA³   Alw 72 Pl'seS⁵at111¾ Th'rdCl'u'xry Spr't'Edit'r 1
Apr13-74¹Aqu 6 f 1:10⅗ft 7 119 7²¾ 64¾ 65¾ 66 Santi'goA⁶   Alw 84 JoMoss115 Gav⁵el Em⁵reton 9
Oct23-73³Aqu ⊤1 1:36⅗fm 16 113 56¼ 76 8¹⁰ 8¹⁰ SantiagoA¹   Alw 82 I'mO⁵rb⁵oy113 Green⁵Car⁵bado Sr⁵ate 1
Sep27-73³Bel 1 1:37¼ft 8¾ 121 1½ 66¼ 67 69¾ SantiagoA¹   Alw 72 Cannonade121 L'AmourRullah Throne
Sep18-73³Bel 7 f 1:24⅘sy 10e 121 11¹¹ 89¼ 33¼ 15 Sant'goA⁴   Mdn 79 King'sDay121 Accipiter BuckHill
Aug15-73³Sar 6 f 1:10⅗ft 14 119 6⁶ 67¼ 67¼ 58¾ SantiagoA¹   Mdn 77 Dr.Zegarelli 119 Lea'sPass BuckHill
July 31 Sar 5f ft 1:00h   **July 27 Bel 5f ft :59⅗hg**   **July 24 Bel trt 4f ft :48h**

antagenet **119** B. g (1971), by First Landing—Royal House II., by Crepello.
Breeder, H. O. H. Frelinghuysen (Fla.). 1974 . 1 1 0 0 $9,000
er, Wilrun Farm. Trainer, E. Yowell. 1973 . 3 1 0 1 $5,880

7-745Aqu	6 f 1:09⅘ft	25	109	1¹	1½	2ʰ	1ⁿᵒ	Ve'ziaM²	31500 94	Plantagenet109	Joe Iz	Long Hunt 7
26-733Aqu	6 f 1:12⅕ft	5¼	121	1½	2ʰ	11½	1ⁿᵏ	Vas'zJ²	M35000 82	Plantage 121	BlessedN'te	PlayH'se 12
18-732Aqu	6 f 1:11 ft	7¾	121	3²½	78	71²	710	VasquezJ⁸	Mdn 78	Rid...121	Peleus	Nile Delta 14
26-734Bel	6 f 1:11⅘ft	38	121	2⁶	2²	1½	31¼	VasquezJ⁴	Mdn 83	R'ghM'ch121	S'wOn t'eR'd	Pl'nt'g'n't 12

Aug 9 Sar 3f ft :35b   Aug 5 Sar 5f ft 1:00h   July 24 Aqu 3f ft :37b

dsonian **116** B. c (1971), by Swoon's Son—Bethlehem, by Princequillo.
Br., Tilly Foster Stock Farm (N. Y.). 1974 . 2 0 0 1 $1,140
er, Kenyon Farm. Trainer, R. N. Blackburn. 1973 . 8 1 3 3 $17,830

3-742Aqu	6 f 1:11⅕ft	6½	119	56	56½	42½	3½	BaezaB¹	Alw 83	Lotharlo 119	Aquinas	Hudson'an 9
13-743Aqu	6½ f 1:16⅖ft	2	▲117	64¾	44½	61²	716	TurcotteR⁶	Alw 77	Quebec124	Knight ofHonor	SharpDig 7
18-734Aqu	1 1:37⅘ft	4-5	▲120	2½	2ʰ	2ʰ	23	TurcotteR⁴	Alw 77	Christoforo120	Hudson'n	BuyAm'ric'n 7
6-738Aqu	6 f 1:11⅕gd	9-5e	120	3ⁿᵏ	1ʰ	2ʰ	2ⁿᵏ	BaezaB⁵	Hcp0 87	Fra...ms12.	...un'n	CacD'nc'r 9
27-737Aqu	1 1:36⅘gd	3	122	21½	1ʰ	2½	2¹	TurcotteR⁶	Alw 82	Glo...22	Hudson'n	Beau Legend 8
7-736Aqu	6½ f 1:17⅘ft	6½	122	3¹	3²	34	36½	SantiagoA⁷	Alw 80	R'...rene122	...mb Hudson'n 7
9-735Aqu	7 f 1:25⅘ft	20	122	74	62½	41	34¼	SantiagoA⁹	Alw 70	HeavyMayonn'se119	PiaKid	Hudson'n 12
29-732Aqu	6½ f 1:21⅘sy	8	121	64¼	56	23	1¹	Sant'goA⁸	Mdn 82	Hudsonian121	WhoaBoy	Pass theGlass 14
8-733Bel	6 f 1:11⅖ft	10	121	38	47½	52	33½	Sant'goA⁷	Mdn 81	Camangie 111	Criterion	Hudsonian 12

Aug 8 Sar 4f ft :49b   July 28 Sar 5f ft 1:02b   July 22 Bel tc 7f fm 1:30b

quinas **116** B. c (1971), by Never Bend—Copper Canyon, by Bryan G.
Breeder, Cragwood Estates, Inc. (Ky.). 1974 . 9 1 2 1 $10,250
er, Cragwood Stable. Trainer, M. Miller. 1973 . 3 M 0 1 $1,650

3-742Sar	6 f 1:11⅕ft	5	109 ▲▲1½	1¹	1¹	2ʰ	DeM'oCJr⁶	Alw 84	Lotharlo 119	Aquinas	Hudson'an 9
20-747Aqu	6 f 1:10⅘ft	15	104 ▲▲4¹½	2½	23	32¼	DeM'oCJr⁴	Alw 88	H'ppyDeleg'te117	RisingCr'st	Aquin's 10
27-747Aqu	7 f 1:23 ft	8½	115	65	67	55½	47	NemetiW⁵	Alw 79	Menocal 115	Pia Kid	Bitache 8
19-742Mth	6 f 1:09⅜ft	3	115	3²	3½	1½	14	NemetiW⁷	Mdn 92	Aq...116	...Star	...n 12
6-742Bel	6 f 1:11 ft	2½e▲105 ▲▲1ʰ	13	2ʰ	46¼	DeM'rcoC⁴	Mdn 82	Pi...113	J...J	S...rat 11
25-742Bel	6 f 1:10⅖sy	2½e▲108* 43	42½	43½	56¼	MontoyaD⁶	Mdn 85	B...113	...Search ...tion 11
15-742Bel	6 f 1:11 ft	11	103 ▲▲3²	1½	1½	2½	DeM'coC¹⁰	Mdn 87	Deirouillard113	Aquinas	HatchetM'n 11
22-742Aqu	6 f 1:10⅜ft	6½	113	31½	3²	3²	47¾	Velasq'zJ⁴	Mdn 82	Storm 113	Lassington	Blue Devil 8
8-742Aqu	6 f 1:11⅖ft	9¾e	113	2¹	2ʰ	1ʰ	52¼	Velasq'zJ⁴	Mdn 83	Sh'tUp andD'l 114	Tuxedo	Tr'pic'IB'y 14
24-732Aqu	6 f 1:11 ft	6¼	122	11¹²12¹⁵	61²	59¼†Velasq'zJ⁷	Mdn 79	NileDelta122	LittleCurrent	WhoaBoy 14

†Placed fourth through disqualification.

Aug 9 Sar 3f ft :39⅘b   July 31 Sar trt 4f ft :54b   July 17 Bel 4f ft :49⅖b

oup Plan **121** B. g (1970), by Intentionally—Nanticious, by Nantallah.
Breeder, Eaton Farms, Red Bull Stable 1974 . . 1 0 0 0 $570
& Mrs. G. Proskauer (Ky.).
er, Hobea Farm. Trainer, H. A. Jerkens. 1973 . 6 1 1 1 $9,420

3-742Sar	6 f 1:11⅕ft	19	124	68	68	55½	4½	Cast'daM⁹	Alw 83	Lotharlo 119	Aquinas	Hudsonian 9
8-733Aqu	6 f 1:10 ft	6¼	122	1ʰ	31½	35	48	Vel'quezJ¹	Alw 85	SpikedApple124	St'ryKnight	Schroon 8
29-733Aqu	6 f 1:11⅖m	7	122	76¾	61¹	66½	12	BaezaB⁸	Mdn 84	Gr'p...122	M'j'sticN'tive	Inv'stig't'n 8
16-734Aqu	6½ f 1:19⅕ft	6	122	76½	65	42½	33½	Vel'q'zJ¹⁰	Mdn 76	Drea...WitMe122	Inv'tig't'n	Gr'pPl'n 10
5-732Aqu	6 f 1:13 ft	6¼	122	78	67	55½	55¾	Velasq'zJ⁸	Mdn 72	Spa...Dev112	Investigat'n	JewelBag 8
9-731Bel	6½ f 1:17⅖ft	7-5	▲121	63½	85½	87½	81²	Velasq'zJ⁹	Mdn 77	G'tl'm's'W'd121	Inv':ig't'n	D'mW'hMe 10
1-733Bel	6 f 1:11 ft	6	120	53	1½	1¹	2¾	VasquezJ⁷	Mdn 87	Downtown120	GroupPlan	Investigation 7

Aug 8 Sar 3f ft :36⅘b   Aug 1 Sar 4f ft :47h

y and Pleasure **119** Dk. b. or br. g (1971), by What a Pleasure—Faint for Joy, by Swoon's
Son. Br., Waldemar Farms, Inc. (Fla.). 1974 . 4 1 0 1 $7,110
er, S. I. Joselson. Trainer, P. G. Johnson.

1-741Sar	6 f 1:11⅖ft	3	117	2ʰ	1ʰ	12	13½	Bel'nteE²	Mdn 73	J'y a...Pl're117	HiʰC'm'r	J't toN'...O's 14
24-741Aqu	6½ f 1:17⅖ft	3½	121	2ʰ	1¹	41½	Bel'nteE⁸	Mdn 87	Face...117	F'...p'm't T...n 12
7-741Aqu	6 f 1:11⅖ft	26	117	1½	1½	21½	34½	Cas'daM¹⁰	Mdn 81	C'n...114	J't N...0'ns	J...e 12
2-742Aqu	6 f 1:10⅘ft	16	117	3¹	31½	45	78¼	Cast'daM³	Mdn 80	H'yD'g'te117	C'n'gL'd	J't toN'wOr'ns 11

July 12 Bel trt 4f ft :50⅕h   June 28 Bel 5f ft :59⅖h   June 18 Bel 6f ft 1:14hg

(cont'd on next page)

Rough March   109   B. c (1971), by Go Marching—Deb Dance, by Rough'n Tumble.
Breeder, H. Massey (Ky.).   1974   3 0 0 0   (—
Owner, Grandview Stable.   Trainer, J. S. Nash.   1973   11 1 1 2 $10

Aug 3-74²Sar	6 f 1:11⅕ft	23	119	7¹⁰	8¹³	88	6³¾	HoleM³	Alw 80	Lothario 119	Aquinas	Hudsonia
Mar 6-74⁷Hia	6 f 1:10⅖ft	4¼	117	69	65½	57	65½	W'dh'seR⁸	Alw 86	StarLance 122	JoJoTex	Knowerneve
Jan17-74⁹GP	6 f 1:09⅕ft	108	110	98¾	9¹²	8¹⁵	79¾	W'dh'seR⁸	AlwS 83	Rea'S'r'me110	Eric'sCh'mp	L'dReb'l
Nov10-738Atl	1₁₆ 1:46⅖sl	8¾	113	3⁴	38	69½	62⁰	BarreraC⁵	AlwS 55	Hegem n 4	Mark theP'rce	HinkyDee
Oct30-73⁶Aqu	1 1:36⅖sft	4¼	119	5³	6¹¹	58¼	41¾	PincayLJr⁴	Alw 83	S'r't' aPr e121	LordF'r'stn'r	Fl'gS'
Oct23-73³Aqu	Ⓣ 1 1:36⅜fm	12	113	66¾	87½	69¼	68¾	Cord'oAJr⁵	Alw 83	I'mO Top 13	GreenGambados	Relent
Oct 6-73⁴Bel	6 f 1:10⅝ft	8½	121	78½	79	65	43¾	PincayLJr¹	Alw 86	FlipSal 121	FrankieAdams	W'dMcAl'
Sep26-73⁴Bel	6 f 1:11⅘ft	8-5	121	5⁸	55½	31½	1½	Pinc'yLJr⁸	Mdn 84	R'ghM'ch121	S'wOn t'eR'd	Pl'nt'g'n'

Aug 9 Sar 3f ft :36h   July 17 Bel 5f ft 1:02h   July 13 Bel 3f ft :34⅕h

Face Mask   119   B. g (1971), by Forward Pass—Bemuse, by Princequillo.
Breeder, King Ranch, Inc. (Ky.).   1974   1 1 0 0 $5
Owner, King Ranch.   Trainer, W. J. Hirsch.

Jly 24-74¹Aqu	6½ f 1:17⅖ft	17	117	79½	79	66½	1¾	Sant'goA³	Mdn 89	Face ask117	F'r'm'tDip'm't	Prom't'

Aug 8 Sar 3f ft :37b   Aug 3 Sar 5f ft 1:00h   Aug 1 Sar 4f ft :52b

Cunning Lad   119   Ch. g (1971), by Bold Lad—Treacherous, by Ambehaving.
Breeder, Lazy F Ranch (Ky.).   1974   3 1 1 1 $8
Owner, Lazy F Ranch.   Trainer, S. W. Ward.   1973   1 M 0 0   (—

Jly 17-74¹Aqu	6 f 1:11⅖ft	4½	117	2½	3¹½	1½½	13½	Gustin'sH⁹	Mdn 86	C'n' J' N' O'ns	P 'r' Dip'
Jly 2-74²Aqu	6 f 1:10⅖ft	5	117	2h	2½	23	23¾	GustinesH⁵	Mdn 85	H'y 17 C g	J't t'g
Jun22-74²Bel	6 f 1:11⅜ft	10	115	1½	1h	1½	31¾	GustinesH²	Mdn 83	D' c'115 t nWOrl'
Sep26-73³Bel	6 f 1:11⅕ft	17	121	10¹⁰	99½	9¹⁸10²⁸	G'stinesH⁷	Mdn 69	W'oMcAP' r121	S'v'rB'dge	Q'nC'yL'

Aug 7 Sar 6f ft 1:15⅜b   Aug 3 Sar 4f ft :47⅖h   July 29 Sar 5f ft 1:00⅘b

A handicapper who evaluates horses according to their class might well be baffled by this allowance race. Four horses were beaten by less than a length against similar allowance company in their last starts. Three other members of the field won maiden races recently. And another won a high-priced claiming event.

But a man armed with speed figures would know that the claiming horse, Plantagenet, is toweringly superior. He ran six furlongs in 1:09⅘, over a track with a variant of − 17, to earn an impressive figure of 109. That was Plantagenet's first start of the year; with the race and subsequent good workouts under his belt, he should be able to duplicate or improve upon that performance. If he does, none of his rivals should be able to touch him.

Pokers Brush, whose figure of 100 is the second-best in the field, is four lengths slower than Plantagenet. The lightly raced horses who seem eligible to improve — Face Mask, Group Plan, and Cunning Lad — would have to improve by about 20 points (or eight lengths) in order to win.

Despite Plantagenet's obvious merits the bettors at Saratoga didn't know quite what to do with this race. Because Plantagenet had beaten only claiming horses, they doubted his class and made him a very tepid favorite at 3 to 1. He won and paid $8.80, with Face Mask second and Pokers Brush third.

Speed figures not only help a horseplayer pick winners, but they give him an understanding of the sport that even many supposed experts lack. Because I am a speed handicapper, I felt that I could comprehend and appreciate the career of Secretariat more fully than almost any racing fan — and perhaps as much as his owner, trainer, and jockey.

Long before the world was hailing Secretariat as a superhorse, I knew — as did my fellow figure men — that the colt was something special. In the third race of his career, a routine allowance event at Saratoga, he had run a figure of 120. It was by far the biggest figure I had ever made for a two-year-old, and it was not far from the biggest figure I had ever made for any horse, 129. Secretariat lived up to his initial promise, running in the 115-to-120 range for the rest of the year, winning ten races in a row.

When his winning streak was broken in his final prep race for the Kentucky Derby, the Wood Memorial Stakes at Aqueduct, it was obvious that something was wrong with Secretariat. His figure was a dismal 108, the worst he had run since the first race of his career. But he rebounded in the Derby and the Preakness to run figures of 129, and this would be his usual level of performance for the rest of his career, with one glorious exception — the Belmont Stakes.

Any sports fan could appreciate Secretariat's 31-length victory, but only a speed handicapper could measure just how extraordinary it was. Secretariat earned a figure of 148 that day — so much higher than any race I had ever seen that the horse had seemed to step into a different dimension. As so often happens with horses, even cheap ones, who run one extraordinary race, Secretariat resumed running his usual figures in the high 120s. When he was upset by Prove Out in the Woodward Stakes at Belmont, his apologists made a thousand excuses for him and blamed the jockey, Ron Turcotte, but the figures disclosed what had happened. Secretariat ran a 128, his usual race, and had simply been beaten by a horse who was better on that day.

Romanticists could appreciate Secretariat for his strength, his grace, his exciting style of running. But for me the most awesome moment of his career came two days after the Belmont Stakes, when I sat down with paper, pencil, and the Belmont charts, calculated my track variant and wrote down the number 148 for the eighth race that day. For a true addict, speed figures are the most beautiful part of the game.

10

Class

IN THE FALL of 1973, I made a special trip to Belmont Park to bet a two-year-old named Stonewalk in the Cowdin Stakes. Although he had previously beaten only mediocre horses in a maiden and an allowance race, Stonewalk had earned speed figures worthy of a champion. I was unconcerned that he had not yet demonstrated his class by facing strong opposition. Because I am committed to the belief that time is the one way to measure a horse's ability, I consider class to be relatively unimportant.

Before the races that day I had lunch with Mannie Kalish, the well-known New York handicapper and a man who believes in class. I expressed my enthusiasm for Stonewalk and he replied, with a touch of condescension, "Oh, so you're another one of those speed guys." Kalish said he liked Protagonist in the Cowdin. The colt had recently raced in the Futurity Stakes, had been bumped and knocked off stride, but still managed to finish third. In Kalish's eyes, this performance in stakes competition verified Protagonist's class and his superiority over Stonewalk.

That was absurd, I argued. Stonewalk had run ten lengths faster than Protagonist, and this precise measurement of their capabilities was a lot more meaningful than some vague, elusive, undefinable thing called class. Kalish thought I was a naive kid who hadn't matured enough to understand the complexities of the game. I thought he was a doddering fool who, like most of the sport's traditionalists, are blinded to the importance of speed. There was no middle ground on which we could compromise. Speed handicappers and classifiers rarely have a meeting of the minds.

When Protagonist rallied to beat Stonewalk by two lengths, I could not explain the outcome of the race in any way that was consistent with my own philosophy. Although most races can be best handicapped and understood with speed figures, there are many exceptions like the Cowdin when class prevails and speed proves to be meaningless. To me, this is the greatest mystery of the game. If I could some day discover and define the interrelationship between the two factors, I would consider it an intellectual breakthrough of the first magnitude.

I do not have the complete answer. But I have learned some applications of the class factor that will provide indications of a horse's ability when speed figures will not. In situations where speed figures are useless — in grass races and at tracks that do not have an electric timer — they are indispensable.

The class level at which a horse is entered will often provide clues about his trainer's intentions. The opinion of a trainer about his animal can be self-fulfilling. If he thinks the horse is entered in a spot where he can win, the trainer will probably do everything possible to get him into razor-sharp condition. If he believes the horse is overmatched, the trainer may not bother to prepare him for his optimum performance and may tell his jockey not to abuse the horse. Such manipulations seem to explain, as speed figures could not, the in-and-out past performances of Covered Hoop.

vered Hoop   **114**   B. g (1971), by Gyro—Miss Lawdy, by Hoop, Jr.
Breeder, L. & E. Jackson (Ky.).   1974   11   3   0   0 $12,755

r, N. A. Martini. Trainer, J. G. Moos.   **$13,000**

-743Aqu	1 1-8 1:54½ft	6½	118	1½	11½	12	13½	VeneziaM[2]	9000	64	CoveredHoop1[18] St'lArch Hitch'gPost 7
-741Aqu	7 f 1:25⅘sy	7	116	6⁴½	8⁹½	81³	71⁵	Ve'ziaM[5]	12500	57	Manly One 116 Warbum Pete Simon 8
-745Aqu	1 1:39 sy	7	116	12	11¼	13	12¾	VeneziaM[7]	9000	72	C'v'r'dH'p116 R'dyM'n'yK'te R'n'gB'k 7
-744Aqu	1 1:40⅕ft	5	112	5³½	6¹¹	61⁶	61⁷	V'n'ziaM[4]	13000	49	TimeTells107 NewsW'tch D'rbyt'nM'n 6
-746Aqu	6½ f 1:19⅕ft	13	116	5⁴	6⁵½	6⁸	57¼	Ve'ziaM[5]	16000	73	PurchaseStreet Bavaria Anecdote 6
-747GP	Ⓣa1 1/16 1:47 fm	16	116	8⁹½	5³¼	4⁶	45¼	MiceliM[1]	16000	74	Onaduel 116 Talk Less Lt. Ted 10
-7410GP	Ⓣa1 1/16 1:47⅖fm	8	112	2³	24	2h	3²	KellyJ[3]	10500	75	Mr.Art116 Thr'st ofCour'ge H'rtHouse 10
-745GP	1 1/16 1:46 gd	7½	105‡	3¹½	14	1nk	GarridoJ[5]	9000	71	CoveredH'p105 Hitch'gPost PatHand 10
-746GP	Ⓣ 1 1/16 1:46½syl	25	113	9²⁰	9¹⁶	81⁴	81¹	BoveT[1]	13000	62	Assagal 112 CosyMan ArmsAndArmor 9

May 16 Bel tc 6f fm 1:15⅖h   **May 7 Bel 6f ft 1:14⅘h**   **May 4 Bel 4f sy :47⅘h**

Covered Hoop won a $9000 race early in 1974, lost four times in higher-class company, then dropped to $9000 and won again. Trainer J. G. Moos was presumably convinced by this time that $9000 was his horse's precise value. When he entered him for $12,500 on April 10, he was probably not making a serious attempt to win. In fact, a bad defeat might benefit Moos when he entered Covered Hoop at his proper level. The horse's odds would be better and, more important, other trainers might be discouraged from claiming him. After Covered Hoop lost by 15 lengths and then was entered for $9000 on April 24, literal-minded speed handicappers might have dismissed him because his most recent race had been so bad. But they should disregard that dismal performance and figure that Covered Hoop will improve dramatically because of his drop in class. A drop from $12,500 to $9000 won't make a horse improve by 15 lengths, but a change in the trainer's intentions will.

If Covered Hoop had been dropped instead to $6500, the situation would be much different. The betting public would undoubtedly make him a heavy favorite, reasoning that an established $9000 horse figures to demolish such cheap opposition. But an astute handicapper would be skeptical, realizing that no trainer would be willing to lose a $9000 animal for $6500 unless something was seriously wrong with him. Whenever a horse's record suggests that he can win at a certain claiming level, and he is entered for a lower price, the drop in class is a negative sign. These dropdowns are the worst bets in racing. They seldom win, and when they do their odds are unappetizingly low. No matter how superior his figures may be, I will not bet a horse who is entered for a suspiciously low claiming price. And if he does not have superior figures, I will bet against him with enthusiasm.

The distinction between a negative drop in class and a useful one can be very subtle. A handicapper trying to pick the winner of the ninth race at Aqueduct on November 22, 1973, practically had to read the minds of the trainers in order to evaluate three horses that were dropping sharply in class — Steal a Dance, He's a Card, and Dealer.

Steal a Dance won his last start for $10,000, and previously performed well for $13,000 and $15,000. In view of his sharp form, he is worth at least $10,000 and should be running at that level. But trainer Johnny Campo has entered him for an $8000 price tag. One should always be suspicious when a horse drops in class after a victory. Campo must know that Steal a Dance is not as good as he looks on paper.

al a Dance ✳   **112**   Dk. b. or br. g (1968), by No Robbery—Witch's Dance, by Bolero.
Breeder, Jonabell Farm (Ky.).
, Arlene Schwartz. Trainer, J. P. Campo.   **$8,000**

								1973 15 1 1 1	$9,700
								1971 18 3 4 0	$66,759

-73¹Aqu 6 f 1:11⅕sy 3 ▲116 87¼ 67 54 11 Pin'yLJr⁴ 10000 87 Steal aDance116 StansStory Chili II. 13
-73¹Aqu 6½ f 1:16⅘ft 53 116 72⅓ 911 916 920 And'onP⁹ 15000 72 DeltaTr'ffic116 B'ldM'rit Ch'fC'chise 9
-73²Bel 6 f 1:10⅕ft 5¼ 116 87 63¼ 22 22 Pin'yLJr² 13000 90 CountCasp'r116 St'l aD'ce ThreeOn'ns 9
-73²Bel 6½ f 1:17⅖ft 2½e▲116 65½ 74½ 42½ 41¾ C'd'oAJr³ 15000 87 IrishMate116 Cerril SilentRoamer 10
-73²Bel 7 f 1:23⅖sy 14 112 1½ 21½ 47½ 8¹³ Vel'q'zJ³ 18000 71 Override114 NeverConfuse RoyalQ'ster 10
-73²Bel 6½ f 1:16⅘ft 10 116 52¼ 74¼ 73 55 C'd'oAJr³ 20000 87 He's aC'd114 Prez'sSon B'k theSyst'm 10
-73⁸Sar 7 f 1:24⅖sy 25 113 67 81011191120 Balta'rC⁷ 35000 65 Y'ungEd107 Cl'seC'mb't Inv'st'dPower 11
-73⁸Sar ⊤ 1⅛ 1:47⅗fm 5 112 57¼ 66¼ 88¾ 8¹³ Tur'tteR³ 40000 81 InCamera118 Avant DonQuixote II. 8
-73⁹Aqu ⊤ 1¹⁄₁₆ 1:44 gd 6⅔ 112 11½ 1¼ 1h 3¾ Turc'teR⁶ 35000 85 Sh'lt'rB'y116 St'n'yB't'ry St'l a D'nce 9
Nov 14 Bel trt 4f ft :50⅘b   Nov 10 Bel trt 4f ft :51b   Sept 25 Bel trt 4f ft :51b

s a Card ✳   **116**   Gr. g (1969), by Bold Lad—Flash Card, by Count Fleet.
Breeder, G. M. Humphrey (Ky.).
, J. Taub. Trainer, J. Parisella.

		1973 10 2 0 0	$10,620
		1972 11 1 0 1	$3,820

-73⁹Aqu 6¼ f 1:17 ft 9-5 ▲116 85½ 85¾ 96¼ 65 Pin'yLJr⁸ 15000 86 Gay Gallant 116 Bostons Boy Brumidi 12
-73²Bel 6 f 1:10⅖ft 8¼ 124 98¼ 86½ 85¾ 54¾ PincayLJr⁸ Alw 86 SirArctic121 Maskos Jim theB'rt'nd'r 9
-73²Bel 6½ f 1:16⅘ft 5½ 114 62⅔ 51⅜ 1h 1ⁿᵏ Turc'teR² 19000 92 He's aC'd114 Prez'sSon B'k theSyst'm 10
-73¹Bel 6 f 1:09⅘ft 13 115 65½ 54¼ 54 42 Turc'eR¹⁰ 18000 92 Corporation112 W'eOldOwl II. B'ldP'p 11
-73⁴Mth 6 f 1:10⅕ft 21 114 65¼ 67½ 66 42 C'pedesR⁹ 19000 89 SocialEnd'v'r113 Dot'sImp Ni'tDr'gn't 9
-73⁶Mth 6 f 1:09⅘ft 2½ ▲117 91² 911 98 97¼ Mic'liM⁶ c15000 86 DoctorArt119 FlyingAh'd Jessie'sJest 10
-73⁷Mth 6 f 1:10⅖ft 5½ 118 99¾ 915 81⁴ 712 BlumW¹¹ Alw 78 Kinzua111 SpearCarrier StudentL'mp 12
Oct 25 Bel trt 4f ft :50⅗b   Oct 23 Bel trt 4f ft :49b

ler ✳   **112**   Dk. b. or br. c (1969). by Swaps—Prize Day. by Royal Charger.
Breeder. L. Combs II. & Cambridge Stable (Ky.).
, S. Sommer. Trainre, F. Martin.   **$8,000**

		1973 19 1 2 3	$21,690
		1972 17 5 1 1	$31,960

-73²Aqu 6½ f 1:18 ft 8 116 22 2½ 2½ 67¼ Cas'daM⁶ 13000 79 B'ddyFr'd'hs116 D'bl'yR'y'l BritishR's 10
-73⁵Aqu 6 f 1:10⅘ft 6 116 1h 42½ 91³ 91³ C'oAJr¹⁰ 20000 76 Bold Pep 116 Sea Bird II. Wauwinet 10
-73⁵Bel 6½ f 1:17 ft 3 116 34 54 89½ 911 Vel'q'zJ⁴ 30000 80 PrimePrince116 Corporation RibR's! 9
-73⁵Bel 6 f 1:09⅖ft 4-5e▲116 3ⁿᵏ 42 44 47¾ Vel'q'zJ⁶ 35000 88 WildcatC'try119 R'neD'p't D'dasPr'ce 8
-73⁸Bel 7 f 1:21⅘ft 13 115 12 3½ 8¹⁰ 8²¹ Pin'yLJr⁵ 50000 72 Accohick120 Tunex GustavusAdolphus 8
-73³Sar 6 f 1:10 ft 8-5e▲118 65 63¾ 64¾ 63½ S'tiagoA² 50000 86 EnglishDancer114 Accohick ScareTag 7
-73⁷Aqu ⊤ 1 1:39 yl 3½ 116 13 23 411 417 Belm'nteE⁴ Alw 69 RockyM'nt116 StarEnvoy Straph'ng'r 4
-73⁸Aqu 1 1-8 1:49 ft 7¼ 108* 11½ 11 32 46½ WallisT⁶ 50000 84 GustavusAd'lph's115 Cheriepe Trupan 7
Nov 5 Bel trt 4f ft :50b   Oct 27 Bel trt 6f ft 1:14h   Oct 10 Bel trt 4f ft :47⅕h

He's a Card won for $19,000, ran creditably in an allowance race against horses worth at least $30,000, then was entered on November 15 for $15,000. That was a negative drop, and He's a Card ran a dull race. Now he drops again, to $8500. Trainer John Parisella paid $15,000 for the gelding earlier in the season and has recouped only a fraction of his investment. Yet he has seemingly given up on He's a Card and is willing to lose him cheap.

Dealer couldn't win for $30,000; he couldn't win for $20,000; he couldn't win for $13,000. But he displayed some signs of life in his last start, showed speed to the stretch before he tired, and may have found his proper level at $8000. Trainer Frank Martin has not entered him here because he is trying to get rid of a cripple; he thinks this is a race that Dealer has a chance to win.

Martin was right. Dealer won by 4½ lengths, paying $15, as He's a Card ran third and Steal a Dance finished ninth.

Drops in class are most easily recognizable when a horse moves from one claiming level to another. But allowance races have step by step gradations just as claimers do. The lowest-grade allowance races are those for "nonwinners of a race other than maiden or claiming." The competition gets progressively tougher in races for "nonwinners of two . . ." "nonwinners of three . . ." up to the high-grade allowance races with conditions that even stakes-caliber horses can meet. When a horse is overmatched in allowance company and then entered in a race where he fits the conditions perfectly, the drop in class may be just as meaningful for him as for a claiming horse who is lowered in price.

There are many circumstances in which the relative class of horses cannot be measured so easily. If a solid $10,000 claimer is entered in an allowance race for "nonwinners of a race other than maiden or claiming," how does his class compare with that of horses who have been running regularly in allowance company? The only answer to the question can come from observation and experience. If the race is being run in Kentucky, the $10,000 claimer is probably superior. In New York, he would be overmatched. How does a New England handicapper evaluate a top-grade New York allowance horse running in a stake at Suffolk Downs? He learns from experience that the New York horse is usually superior. What does a handicapper at Dover Downs do when he encounters a maiden-special-weight horse from Liberty Bell running in a maiden-special-weight race at his home track? He learns that he should mortgage his house and bet it all on the Liberty Bell invader.

Even when their designated class levels don't reflect it, there are certain groups of horses that will regularly beat other groups of horses. When a handicapper can identify these hidden class advantages, he can find some of the best bets in racing. A studious horseplayer at Shenandoah Downs on September 9, 1972, could have found an excellent wagering opportunity by diagnosing that a maiden had a great edge in class over a field of allowance horses (see pages 166–167).

Only three horses in this field — Come On Rabbit, Deep Rang, and Bonus Money — have respectable records in allowance company, and they appear to be the class of this field. They have been running against each other for most of the season, taking turns beating each other; they all seem to be of roughly equal ability. Just how good are they? We can see that Deep Rang was unable to win against $7500 maiden claimers at Pimlico, but was immediately transformed into a star when he came to West Virginia — evidence that the Shenandoah allowance ranks are rather weak. We can get a further indication of the quality of these horses by doing homework in back issues of the *Racing Form*. In the edition of August 28, we can look up the past performances for the race in which Bonus Money beat Come On Rabbit. The horse who finished third behind them, Tumble Bug, had lost his previous start in a $4000 claiming race at Timonium that was run in the dismal time of 1:11⅖ for 5¾ furlongs. Obviously, the so-called allowance horses in West Virginia are no better than cheap claimers in Maryland.

One of the horses in this field is coming from Maryland.

9 SHENANDOAH — 6 FURLONGS — SHENANDOAH DOWNS — START · FINISH

6 FURLONGS. (1.10 4/5) ALLOWANCES. Purse $7,500. 2-year-olds. Weights, 120 lbs. Non-winners of a race other than maiden or claiming since August 10, allowed, 3 lbs. One race since July 10, 6 lbs. Winners of races other than maiden or claiming since August 10 to carry 2 lbs. extra for each such race won.

Coupled—Come On Rabbit and Bonus Money.

Smoked Salmon
Own.—Gray W L

Ch. c. 2, by Loom—Traffic Dream, by Traffic Judge
Br.—Fletcher W D (Va)
Tr.—Edwards W H Jr

114

				St. 1st 2nd 3rd	Amt.
			1972 1 M 1 0	$760

25Sep72- 2Tim fst 5¾f 23½ .47½ 1.09¼ Md Sp Wt 2 3 1½ 11 11½ 2² Barnes T 118 89-12 Prince Wave 118² Smoked Salmon 118nk Piano Top 118⁵ Bore out 7

LATEST WORKOUTS Aug 8 Del 4f sl .49 b Aug 5 Del 3f fst .38 b

Come On Rabbit
Own.—Digiacomo A

Ch. g. 2, by Hedevar—Nimble Patty, by Alsab
Br.—Di Giacomo A (W.Va)
Tr.—Longerbeam M G

1095

				St. 1st 2nd 3rd	Amt.
			1972 10 1 2 2	$3,079

28Aug72- 8ShD fst 6f 23½ .47½ 1.14 Allowance 4 4 7½ 7⁴½ 56 23 Romaine R7 b .70e 81-21 Bonus Money 119³ Come On Rabbit 112nk Tumble Bug 116² Gamely 8
22Aug72- 4ShD fst 5½f 23¾ .47½ 1.08 Allowance 8 8 81⁵ 87½ 76½ 66½ Vasil A b 119 *3.10 79-17 Forgene 119² Triptique 119nk Nashville Champ 119¹ Checked 8
21Jly72- 9ShD fst 5½f 24 .48½ 1.08⅖ Handicap 4 9 99½ 95½ 73½ 63½ Grove P b 114 *2.20e 81-15 Fathers Ace 116½ D Deep Rang 114¹ Lover s Lyre 112hd No Threat 10
15Jly72- 7ShD fst 5½f 23¾ .48½ 1.09⅘ Allowance 9 10 106³ 108 96½ 31½ Vasil A b 119 33.90 76-18 DeepRang 116½ FthersAce 119nk ComeOnRbbit 119½ Rallied Gamely 10
15Jly72-Evening Program

6Jly72- 6CT fst 4½f 22⅗ .46⅗ .53⅗ Allowance 6 10 911 89 49½ 49½ Vasil A b 119 16.50 83-10 Save The Eagle 116³ Lover s Lyre 116⁶ Cupid s Boy 119nk Mild bid 10
21Jun72- 1CT sly 4½f 23⅗ .55 Md Sp Wt 2 6 23 22 12½ 14½ Vasil A b 119 3.60 84-12 Come On Rabbit 119²½ He s Myrullah 119³½ Sailor Max 119¹½ Driving 7
6Jun72- 2CT fst 6½f 24¾ .49½ 1.22⅘ Md Sp Wt 6 3 43½ 44 56½ 48 Vasil A 118 4.90 67-19 Deep Rang 115⁴ Glint Of Gold 115⁴ Speonk 118hd Weakened 8

LATEST WORKOUTS Jly 20 ShD 3f fst .39 b

Deep Rang *
Own.—Mihalick G

Dk. b. or br. f. 2, by Terrang—Deep Love, by Our Love II
Br.—Mihalick G (Va)
Tr.—Palmer J R

114

				St. 1st 2nd 3rd	Amt.
			1972 11 2 3 1	$5,710

2Sep72- 4ShD fst 6f 23⅗ .47½ 1.14½ Allowance 2 1 21½ 21½ 22 21½ Lewis W R Jr 116 *.90 81-17 Forgene 119¹½ Deep Rang 116² Dream Pro 119⁸ Gamely 6
18Aug72- 9ShD fst 6f 22⅘ .47 1.14¾ Handicap 1 1 23 32 32½ 21¾ Sam J 116 3.90 80-16 Fathers Ace 119¹½ Deep Rang 116¹ Bonus Money 114⁴ Gamely 6
21Jly72- 9ShD fst 5½f 24 .48½ 1.08⅖ Handicap 2 1 2½ 42 31 1½ Sam J 114 3.40 D 83-15 Fathers Ace 116½ D Deep Rang 114¹ Lover s Lyre 112hd Bore Out 10
15Jly72- 7ShD fst 5½f 23¾ .48½ 1.09⅘ Allowance 5 1 2½ 31½ 2hd 11½ Sam J 116 3.40 78-18 Deep Rang 116½ Fathers Ace 119nk Come On Rabbit 119½ Driving 10
15Jly72-Evening Program

15Jun72- 4CT fst 4½f 23½ .47½ .54 Allowance 7 2 32 33½ 23 Detiege C 117 6.50e 86-14 Dream Pro 120³ Deep Rang 117hd Lover s Lyre 117⁵ Gamely 8
6Jun72- 2CT fst 6½f 24¾ .49½ 1.22⅘ Md Sp Wt 4 1 11½ 12 12 14 Detiege C 115 *1.10 75-19 Deep Rang 115⁴ Glint Of Gold 115⁴ Speonk 118hd Handily 8
23May72- 4Pim fst 5f 23½ .47½ 1.00⅖ Md 10500 5 1 34 613 613 44½ Hinojosa H 117 7.90 78-19 Strong Side 120¹½ Lady Ara 117½ Royal Carle 117³ Late foot 8
17May72- 3Pim fst 5f 22⅘ .48 1.01 Md 7500 8 7 67½ 12¹⁰ 76½ 54½ Moreno O 117 9.40e 75-16 With Pluck 116² Stewart Little 120½ I m Gonna Fly 108¹ Late foot 12

LATEST WORKOUTS Aug 10 CT 3f fst .37 b

Philbrook
Own.—Mims T B

Dk. b. or br. c. 2, by One Sub—Sea Muffin, by Battlefield
Br.—Mims T B (Va)
Tr.—Windle G B Jr

114

				St. 1st 2nd 3rd	Amt.
			1972 2 M 0 1	$299

29Aug72- 1ShD fst 6f 23⅘ .48½ 1.15⅖ Md Sp Wt 6 5 54 45½ 32 31½ Kloss G 118 4.30 75-17 Merry Flirt 115¾ Weird Harrold 118½ Philbrook 118⁴ No Mishap 10
22Aug72- 1ShD fst 5½f 23⅘ .48½ 1.09 Md Sp Wt 9 9 75½ 75¾ 53 53 Kloss G 119 4.90 78-17 Double Flash 116no Fine Delite 119no Weird Harrold 119½ Late bid 9

LATEST WORKOUTS ●Aug 4 ShD 5f fst 1.02⅗ hg Jly 25 ShD 3f fst .36¾ bg

Berry, Time P J
Own.—Miller P J
Br.—Miller P J (W.Va)
Tr.—Smith F J

																1972	6	1	1	1	$2,806

29Aug72- 1ShD	fst	6f	.23⅖	.48⅖ 1.15⅖		1	22	22	2hd	1½	Sam J	115	5.30	77-17 Merry Flirt 115¾ Weird Harrold 118¾ Philbrook 118⁴	Driving 10
16Aug72- 5Tim	fst	5¾f	.24	.48⅖ 1.11¼	③Md Sp Wt	1	4	3nk	3nk	3nk	43½	Grove P	118	6.90	79-15 Misty Eyes 118no Arizona Witch 118¹ Solindra 118²½	Speed, tired 8
21Jly72- 6Del	fst	5½f	.22⅖	.47 1.06	Md 10500	1	5	3½	45	38	313	Jimenez C	117	4.10	75-17 Take Charge 120¾ Tall Award 120¹² Merry Flirt 117no	Evenly 8
13Jly72- 1Del	sly	5½f	.22⅖	.47½ 1.07¼	Md 7500	4	9	913	814	88½	22½	Hinojosa H	117	7.70	79-14 April Treat 117²¼ Merry Flirt 117no Tuscarawas 120³	Closed fast 10
29Jun72- 3Del	sly	5½f	.22⅖	.48⅖ 1.08¼	③Md Sp Wt	2	5	2½	55½	46½	56	Jimenez C	117	3.00	70-18 Popeyes Proof 117³ Primpies Cutie 118¾ Tiger Magic 120½	Brief speed 10
8Jun72- 2Del	fst	5f	.22⅖	.46⅖ .59	③Md Sp Wt	3	4	53½	46	711	714	Black A N	119	54.20	80-14 Honorable Miss 119¹½ Tuerta 119⁸ Curupi 119²	Early speed 12

LATEST WORKOUTS   Aug 12 ShD 4f fst .49 b

Hug Bug
Own.—Skinner J L
Dk. b. or br. f. 2, by Rash Prince—Accepted Dare, by Prince Dare
Br.—Skinner J L (Md)
Tr.—Skinner J L

																1972	2	M	0	0	Amt.

11Jly72- 3Lib	fst	5½f	.22⅖	.48½ 1.09	Md 6500	6	3	2hd	2½	44½ 107½	Rowland J5	110	62.70	67-23 Morning Shower 118²½ Tucson Twist 115¹ Rays Pet 118½	Tired 12
16Jun72- 5Lib	fst	5f	.23⅖	.49 1.01⅖	⑤Clm 8000	4	6	76½	79½	714 729	Rowland J5	111	31.50	55-21 Poppy Jackie 120⁴½ Western K. 118½ Tight Fight 114³	Trailed 7

Easter Psalm
Own.—Torreyson L E
Dk. b. or br. f. 2, by War Tune—Happy Hobby, by Piet
Br.—Torreyson L E (Md)
Tr.—Torreyson L E

																1972	8	1	2	1	Amt. $2,940

24Aug72- 4ShD	fst	5½f	.23⅖	.48⅖ 1.08⅖	Clm 5000	1	7	55½	53	31	21	Addesa E	b 119	*2.20	81-18 Cupids Boy 119¹ Easter Psalm 119hd Transplant 116½	Blocked, missed 7
10Aug72- 4ShD	fst	5½f	.23⅖	.48 1.08⅖	Clm 5000	5	6	64¾	32½	42½	41½	Addesa E	b 118	2.30	82-15 Till Best 116¾ Lady Ski 116nk Easter Psalm 118⁴	Rallied 6
3Aug72- 6ShD	my	6f	.23⅖	.48 1.15	Clm 5000	1	3	66	42½	31½	43	Addesa E	b 119	3.70	76-15 Chanook 115¹ Till Best 115² Mountain Mamma 115no	Good try 9
20Jly72- 1ShD	fst	5½f	.24⅖	.49⅖ 1.09⅖	Md 5000	2	3	31½	2hd	13	16	Addesa E	b 119	2.10	78-18 Easter Psalm 118⁶ Sailor Max 118⁵ Caralette 115²	Driving 9
6Jly72- 2CT	fst	4½f	.23		③Md Sp Wt	3	7	66	44	43½	18½	Addesa E	118	4.80	85-10 Fathers Ace 118²¼ Gama Queen 116¹ Bonus Money 119hd	No rally 10
19Jun72- 1CT	fst	4½f	.23⅖	.54½	③Md Sp Wt	1	7	79½	66¼	49	49½	Addesa E	119	5.00	77-11 Save The Eagle 119⁷ Moby Doll 119¹ Lady Wakefield 114¹	Late foot 9
8Jun72- 1CT	fst	4½f	.23	.48⅖ .55½	Md 5000	7	7	67	47	41½	43½	Addesa E	119	*2.30	81-12 Lady Ski 116⅝ Cagey Baby 119no Minnie Sue 119½	No rally 10
1Jun72- 1CT	fst	4½f	.23⅖	.48½ .54½	Md 5000	5	7	48½	37	28	Addesa E	119	*2.20	77-12 Lovers Lyre 119⁸ Easter Psalm 119¹½ Minnie Sue 119½	Gamely 8

LATEST WORKOUTS   ● Aug 10 CT 3f fst .36⅗ b

Bonus Money
Own.—Longerbeam Betty
Dk. b. or br. g. 2, by Idyll Money—Monte's Pette, by Monte Cristo
Br.—Longerbeam Mr-Mrs M G (W. Va)
Tr.—Longerbeam M G

																1972	7	2	1	2	Amt. $4,000

28Aug72- 8ShD	fst	6f	.23⅖	.47⅖ 1.14	Allowance	6	5	32	12	13	13	Vasil A	b 119	*.70e	84-21 Bonus Money 1193 Come On Rabbit 112nk Tumble Bug 116²	Driving 8
18Aug72- 9ShD	fst	6f	.22⅖	.47 1.14⅖	Handicap	6	5	13	1hd	2½	3²½	Vasil A	b 114	3.60	79-16 Fathers Ace 119¹½ Deep Rang 116¹ Bonus Money 114⁴	Weakened 6
9Aug72- 4ShD	fst	3½f	.22⅖	.34½ .41	Allowance	3	6			43½ 1½	Vasil A	b 120	*1.40	90-10 ②Bonus Money 120½ Lind 117² Black Go 120nk	Swerved start 6
29Jly72- 6ShD	fst	6f	.23⅖	.47⅖ 1.14⅖	Allowance	3	3	68½	35	33½	22½	Vasil A	119	4.10	79-17 Chatsrullah 1194½ Bonus Money 119⁴ Juss Fishing 116²½	Gamely 9

29Jly72-Evening Program

21Jly72- 9ShD	fst	5½f	.24	.48½ 1.08⅖	Handicap	3	4	88½	85½	86½	88½	Fitzgerald R	115	*2.20e	75-15 Fathers Ace 116½ ②Deep Rang 114¹ Lovers Lyre 112hd	No Factor 10
12Jly72- 1ShD	fst	3½f	.22⅖	.34 .40⅖	Md Sp Wt	5	5		1hd 16½	Vasil A	119	*.70	93-05 Bonus Money 1194½ Sailor Max 1193½ Gin Stone 1091½	Mild drive 10
6Jly72- 2CT	fst	4½f	.23	.47⅖ .54	Md Sp Wt	2	1		43 33½ 33½	Vasil A	119	*1.80	85-10 Fathers Ace 119²½ Gama Queen 116¹ Bonus Money 119hd	Mild bid 10

LATEST WORKOUTS   Aug 3 CT 3f my .38⅖ b

Rob-O-Let
Own.—Houston R B
Dk. b. or br. c. 2, by Restless Cloud—Betaway, by Bossuet
Br.—Houston R B Jr (Va)
Tr.—Thomas M

																1972	3	1	0	1	Amt. $1,600

28Aug72- 8ShD	fst	6f	.23⅖	.47⅖ 1.14	Allowance	8	2	64½	78	716	Grove P	119	5.70	68-21 Bonus Money 1193 Come On Rabbit 112nk Tumble Bug 116²	Stopped 8
15Aug72- 6ShD	fst	6f	.23	.48⅖ 1.15⅖	Md Sp Wt	4	1	13	12	13	12	Fitzgerald R	119	2.20	77-19 Rob-O-Let 119² Fine Delite 119³ Chaptico Challenge 119¹½	Mild Drive 7
10Jly72- 1ShD	fst	3½f	.22⅖	.34⅖ .40⅖	Md Sp Wt	8	1		24 33½	Fitzgerald R	119	5.40	88-08 Cagey Baby 1194½ Hes Myrullah 119no Rob-O-Let 119²½	No mishap 10

LATEST WORKOUTS   ● Aug 10 ShD 3f fst .36⅖ b

Smoked Salmon raced once at Timonium, finishing second in a maiden-special-weight event that was run in the good time of 1:09⅖. He was beaten by Prince Wave. With a little further research, we can find Prince Wave's record and see that he had come to Timonium from the big leagues, Monmouth Park, where he had finished second in a maiden-$14,000-claiming race. Smoked Salmon's performance against this rival suggests that he is much superior to the West Virginia allowance horses, who probably aren't worth more than $5000 or so.

After reaching this conclusion on that day in 1972, I was congratulating myself for my own brilliance. I went to Shenandoah to bet Smoked Salmon, knowing his odds had to be excellent since his superiority could be detected only by the most sophisticated handicapping. After Smoked Salmon won, I collected the princely payoff of $4.40. Horseplayers aren't so dumb.

There is another type of class advantage that is so subtle that the betting public rarely detects it and that provides some of the most solid and lucrative opportunities in racing. Even races with a precise class designation — $10,000 claiming company, for instance — come in great variety. There are weak fields of $10,000 claimers and highly competitive fields of $10,000 claimers. A horse moving from an unusually strong field into an average one would be taking what amounts to a drop in class. Steve Davidowitz discovered a way to identify these strong fields, which he christened the Key-Race Method.

On August 5, 1972, Steve and I watched Scrimshaw defeat Gay Gambler by four lengths in an allowance race on the grass at Saratoga. There seemed to be nothing exceptional about the race. Its time was not particularly fast. The horses in the field did not have dazzling credentials.

A week later the Bernard Baruch Handicap was run at Saratoga and drew so many of the nation's star turf runners that it was split into two divisions. Scrimshaw won the first division impressively. The second division was captured in track-record time by Chrisaway, a 50-to-1 shot who had finished ninth behind Scrimshaw in that allowance race. The performance of these two horses suggested that the field on August 5 had been very strong — of stakes caliber, in fact. When Gay Gambler was entered in an average allowance race a few days later, we knew that we could view him as if he were a stakes horse dropping sharply in class. He won and paid $5. Chartered Course, who had finished a distant last on August 5, won his next start and paid $25. Mongo's Image, another of the also-rans in that field, came back to win and returned $17.

To detect these key races, I keep a set of all the result charts at the track I am following. Whenever a horse wins, I note on the chart of his previous start his victory and the class in which he accomplished it. When two horses come out of the same field and win, I will pay careful attention to any horse in that field when he makes his next start. During the winter of 1973, I was looking for key races at Shenandoah Downs and found one in the first race on November 15.

The winner, Wild Journalist, had come back to finish second in an allowance race. Meadow Lady subsequently won in maiden-special-weight company. Lee Bee won for $5000. Bien Chica and Rough Powder, the seventh- and eighth-place finishers, won their next starts in maiden-claiming company. Then the sixth-place finisher, Godie's Lady, was entered in a $2500 maiden-claiming event. Her past performances couldn't have been more dismal.

Godie's Lady was such a hapless creature that she had never finished in the money during her ten-race career. But

FIRST RACE
3 ½ FURLONGS. (.39) MAIDEN SPECIAL WEIGHTS. Purse $2,100. 2-year-olds. Weight, 11

Shenand'h

NOVEMBER 15, 1973

Value of race $2,100, value to winner $1,260. second $420, third $210, fourth $105, fifth $63, sixth $42. Mutuel pool $1

Last Raced	Horse	Eqt.A.Wt	PP St	$\frac{1}{4}$	Str	Fin	Jockey	Od
8Nov73 ¹ShD³	Wild Journalist	b 2 115	5 1	1^3	1^4	$1^{3\frac{1}{2}}$	Sanders M L	
3Nov73 ⁹ShD⁸	Meadow Lady	b 2 115	10 3	$2^{\frac{1}{2}}$	2^3	2^{7k}	Kirk D	
30Oct73 ¹ShD²	Lee Bee	2 111	8 5	5^1	5^2	3^1	Shelton P⁷	
31Oct73 ³ShD	Berk Motley	b 2 118	4 2	3^4	3^3	$4^{\frac{1}{2}}$	Dalgo M J	
	Captain America	2 118	1 9	7^1	7^2	5^2	Detiege C†	
24Oct73 ³ShD⁷	Godie's Lady	2 117	9 4	6^3	$6^{\frac{1}{2}}$	6^{nk}	Reynolds L	
1Nov73 ¹ShD⁹	Bien Chica	2 115	7 6	4^{hd}	$4^{\frac{1}{2}}$	7^2	Canizo V	
	Rough Powder	2 118	6 8	9^{10}	8^{hd}	8^1	Castaneda O	
24Aug73 ²CT¹⁰	Trail Fire	2 115	3 7	$8^{\frac{1}{2}}$	9^{10}	9^8	Smith D D	
18Oct73 ¹ShD¹⁰	Robin Diane K.	2 115	2 10	10	10	10	Grove P	

Time, :22⅘, :34⅖, :40⅘s Track fast.

Official Program Numbers

$2 Mutuel Prices:

5-WILD JOURNALIST		4.60	3.00	2.40
10-MEADOW LADY			3.40	2.80
8-LEE BEE				2.60

dk b or br. f, by Journalist—Wild Harp, by Royal Lover. Trainer Adams J P. Bred by Soule C I Jr (Md).

IN GATE AT 7:20 OFF AT 7:20 EST Start Good Won Easily

Owners— 1. Adams Jr & Stokely; 2. Wood R W; 3. O'Neill W D Jr; 4. Letourneau B; 5. Wood H G; 6. McCanns 7. Armstrong P; 8. Michael C W; 9. Reid G W; 10. Krebs V.

† Apprentice allowance waived: Captain America 7 pounds.

Overweight: Godie's Lady 2 pounds.

Scratched—Distaff Dilly; Old Man Even Up; Capitol Love; Len Hauss (3Nov73¹ShD⁹).

in the November 15 key race she had beaten two horses who subsequently won for $3000 and $3500. In a $2500 race, Godie's Lady was theoretically a standout on the basis of class. A handicapper with the courage of his convictions would have collected a $16.20 payoff.

The various applications of class that I use in handicapping are extremely valuable, but they do not explain all the situations in which class will determine the outcome of a race. I am sure there are many other facets of the class factor that I have not yet dreamed of. No matter how smart a horseplayer would like to think he is, there are always new things to learn, new areas to explore.

11

Money Management

I WAS BUBBLING with optimism and self-confidence when I went to Laurel Race Course on opening day of the 1973 season. There were two horses on the program — Samoht in the fifth race and Amorio in the ninth — who looked like superb bets. If one of them was successful, I would have a good day. If both of them won, it would be a spectacular afternoon.

Samoht lost and Amorio won at 3-to-2 odds, so I should have made a modest profit. I didn't. Instead, I managed to lose $700. Arranging this debacle did not require any unusually aberrant behavior — just the sort of erratic money management that is a common racetrack disease and prevents many sound handicappers from beating the races.

I wanted to make a strong bet on Samoht in the fifth and thought it would be nice to make a modest score early in the day so that I could be betting the track's money by that time. I took a few chances, therefore, on the daily double and the third-race exacta, and by the fifth race I was losing $100. I briefly considered cutting down my wager on Samoht but when he went off at 11 to 1, I decided that any such restraint would be an act of cowardice. I bet $300, and when he finished out of the money I was beginning to worry. I didn't want to go into the Amorio race in a position where I would have to make a big bet just to get even. So I tried to recoup quickly. I took a shot at the seventh-race exacta and when that failed I convinced myself I had found a promising horse in the eighth race. I bet $100 on Return to Reality, and when he finished second I was minus $550 going into the Amorio race. My horse's odds were 3 to 2 — a generous price considering his credentials — but even a maximum bet of $300 wouldn't get me even. And I was feeling so shaky by this time that I didn't want to risk so much. So I compromised. The ninth race was another exacta event, and I decided to play three exactas for $50 apiece, combining Amorio with the horses I considered likely to finish second. Amorio won easily, but an impossible longshot ran second and wiped me out. It was the worst day of my life at a racetrack, not only in terms of money but in terms of stupidity. If I had just done roughly what I had intended to do at the start of the day — bet $300 to win on each of the two horses I liked — I would have shown a $150 profit for the afternoon.

Every horseplayer has had similar experiences, probably more often than he would care to remember. He may plan his course of action meticulously before he goes to the track, but when he is there he will be subjected to such an onslaught of emotions — overconfidence, lack of confidence, greed, conservatism, complacency, desperation, panic — that he will not be able to function like a machine. But he must try. Even when a man has mastered the art of handicapping, he has not learned how to beat the races. Money management is, with no exaggeration, 50 percent of the game. I know many excellent handicappers who seldom show a profit because they cannot properly discipline their betting and control their emotions. And I know people with seemingly inferior handicapping skills who manage to win because they know how to bet intelligently.

Most handicapping books suggest, and many horse-players share the belief, that the one secret of successful betting is extreme patience. The stereotype of the professional gambler is a man who makes only a few bets a week. He sits immobile, race after race and day after day, waiting for the occasional spot that offers a golden opportunity. With all the discipline of a Calvinist spurning the temptations of the flesh, he resists the siren call of daily doubles, exactas, trifectas, 50-to-1 shots, and any race in which his convictions are less than total. Then the moment comes: he finds a solid 8-to-5 shot who meets all his requirements; he walks to the window and bets his bankroll. Whether he wins or loses, his equanimity is unaffected. He returns to his seat to wait, wait, wait for the next solid situation.

Many of the people who believe that this is the way to beat the races are losers who are deceiving themselves about their own abilities and ignoring the psychological realities of the racetrack. A horseplayer may go to the track, bet a succession of losers, and then cash one solid winner that gets him even for the day. Afterward he rationalizes, "That winner was a real standout. If I could just wait for horses like that and sit out all the other races, I'd be a winner."

But this is easier said than done, as one of my racetrack

acquaintances learned not long ago. Ray Fritz was a waiter in a Georgetown restaurant who went to the races on his days off. He was too eager for action, too prone to bet every race, but he believed that if he ever became a full-time gambler he would be motivated to exercise the necessary restraint. One day at Bowie he parlayed a borrowed $200 into $2000 and decided to fulfill every casual horseplayer's dream. He quit his job and became a professional gambler. His calling came naturally enough. Ray's father was a big bettor and his whole family loved to gamble. A year before, he had made a junket to Las Vegas with his grandmother, his father, two aunts, and two uncles. Having had so much exposure to betting, Ray knew the secret of success: self-discipline. If he was going to beat the horses, he had to pick his spots carefully. He couldn't bet nine races a day with gusto and hope to survive.

Ray started his new career by wagering $200 on solid, conservative selections; he passed many races and made only token bets on most of the others. The strategy worked beautifully. After two weeks he was more than $4000 ahead.

But difficulties were arising. When a horseplayer is trying to operate with extreme patience and caution, what does he do when he finds a 10-to-1 shot who looks very promising but does not quite meet all his requirements for a strong wager? If he doesn't bet and the horse wins, he is going to be haunted by the missed opportunity and start cursing his own conservatism. After his initial flurry of success, Ray became so confident about his own handicapping ability that he started playing these marginal horses. If an animal didn't quite qualify for his maximum $200 bet, he might venture $100 or $150.

As he began to deviate from his original policy of restraint, Ray began to lose. He knew he should retrench and renew his determination to wait for the solid opportunities. But it is painfully difficult for any gambler suffering through a losing streak to resist trying to recoup immediately. Ray was betting more than ever in an effort to recover his losses. As these losses continued to mount, he was shooting for the moon every day. Instead of hoping to cash one $200 bet on a 2-to-1 shot, he was thinking, "If I hit this horse I'll parlay it onto the next race, and then if I hit the exacta I'll win ten grand."

Betting wildly, desperately, Ray was losing $500 a day but kept going back to the track, figuring his lucky day might be imminent. It never came, and Ray was wiped out. He now has a job as a salesman and goes to the track on his days off.

The "professional" approach of playing very few races rarely works in actual practice for anyone who lacks the self-control of a Hindu holy man. But the concept behind this approach is undeniably sound. Any horseplayer who hopes to win consistently must do it on the few races that he can decipher clearly and bet with confidence. After my $700 fiasco at Laurel, I was convinced for the last time that I needed some system of betting that would force me to take maximum advantages of the races I knew offered good opportunities. At the same time I needed a method that would permit me to be a human being who likes action, who likes to take stabs on 50-to-1 shots and shoot for a fortune in exacta races. I finally developed a realistic set of guidelines that simultaneously disciplines me and allows me the latitude for some self-indulgence.

I divide all possible wagers into two categories: prime bets and action bets. Primes are the crème de la crème. They are the horses who meet all my important handicapping requirements, who I realistically think have a better than 50 percent chance of winning, and who are going to the post at odds of 7 to 5 or higher.

Many horseplayers would disdain such low odds. When I was a $2 bettor, I thought anyone who played favorites was revealing a lack of imagination in his handicapping or a weakness in his character. And I was right not to wager on favorites then, because I lacked the skill to pick the high percentage of winners that is necessary to make them worthwhile.

Nobody can pick even short-priced winners with unfailing success, of course, because certainties do not exist in racing. A horse who looks unbeatable on paper often loses because of bad racing luck, larceny, or imperceptible changes in his condition. But a handicapper equipped with good figures and good judgment should be able to hit at least 50 percent of his most solid selections. If he wins with half of the 7-to-5 shots he bets, he will make a profit of 20 percent on his investments. That is a healthy rate of return.

Any nonprime bet is an action bet. It may be a 50-to-1 flyer. It may be an exacta in which I hook up three or four horses. It may be a solid horse who narrowly misses qualifying as a prime. It may be a virtual sure thing whose odds are inadequate.

The starting point in my betting system is to set a fixed amount for prime bets. This amount should equal somewhere between 5 and 10 percent of a horseplayer's total betting capital. If he has $3000 earmarked for gambling, he might make $150 prime bets. This amount should be high enough to make losing hurt just a little and restrain a horseplayer from making a prime bet unless he is very confident. It should be high enough so that a man who hits one 7-to-5 shot will consider his profits a very adequate day's pay. But the amount should not be so high that it will make a horseplayer too conservative or uncomfortable and wreck his equilibrium if he loses two or three bets in a row.

Having set the amount of a prime bet, I permit myself to lose no more than two-thirds of this sum on all my action bets during the course of a day. And I may bet no more than one-third of a prime on any race. If a horseplayer making $150 prime bets goes to the track on a day when he can find no outstanding wagers, he may bet no more than $50 on any race and lose no more than $100 during the course of a day. If he does make a prime bet, he still may lose $100 in action bets in addition to his $150.

I think these guidelines are sane and realistic. The prime bets insure that a horseplayer will be putting his big money where it belongs. The action bets give him an outlet for his gambling instincts and give him the chance to make a substantial profit even if he happens to be wrong on the one race where he has a strong conviction.

The chief difficulty of this method is making the fine-line decision whether a very promising horse should be a prime or merely an action bet. This is never easy. When I handicap the races before going to the track, I look for horses who may deserve a prime bet, but I never make a final decision until the race itself. Sometimes the track condition, the appearance of the horse, the odds, or other factors will sway me. Sometimes I will be agonizing until five minutes before post time and be guided by my instincts.

But no matter how excruciating the decision may be, a horseplayer must make it one way or another. If he is operating with $150 prime bets and $50 maximum action bets, he will invariably be tempted to compromise and wager $100 or so when he can't make up his mind how much he likes a horse. This is the surest road to ruin at the racetrack: betting fairly large sums of money on horses who are fairly good. When he starts blurring the distinction between prime and nonprime bets, a horseplayer is taking a step that will inevitably lead toward helter-skelter betting with no proper balance between his strong and weak selections. And eventually he is going to have days when he comes home depressed and wondering, "How did I lose five hundred dollars today? There wasn't a single horse I really liked."

Horseplayers ought to get into the habit of betting to win only, and avoiding the false security of place and show wagers. The mathematics of betting is such that the tracks and the state extract a slightly higher percentage from the place and show pools. This adds up in the long run. If a gambler maintains a list of all his prime bets during the course of a year, he will almost surely find that betting to win only will produce the greatest return.

Betting horses both to win and place offers one psychological advantage. When his selection finishes second, a horseplayer will get his money back and perhaps make a small profit. Some horseplayers become so distressed when they lose by a nose that their confidence is undermined and their subsequent judgment is warped. Win and place betting makes them feel more comfortable. But ideally a horseplayer should be willing to take the consequences when he makes a serious bet. He should recognize that in the long run the good and bad breaks will even out and he will make more money if he has the courage to stick to win betting only.

The stick-in-the-mud purists who write most handicapping books usually counsel their readers to avoid not only place and show bets, but also the temptations of gimmicks like the exacta, in which the object is to pick the first two finishers in a race in correct order. Exactas have become very popular at American tracks during the last few years, and I personally find them irresistible. They offer a way to bet sound, logical horses and still make large profits with a fairly small investment. There is nothing sinful or unprofessional about that.

When I encounter a prime bet in an exacta race, my enthusiasm for the exacta usually depends on the odds of my horse. If he is 2 to 1 or better, I am inclined to bet most of my money to win. When I locate a solid horse at a good price, I want to be sure that I am going to make an ample profit if he wins, without having to worry about who will run second. If I have a conviction about the horse who is likely to run second, I may place a small portion of my prime bet on a single exacta combination.

But when a prime bet is going to the post at unappetizing odds — 7 to 5 or less — I may be inclined to gamble. If I can narrow down the other contenders, I may invest my whole prime bet in a few exacta combinations. If my horse wins and I lose money on the race, I am prepared to feel very stupid.

Exactas are most attractive in nonprime situations. There are many times an astute handicapper will not be able to isolate the likely winner of a race but can separate the contenders from the noncontenders. By combining three or four horses in the exacta, he can bet with some confidence. I know a horseplayer named André who developed this technique to the point of near perfection.

André is a racetrack jetsetter who spends his winters at Hialeah and Gulfstream, his summers at Longchamp in Paris, and his autumns at Belmont Park. When he is not gambling he does not deign to engage in gainful employment, though he does write a little avant-garde prose. (When he employed his ornate style on an examination at

Yale, the professor gave him an F with the notation, "If English is not your native language, please see me.") So André's friends, most of whom work for a living, have always viewed him as something of a wastrel. But two years ago they were forced to start treating him with more respect. After conceiving his system, André won more than $8000 in a single Florida season while betting almost exclusively at the $2 exacta window.

During his periodic stays in France, André followed with admiration the exploits of the legendary horse bettor known as Monsieur X. The tierce, a bet in which the object is to pick the first three finishers in a race, is a national mania in France, and Monsieur X won it so often that the country's racing authorities had to change the rules of the game to foil him. Monsieur X's technique was to study the tierce field, which would usually contain about twenty horses, and eliminate roughly half of the entrants, the ones he figured had no chance at all. Then he would play all the combinations involving the contenders. He had to invest a small fortune, but he won a large fortune.

André believed that he could adapt this method for use at the Florida tracks. He had observed that a powerful bias existed at Hialeah and Gulfstream: horses with early speed and inside post positions were dominant. And horses who had been competing during the first segment of the Florida season at Calder Race Course had an advantage over seemingly classier rivals that had been rested since the end of the New York season.

André would unhesitatingly eliminate stretch runners, horses in outside post positions, and horses who had not raced recently, and then combine four or five contenders in the exacta, investing about $50 a race. His purist friends were horrified. One of them scolded him: "Five horses in a race! You're betting like you're at the supermarket." But André collected so many astronomical exactas that he silenced all the skeptics.

When a horseplayer has developed a workable method of handicapping and adopted a rational system of money management, he may hope that he will now be able to live without the drastic, unsettling rises and falls of fortune that most gamblers must endure. But he won't. He will still experience the dizzying exhilaration of occasional winning streaks that make him think he is God, and, much more often, the excruciation of losing streaks that threaten to unhinge him completely.

Long winning or losing streaks can make or break a horseplayer's year. He must learn to understand and cope with them. Most so-called runs of luck at the racetrack are caused not by fate but by the bettor himself — by the astuteness of his handicapping and by his own mental attitude. Nongamblers may think that this sounds ridiculous: one individual's state of mind has no influence on the performance of a group of dumb animals. But an experienced horseplayer knows that when he goes to the track with a negative attitude, thinking, "I can't afford to lose more than one hundred dollars today," he is foredoomed to lose at least $100. And when he goes to the track with an air of quiet assurance, realizing that there are no certainties in racing but also feeling supremely confident of his own abilities as a handicapper, he is likely to be a winner.

This may sound as if it borders on the occult, but a horseplayer must try to develop a sense of when he is likely to lose and when he is likely to win. One season at Bowie I was suffering through a run of what seemed to be legitimate bad luck. My handicapping was sharp, but I had lost six straight photo finishes on horses I had bet seriously. Then, finally, I made a healthy wager on a 16-to-1 shot, sweated out an interminable three-horse photo, and won it. That night I celebrated by taking my girl friend to Duke Zeibert's Restaurant for lobster and told her excitedly, "This is just the beginning. I'm going to win a lot of money in the next few weeks." I recounted the tale of Sun in Action, when one winner so changed my mental attitude that a months-long losing streak was transformed overnight into a monumental winning streak. She was still doubtful. Two weeks later, after an unbroken string of successes for me at Bowie, we were celebrating over crab imperial at La Bagatelle and she asked me, "Did you really know you were going to win?" I did. A horseplayer can feel it, know it as well as he knows himself. When he is in command of the handicapping techniques that are working at a particular time and place, when he is brimming with confidence in his own skills, he knows. These great winning streaks usually do not last very long, but while they do they are the high points of a gambler's life. During the time they are running their course, a horseplayer must consciously try to capitalize on them. He should go to the track every day he can and be much more aggressive than usual in his betting, perhaps raising the scale of his wagers until the streak ends.

Losing streaks are much more difficult to recognize because nobody wants to recognize them. But a horseplayer who has the experience and honesty to sense when he is about to lose can save himself a lot of money.

A few years ago at Saratoga I watched a professional handicapper operate throughout the four-week season and witnessed a display of perception and discipline that was almost superhuman. The man's handicapping was consistently brilliant; during the first two weeks of the meeting he won more than $6000. Then he encountered a race in which he was torn between two horses. He had been leaning toward one but a few minutes before post time changed his mind and bet $400 on the other. The wrong horse won, and he left the track uncharacteristically shaken and depressed. The next day he told me, "That race really messed up my head. I'm going to take it easy betting for a while." For the next week he wagered on a piddling scale, rarely venturing more than $20 on a race. I was appalled. Here was a man riding on the crest of a winning streak that most horse-players could only dream about, and he virtually stopped betting after just one tough loss. After a week of this restraint, my friend told me he had found the horse who was going to restore his confidence — a filly named Table Flirt who was a superior mudder and would be competing over a sloppy track. He bet $500 to win, and Table Flirt romped home by seven lengths at odds of 9 to 5. My friend immediately resumed betting with his usual gusto and finished the Saratoga meeting with a $9000 profit. Yet if he had not taken that week's breather, if he had allowed that one unsettling defeat to plunge him into a state of depression and a losing streak, Saratoga might have been a disaster for him.

Every horseplayer should learn to recognize the harbingers of a losing streak. I have detected three reliable signs that disaster is just around the next bend.

A few painful or unlucky losses — caused by photo finishes, disqualifications, or jockeys' errors — can wreck a bettor's mental attitude. He starts thinking, subconsciously, that he is fated to lose, so it doesn't matter what he does. In this frame of mind he will inevitably start handicapping sloppily and betting masochistically.

A horseplayer will often get into trouble when the conditions change abruptly at the track where he is operating. If he has been using a track bias to his advantage, he will have a great deal of trouble adjusting when the track returns to normal and the bias ceases to exist.

The most disastrous losing streaks usually come immediately after a horseplayer has enjoyed a great winning streak. His self-assurance gradually changes into cockiness and overconfidence. He begins to think that anything he does will turn out right, and without realizing it he becomes careless and undisciplined in his handicapping and betting. Danny Lavezzo, a bettor who owns the fashionable New York bar P. J. Clarke's, terms this phenomenon the "Messiah complex." Lavezzo had been spending a winter in Florida and had a phenomenal hot streak at Gulfstream and Hialeah. "It was one of those periods when speed on the rail was winning everything," he recalled, "and I was betting speed on the rail. I picked all the winners. Best bets at fifteen to one, things like that. After a while, I thought I was infallible. I was getting a Messiah complex. I should have realized that was the beginning of the end. I was lucky to break even for the season."

The turning point from a winning streak to a losing streak usually comes at approximately the moment when a horseplayer utters the words, "How long has this game been going on?" It happened to me in the fall of 1972 at Laurel. For six weeks I had been picking long-priced winners at a phenomenal rate. When I touted all my friends onto Dismas and watched him win easily and pay $39.40, I was overcome by the Messiah complex. Even with colleagues like Clem Florio, who had taught me much of what I know about horse racing, I was exuding an air of smug, obnoxious superiority. I was God's gift to the art of handicapping. Of my next twenty prime bets, nineteen lost. "This game," Clem reminded me, "will keep you humble."

Losing streaks, like many illnesses, can usually be cured if they are detected early. When a horseplayer recognizes the signs of a losing streak he may continue going to the track and cut his bets down drastically. If he succumbs to temptation too easily, he should stay away from the track for a few days, recycle his thinking, and return to action on a day when he sees a solid prime bet or at least finds the races generally promising. These periods of abstinence may save him hundreds or even thousands of dollars during the course of a year. And at the end of the year, when a horseplayer is totaling his net profits or losses, a thousand saved is as good as a thousand earned.

All horseplayers, even the monomaniacs like me, live a portion of our lives away from the racetrack, and sometimes external forces will adversely affect our performance as gamblers. One such factor is money. When a man is beset by financial pressures in his personal life, he cannot hope to function well at the track; it is an old gambling axiom that scared money never wins. Walter Haight, the late racing columnist of the Washington *Post*, gave me a piece of advice about money when I was a fledgling horseplayer, and I have never forgotten it. "When you're at the track," he said, "you've got to think of money as if it were chips or pebbles that are only used to keep score of how well you're doing. When you start thinking that you could be using your gambling money to pay the rent, or buy a new suit, you'll never be able to win." A horseplayer ought to maintain a betting fund completely separate from the money he lives on. This is especially important if he is married, so that his wife does not have to worry that every trip he makes to the track may be taking food out of the kiddies' mouths.

While horseplayers sometimes cannot control the financial pressures in their personal lives, they have no excuse for letting alcohol interfere with their gambling. Unfortunately, many racetrackers occasionally mix booze and betting. The results can be disastrous. A Washington horseplayer named Carlos Meyer holds what may be the all-time record for money not won because of drinking: $13,920.

A few years ago Carlos was working as a bartender in Georgetown. His boss, an inveterate horseplayer, had received some information from usually reliable sources about a three-year-old ready to win his next start at Hialeah. When the horse's name appeared in the overnight entries, he was listed at 20 to 1.

The boss's bookie had been arrested the week before and there was no way he could place a substantial wager in Washington. So he and his friends who wanted to bet the horse pooled their money and bought a ticket on a 10 A.M. flight to Miami the next day. They gave the ticket to Carlos, along with their betting money of $600. With $600 in his pocket, especially if it is somebody else's money, Carlos is likely to misbehave. Which he did that night. He hit most of the bars on M Street, celebrating as if the horse had already won, drinking rum and Cokes until four in the morning. He didn't know how he got home, but he did manage to set his alarm for 9 A.M. He woke up at two in the afternoon. The alarm clock was lying on the floor, where he had hurled it five hours earlier when its buzzing disturbed his slumber. Carlos called his boss and told him what had happened. His boss was mad. He was a little madder that evening after he learned that the horse had won and paid $46.20. Carlos did not come out of hiding for several days.

As harmful as money problems and alcohol may be, the most deleterious effects on a horseplayer's concentration are caused by women. When a gambler has had an exceptional day at the track, or is in the midst of a great winning streak, he may exude a sense of self-esteem and confidence to which women respond. If this occurs the horseplayer is dangerously apt to fall in love, and the distraction is sure to wreck him at the track. This has happened to me twice. Once I took a date to Bowie and picked five straight winners; the day was so marvelous that it started an immediate romance. I had losing days on my next twenty-one trips to the track. The other time it happened at Saratoga. I won $2000 on an exacta and a few hours later happened to meet a fascinating woman. The reaction was such that I promptly lost more than $2000 in the next week.

Pittsburgh Phil, the legendary gambler who won nearly $2 million in his racing career, had strong opinions about the opposite sex. "A man who wishes to be successful," he wrote, "cannot divide his attention between horses and women. A man who accepts the responsibility of escorting a woman to the race track and of seeing that she is comfortably placed and agreeably entertained cannot keep his mind on the work before him. A sensible woman understands this and cannot feel hurt at my words."

In my youth I once thought that the remedy for the inevitable problems that are posed by women would be to find a woman who was a full-fledged horseplayer herself. She would be sympathetic to my compulsion and might even be able to help me handicap. I was a junior at Harvard when I discovered her. I read a column in a Detroit newspaper about a girl at Michigan State University who had been playing the horses since she was twelve, betting with her hairdresser who also happened to be a bookmaker. I showed the story to my friends, who agreed that this was probably the woman of my dreams and took up a collection so that I could invite her to Boston for a weekend. I wrote her a letter that began:

Dear Roberta,
When I read the story that said you had been
playing the horses since you were twelve, I knew
I had found love . . .

Roberta accepted the invitation and I planned a big day of
gambling for our blind date: Suffolk Downs in the afternoon,
Lincoln Downs at night. Roberta proved to be a capable
handicapper and we both won modestly at Suffolk. I started
studying the evening card at Lincoln and was getting
enthusiastic about a longshot named Kentucky Cousin in
the fifth race. But Roberta folded her *Racing Form* emphati-
cally and said, "I'd rather go to dinner." I could not
understand how a person of sensitivity could pass up an
hour and a half trip to see a bunch of battle-scarred $1500
claimers running at a dumpy Rhode Island track, but I
capitulated and blew the afternoon's winnings on dinner.
The next morning I checked the Lincoln results and saw that
Kentucky Cousin had won and paid $103.60. I had learned
my lesson about mixing women and horses.

12

Putting It All Together

EVEN AFTER A HORSEPLAYER has learned all the important principles of handicapping, he may feel lost and bewildered when he tries to put his knowledge to practical use. As he analyzes a race, he will be dealing with literally thousands of pieces of information in the *Racing Form*. Ideas about speed, class, consistency, and condition will be swirling through his head. Where does he begin? How does he proceed?

I begin by writing down the speed figures that each horse has earned in his last few starts. I focus my attention on the horse with superior figures who could win today's race if he were to only duplicate his most recent performance. Then I ask myself questions about the horse, trying to judge if he is likely to run well again.

Is he reliable? I hesitate to bet a horse seriously on the basis of just one good race or big figure. Ideally, a horse should consistently run figures that are good enough to win today. Regardless of his figures, I demand that a horse show some ability to win. If he displays sucker-horse tendencies, if he has previously been entered in races that he should have won but didn't, I will view him with skepticism.

Is he in condition? A horse's physical condition can vary greatly from race to race. Even if he ran sensationally fast in his last start, I need some positive evidence that he will do it again today. I will usually assume that a horse is fit if he is trained by an extremely competent, reliable man. Otherwise, his record should show a recent race — within the last week or so — or good workouts. The final measurement of a horse's condition is made when he comes onto the track. No matter how good he looks on paper, he must also look good in the flesh.

Is he entered under suitable conditions? A horse must be entered at an appropriate distance, or all his other handicapping virtues may be irrelevant. If he is running on a muddy track, he must not have shown a previous dislike for the mud. If he is racing on a track with a pronounced bias, that bias should be in his favor.

Even if a horse with superior figures fulfills all these criteria, he may still be a risky bet. A handicapper must evaluate the other entrants in the race, not only by looking at their figures, but by judging if any of them is likely to wake up and improve dramatically upon his recent performances. He should pay careful attention to certain types of horses whose bad figures may be irrelevant or misleading:

1. A horse who has just been acquired by a leading trainer or that has been prepared in a manner the trainer has used with success in the past.

2. A horse who has been manipulated for purposes of a betting coup and receives strong betting action.

3. A horse who has been running recently under inappropriate or disadvantageous conditions: at the wrong distance, in the wrong class, with a bad jockey, on the turf, on a muddy track.

4. A horse who was hindered by a track bias in his last start.

5. A horse with the change-of-pace pattern.

6. A horse coming out of a "key race."

The ideal betting situation is a race in which one horse possesses clearly superior figures, gives all the indications that he will reproduce his good form, and meets no opponents who seem likely to improve sharply. These clear-cut prime bets seldom materialize more than once a week.

Sometimes the horse with the top figure can be eliminated on fundamental handicapping grounds, and the horse with the second-best figure will be a solid bet. Other times all the horses with established form will be so weak that a wake-up horse can be played with confidence.

It is dangerous to generalize too much about what constitutes a good betting opportunity. The game offers infinite variety. Handicapping is not a test of a man's ability to apply the right formula to the right situation. It is a test of his creative intelligence.

To demonstrate how the handicapping process works, I have selected a few races that were run in Maryland and New York during 1973 and 1974. Some are complex and some are easy, but each of them involves several important principles. Of course, no set of illustrative races, however large, could raise all the questions that a handicapper must resolve in actual practice. Even horseplayers with decades of experience are constantly facing new problems and new intellectual challenges.

8th Bowie Race Course

MARCH 6,

6 FURLONGS (chute). (1:08⅗). ALLOWANCES. Purse $7,000. 4-year-olds and up which have never won a race other than maiden, claiming, starter or hunt mee Weight, 122 lbs. Non-winners of a race other than claiming in 1974 allowed 3 such a race since Nov. 30, 5 lbs.; since Oct. 22, 7 lbs.; since Sept. 10, 10 lbs.

Cary Street 117 B. c (1970), by Ambernash—Bloomin Alibi, by Alibhai.
Br., Hilltop Stable & J. L. Reynolds (Md.).   1973 7 1 0 2

Owner, J. L. Reynolds. Trainer, H. R. Fenwick. 1974 4 0 1 1

Feb14-74⁵Bow	6 f 1:12⅘ft	5¾	114	3²	3²	4ᵘᵏ	2ⁿᵒ	Cusim'noG¹	Alw 79	Impr'sive Imp112 C'ryStr't B'kSt'e
Feb 6-74⁸Bow	6 f 1:10⅖fr	7	115	5⁴	42½	3²	32¾	GinoL¹	Alw 88	KingHotTot112 B'leStr'tBoy C'rySt
Jan18-74⁸Bow	6 f 1:12 ft	49	114	5⁵	64¼	73¾	73½	CusimanoG²	Alw 79	ComplyHur119 C'ryStr't n'rt
Jan 2-74⁶Bow	1 1/16 1:47⅜ft	12	119	1²	2ʰ	47½	57¾	Cusim'noG¹	Alw 62	Impula112 P'f'Scene n't
Dec10-73⁷Lrl	6 f 1:12½gd	37	120	8²¹	88½	87¼	55½	CannesaJ⁹	Alw 83	Violadfield120 B'dy'LT'n'rt
Nov19-73⁷Lrl	⊤ 1 1:37⅜fm	4¾	119	2½	1½	2²	55½	WalshE⁴	Alw 77	S'n'sB'th'rJim112 Gr'tR'lty Th't'sN
Nov13-73⁴Lrl	⊤ 1 1:39⅝fm	5¼	119	1³	13½	13	13¼	Cusim5oG⁷	Mdn 71	CaryStr't119 Princ'sFree West'nW

March 2 Pim 5f gd 1:04⅗h Feb 2 Pim 5f ft 1:02h Jan 26 Pim 5f sl 1:05b

Midnight Caller * 112 Gr c (1970), by Count Brook—Susie Gray, by Trojan Monarch.
Br., R. E. Vogelman, Jr. & R. R. Hunt (Md.1974 2 0 0 0

Owner, R. E. Vogelman, Jr. Trainer, R. E. Vogelman, Jr. 1973 11 4 1 1

Feb26-74⁸Bow	6 f 1:12⅘ft	12	112	1ʰ	3½	53½108¼	WrightDR⁴	Alw 73	KinwoldsD'ke122 H'dyHit T'ch ofP
Feb14-74⁵Bow	6 f 1:12⅘ft	15	112	2ʰ	2ʰ	1ʰ	67½	WrightDR⁵	Alw 71	Impr'sive Imp112 C'ryStr't B'kSt'e
Jun30-73⁶Del	6 f 1:11⅜ft	7½	112	62¾	7⁷	7⁸	89½	W'ghtDR⁷	Alw 77	KimwH'ch Pay Pap
Jun13-73⁸Del	6 f 1:12½ssl	5½	114	74¼	68½	56¼	6¹¹	WrightDR³	Alw 73	Mini-R'ng 112 S'yinch Hip H
Jun 3-73⁴Del	6 f 1:12 ft	15	114	3½	1ʰ	1ʰ	11½	Wr'htDR⁶	Alw 46	P'ryCaller112 Hostile Key R
May28-73⁵Pim	1 1/16 1:48⅜ssy	8½	112	2½	24½	48	5¹⁹	WrightDR⁷	Alw 46	KitchenG'sip112 That'sHim H'zary
May14-73⁵Pim	6 f 1:12⅘ft	7½	114	2¹½	2¹	1¹	1ⁿᵏ	W'htDR³	Alw 11500 82	Midn'tC'll'r114 M'sicCity St'rMon'
Apr26-73²Pim	6 f 1:12⅖sy	4	112	11½	1³	1⁶	1⁸	Br'leVJr⁹	c6500 84	MidnightCall'r114 ValleyBoss Arch

Feb 24 Bow 4f ft :50⅖b Feb 23 Bow 4f ft :48h Feb 12 Bow 4f ft :49b

Thayer * 112 B. g (1968), by Tudorka—Simoom, by Level Lea.
Breeder. J. P. Thayer (Va.).   1974 4 1 1 0

Owner, F. A. Greene, Jr. Trainer, H. Steward Mitchell. 1973 24 5 4 3

Feb21-74⁹Bow	1 1/16 1:44⅜ft	2½	112	1³	1³	2½	2⁵	GinoL⁴	Alw 80	Sentimentalist 112 Thayer Brun
Jan29-74⁴Bow	7 f 1:25⅜m	1	*112	1ʰ	1ʰ	5⁴	5⁸	GinoL¹	Alw 69	Meformore115 Impular Famous
Jan19-74⁷Bow	1 1/16 1:45⅘ft	4½	114	12½	12½	14	1⁹	GinoL³	13500 79	Thayer114 Picolata Whir
Jan 4-74⁶Bow	1 1/16 1:47⅖ft	2½	*114	1ʰ	13½	1ʰ	52¾	GinoL⁷	16500 68	Dame116 Fame Tim
Dec29-73⁶Lrl	7 f 1:27⅜sl	4	112	2ʰ	1ʰ	1⁶	1⁷	GinoL⁷	13000 72	Thayer112 Timeplus LandersMule
Dec10-73⁵Lrl	1 1:38⅖m	2½	112	11½	13	13	12	GinoL¹	9000 81	Thayer 112 Arlo Man Dark St
Nov29-73⁴Lrl	6 f 1:12 gd	5½	120	3²	2¹	1½	13¾	GinoL⁶	8000 78	Thayer120 DonHernando KingEli

March 2 Bow 5f ft :59⅘h Feb 18 Bow 5f ft 1:00h Feb 12 Bow 6f ft 1:13⅘h

Back Stage Talk 115 Ch. g (1970), by Stage Door Johnny—Patty's Song, by Spy Song.
Breeder, Walnut Hall Farm, Inc. (Ky.).   1974 7 1 0 2

Owner, Spartan Stable. Trainer, A. J. Hemmerick. 1973 2 M 1 0

Feb26-74⁸Bow	6 f 1:12⅘ft	14	115*109½1013	9⁷	6²	RhodesD⁹	Alw 79	KinwoldsD'ke122 H'dyHit T'ch ofP'
Feb14-74⁵Bow	6 f 1:12⅘ft	33	112* 4⁴	53½	52½	32½	RhodesD²	Alw 76	Impr'sive Imp112 C'ryStr't B'kSt'e
Feb 6-74⁸Bow	6 f 1:10⅖fr	31	112* 7⁶	88½	88½	55½	RhodesD⁶	Alw 85	KingHotTot112 B'leStr'tBoy Pay
Jan30-74¹Bow	6 f 1:13⅖gd	12	110*	RhodesD⁸	Mdn 74	Back Stage Talk110 Run Eb
Jan23-74⁵Bow	1 1/16 1:47⅛gd	16	110* 2ʰ	56¼	8151020	RhodesD³	Alw 52	Samoflet22 HipHigh DreamV'nit
Jan16-74¹Bow	7 f 1:24⅘ft	85	110**75¾	5²	33¼	31½	RhodesD¹¹	Mdn 79	T'l'aLie120 Kinw'ldsD'ke B'kSt'geT
Jan 4-74⁵Bow	6 f 1:12 m	17	110**112011191016915	RhodesD⁸	Mdn 68	Mr. Q.120 TopThis KinwoldsD

Feb 23 Bow 4f ft :48⅖h Jan 29 3f my :38b Jan 11 Bow 4f sy :50⅖bg

(handwritten notations in right margin: 71 72 8-, 60 59, 92 84 10, 76 70 65)

th o' Ray ✱ **112** Dk. b. or br. g (1969), by Reneged—Le Muy by Education.
Br., P McLean & W. G. Robins (Ky.). 1974 4 1 0 1 $4,560
er, Beelu Farm. Trainer, Dean Gaudet. 1973 9 0 1 1 $2,040

5-748Bow	6 f 1:12⅖ft	6¾	113	61¾	63¼	74½	41¾	Cusim'oG10	Alw 79	KinwoldsD'ke122 H'dyHit T'ch ofP'p'r 10
4-746Bow	6 f 1:12 ft	2½	▲114	2h	1½	14	13½	WalshE1	c7500 83	PathO'Ray114 FastH'ry RoyalEmp'ror 7
4-746Bow	1 ₁ₜ 1:42 ft	6	114	66½	56½	613	614	Cusi'oG7	c10500 84	Huss'rguvre119 OldH'yWhisk'po o 8
5-749Bow	1 ₁ₜ 1:48⅘sm	7¾	114	43½	42	31½	32½	KurtzJ2	11500 65	Charlie119 garrade PathO'Ray 10
6-733Lrl	1 1:42⅗sy	4½	116	54	42½	810	813	KurtzJ5	12500 46	PictureFrame116 Outet DarkStone 11
0-736Lrl	1 1-8 1:52⅗ft	6-5	▲116	13	12½	12½	21½	KurtzJ1	12500 83	FirstColumn116 PathO'Ray BoldGent 6
2-737Lrl	1 1:38½ft	19	116	55	2h	11	31½	Fel'oBM7	12500 80	Compatriot120 TimothyO. PathO'Ray 8

Jan 11 Bow 3f sly :37b

uch of Pepper **117** Gr. c (1970), by Idolater—Slacks, by Saggy.
Breeder, Fred Howard (Pa.). 1974 3 0 1 1 $2,380
er, G. W. Dalphon. Trainer, W. E. Hairfield. 1973 4 1 1 2 $5,345

6-748Bow	6 f 1:12⅖ft	2½	▲119	51¾	53	43½	31	LeeT8	Alw 80	KinwoldsD'ke122 H'dyHit T'ch ofP'p'r 10
3-745Bow	1 ₁ₜ 1:47⅕gd	2½	114	69	69½	55	54½	Cusim'noG2	Alw 67	Samoht112 HipHigh DreamWithMe 10
7-748Bow	1 ₁ₜ 1:48⅗gd	2½	▲119	1½	2h	2h	2h	BlackAS2	Alw 65	Dark'nyH11 T'chofP'per M'm 8
9-737Lrl	6 f 1:14⅘sl	2½	▲120	86½	85¼	43	21½	BlackAS8	Alw 73	BigH'lH 111 T'chofP'p'r on 10
0-737Lrl	6 f 1:12½gd	3½	120	12251214	65½	31	BlackAS3	Alw 87	V'Hadfield12 BoldF'l P'p'r 12
2-735Lrl	6 f 1:12 ft	3½	120	1h	1h	1h	11	BlackAS6	Mdn 89	T'chOfP'p'r120 Kinw'dsDuke Aft'D'n'r 7
3-734GS	6 f 1:13⅘sy	4½	113	87	68½	33½	32¾	M'leyJW4	Mdn 72	BoldF'wn114 SturdyUn'n T'ch ofP'p'r 11

March 4 Bow 4f ft :48hg · Feb 25 Bow 3f ft :36⅗b · Feb 21 Bow 5f ft 1:01h

ndy Hit **112** B. g (1970), by John William—Handy Sandy, by Tuscany.
Breeder, E. Howell (Md.). 1974 5 0 2 1 $4,184
er, J. J. Carpenter. Trainer, R. E. Dutrow. 1973 9 1 1 1 $4,314

26-748Bow	6 f 1:12⅖ft	2¾	112	2h	1h	2½	21	HawleyS5	Alw 80	KinwoldsD'ke122 H'dyHit T'ch ofP'p'r 10
9-744Bow	6 f 1:11⅖sy	12	114	34½	24	22	22	W'htDR6	c10500 84	Little Seth 114 Handy Hit Swoonbeam 9
31-748Bow	6 f 1:11⅖sy	9½	114	64½	64½	43	41½	Wr'htDR9	12500 81	Wr'htDR114 Hud'h T'ny HnyBoss 11
8-747Bow	6 f 1:12 gd	16	112	1h	1h	12	82½	Wr'htDR1	12500 81	Bea'k104 R'm'ce n'eM'n 12
1-749Lrl	6 f 1:14 m	11	116	27	23	21	42†‡	W'ghtDR4	12000 77	LittleSeth116 Catchment Mr.Titus 6
‡Placed third through disqualification.											
6-735Lrl	6 f 1:11⅖gd	7	116	1h	1h	21½	26	Wri'tDR9	10000 84	NightTr'nL'ne116 H'ndyHit JimArthur 12
9-735Lrl	6 f 1:11⅜ft	23	116	22½	24	22	2½†	WrightD5	10000 90	John deGreat120 HandyHit Jok'rsWild 12

†Disqualified and placed third.
Feb 7 Lrl 4f m :50b · Jan 29 Lrl 4f m :49⅗b

Thayer's credentials appear impeccable. Not only has the horse won four of his last seven starts, but his speed figures are consistently superior. His worst performance of the season — a figure of 84 in his next to last race — looks good enough to beat this field. A duplication of his best performance would demolish it.

There are no questions about Thayer's current condition. He is trained by a very competent man, H. Steward Mitchell. He raced only twelve days ago. Since that effort he worked five furlongs in a torrid :59⅕.

Thayer has been running in route races recently, and if he were a slow-breaking plodder there might be questions about his suitability at today's six-furlong distance. But he is a speed horse and he should relish the distance. He was leading by three lengths at the six-furlong mark of his last race. His past performances show that he won two of his three previous starts at three-quarters of a mile.

The only horse in this field with a figure that might menace Thayer is Path o' Ray, who earned an 89 in his next to last start. Path o' Ray was trained by King T. Leatherbury, one of the best horsemen in Maryland, in that race. He was claimed by a lesser trainer, Dean Gaudet, and subsequently ran much worse. There is no reason to expect that he will revert to his best form today.

Thayer's most formidable rival is Handy Hit, not so much because of the qualifications of the horse, but because of the qualifications of his trainer. Dick Dutrow is the superstar of the Maryland circuit. His horses frequently come to life and win under more improbable circumstances than these. If Dutrow had claimed Handy Hit in his last race, a bettor might reasonably fear that the horse was capable of improving five or ten lengths. But Dutrow has already raced Handy Hit once and his performance was nothing extraordinary. There is no evidence to suggest that Handy Hit will wake up today.

Thayer's credentials qualify him as a classic prime bet. He is the best horse; he is in excellent condition; he is trained by a good man. If Dutrow's horse should improve greatly to beat him, we can assuage our grief by rationalizing that we are bound to win money in the long run on horses like Thayer.

Thayer got his competition from an unexpected source, the long shot Midnight Caller, but raced him into defeat after a head-and-head battle and won by 1¾ lengths. Handy Hit, untouched by Dutrow's customary magic, was nowhere. Thayer paid $5.80 to win, a price that probably wouldn't allow a handicapper to retire to Aruba but was extremely generous under the circumstances.

GHTH RACE
Bow
arch 6, 1974

6 FURLONGS (chute). (1:08⅗). ALLOWANCES. Purse $7,000. 4-year-olds and upward which have never won a race other than maiden, claiming, starter or hunt meeting. Weight, 122 lbs. Non-winners of a race other than claiming in 1974 allowed 3 lbs.; such a race since Nov. 30, 5 lbs.; since Oct. 22, 7 lbs.; since Sept. 10, 10 lbs.

ue to winner $4,200; second, $1,540; third, $840; fourth, $420. Mutuel Pool, $98,230.

Last Raced	Horse	EqtAWt	PP St	¼	½	Str	Fin	Jockeys	Owners	Odds to $1
21-749 Bow²	Thayer	b6 112	3 3	2¹½	2¹½	1h	1¹¾	LGino	F A Greene Jr	1.90
26-748 Bow¹⁰	Midnight Caller	b4 112	2 4	1h	1½	2²½	2no	DRWright	R E Vogelman Jr	33.70
26-748 Bow⁴	Path o'Ray	b5 112	5 5	4¹½	3h	4²½	3²	EWalsh	Beelu Farm	7.80
26-748 Bow³	Touch of Pepper	b4 117	6 2	5²	55	55	4h	TLee	G W Dalphon	2.30
26-748 Bow²	Handy Hit	b4 112	7 1	3h	4²½	3h	5⁴¼	SHawley	J J Carpenter	3.20
14-745 Bow²	Cary Street	b4 117	1 6	6²	6²	6¹½	6¹	GCusimano	J L Reynolds	7.10
26-748 Bow⁶	Back Stage Talk	b4 115	4 7	7	7	7	7	DRhodes⁷	Spartan Stable	28.70

OFF AT 4:19 EDT. Start good. Won driving. Time, :23⅕, :46⅖, 1:11⅖. Track fast.

$2 Mutuel Prices:
3-THAYER		5.80	4.60	3.60
2-MIDNIGHT CALLER			18.20	8.80
5-PATH O'RAY				5.80

B. g, by Tudorka—Simoom, by Level Lea. Trainer, B. Steward Mitchell. Bred by J. P. Thayer (Va.).
THAYER vied for the lead from the outset, secured the lead approaching the eighth pole and drew clear
der vigorous urging. MIDNIGHT CALLER took the early lead under a hustling ride and gave way grudgingly
the drive to narrowly hold for the place. PATH O'RAY, never far back, finished with good courage between
ses. TOUCH OF PEPPER, hustled to remain within striking distance early, lacked a late response. HANDY
, prominently placed, weakened while lugging in through the drive. CARY STREET was outrun.
Scratched—Beale Street Boy.

th Bowie Race Course

FEBRUARY 26, 1974

1¹⁄₁₆ MILES. (1:41⅗). CLAIMING. Purse $3,700. 4-year-olds and upward, registered Maryland-breds. Weight, 122 lbs. Non-winners of two races since Jan. 15 allowed 3 lbs.; a race, 6 lbs.; a race since Jan. 8, 9 lbs. Claiming price, $3,000.

PLED: MARYLAND PRINCE and ROSARYVILLE.

r Tab ✱
er, Bear Creek Farm. Trainer, J. N. Skinner.
119 B. g (1964), by Trojan Monarch—Tabarina, by The Yuvaraj.
Breeder, J. L. Skinner (Md.). $3.000
1974 4 1 0 0 $2,916
1973 16 3 2 1 $12,276

19-749 Bow	1 1-8 1:55⅕ft	12	119	42½	55	55½	47½	Row!'ndJ⁷	4000 63 Potestas114 King of Fr'ce V'd'rbiltAve. 9
12-749 Bow	1¹⁄₁₆ 1:48⅖ft	2½	⁴114	6¹¹	43½	3ⁿᵏ	14½	Row!'ndJ³	3000 66 BarTab114 PullNoP'nches Pr'tyLaura 12
1-749 Bow	1¹⁄₁₆ 1:48⅘ft	4½	113	65½	69½	57½	44½	RowlandJ⁷	3000 59 Westhampton10⁵ Rosaryville Miersen 9
17-749 Bow	1¹⁄₁₆ 1:48½ft	14	113	6¹³	47	44½	46½	RowlandJ⁶	3000 61 Afonis113 Sechelles rook'Vest 12
13-739 Lrl	1 1-8 1:55 sy	11	114	87	10¹⁷	10²⁵	10²⁶	Row!'ndJ¹¹	3000 46 KofFrance113 C'dJudeHebr'ly 12
4-739 Bow	1¹⁄₁₆ 1:47⅕sy	4½	114	92¹	92¹	95	920	RowlandJ⁸	3000 52 CuttheDick113 StarBama TripleP'ride 9
16-737 Tim	1 1:39⅖ft	19	119	7¹⁴	6¹⁶	6¹⁷	5¹⁵	Row'dJ⁴	A2500 65 Last Hill 119 Timmy Willie Gun Gold 7
5-733 Del	1-70 1:43⅘ft	4	117	7¹³	8¹³	8¹⁴	7¹⁵	RowlandJ⁴	5000 65 FearABit117 Aboriginal ColonelJerry 8

Jan 15 Lrl 6f fr 1:17b   Jan 5 Lrl 6f sl 1:22b   Dec 29 Lrl 6f hy 1:21b

an's Sister
er, J. Eshelman. Trainer, H. Ravich.
101 Dk. b. or br. f (1970), by Telekinesis—Wayward, by Double Brandy.
Breeder, Dr. D. L. Price (Md.). $3.000
1974 4 2 1 0 $2,914
1973 19 1 2 0 $3,660

4-749 Bow	1¹⁄₁₆ 1:49⅘ft	3½	107⁴*²¹½	22	22	2¹	McC'onCJ³	3000 58 Therapist114 Dean'sSister DizzySag 12
7-749 Bow	1¹⁄₁₆ 1:48⅗gd	9	122	13	2h	33½	88	WrightDR²	3000 57 ⒻTi'e frAd't're M'sPr'v'ra M'b'lM'b'l 12
2-748 Dov	1¹⁄₁₆ 1:48 ft	9-5	⁴113	13	18	1¹⁰	120	Thornt'nJ¹	2500 96 Dean'sSist'r113 Eclipsed Doll ofSatin 7
6-748 Pen	5½ f 1:08 m	14	112	74½	43	2¹	2ⁿᵒᵗHinojosaH⁵	2500 83 ⒻD'ss155 DeansSister Sampere 12

†Placed first through disqualification.

12-731 Lrl	6 f 1:12 ft	20	109	54	53½	97¾	99½	Felic'noP¹	3000 79 ⒻPH'rn112 P'l'm'c Ike Mys'IM's 12
1-739 Pen	5½ f 1:06 ft	3⅗	112	106½	99½	77¾	DennieD⁹	3200 87 ⒻP'ssTime118 Cr'kpotL'dy B'shf'lSue 11
1-731 Pen	6 f 1:12 ft	27	111	64½	88	10¹⁵10¹²	HowardR¹	Alw 74 ⒻShunned111 PennyFlight Solindra 10
1-731 Pim	6 f 1:14 ft	12	110	1h	1h	13	11½	McC'nG²	M5000 76 Dean'sSister110 S'plyTouch KeepPete 12

Feb 24 Bow 4f ft :51⅗b   Dec 28 Lrl 5f hy 1:07b

(cont'd on next page)

Quill Pen
108 B. m (1969), by Victorian Era—Gold Quill, by Sunny Boy.
Breeder, E. P. Taylor (Md.).
1974 3 0 0 0
1973 25 2 0 3
Owner, Vin Lo Stable. Trainer, A. Bertando. $3,000

Feb21-74²Bow	7 f 1:26¾ft	28	113	12⁹	10⁸¼	9¹¹	9⁷¼	Cusim'oG⁹	4000 65	FearABit112	RoadToRock Peach
Feb 5-74³Bow	1 ¹⁄₁₆ 1:46⅘fr	8¾	108	7⁹¼	6⁹½	7¹⁰	7⁶½	JimenezC⁵	5000 67	Spice Ashore	...idbro..k Sea
Jan21-74⁴Bow	1 ¹⁄₁₆ 1:49⅕sy	2⅔e	116	7⁹¾	7⁶	7¹³	7¹⁶	WalshE⁵	5000 46	Nite..ce'sW...
Dec15-73²Lrl	7 f 1:26⅖ft	7¹	116	6⁸	6⁶½	2²	1¹½	KurtzJ²	4000 79	Quill..e116 ...Sea Nite..
Dec 3-73³Lrl	1 1:39⅖ft	15	113	6¹³	6³½	3¹½	5²½	KurtzJ¹	5000 74	...KAng'l 116 M'd'yPrize M'sL'd..
Nov19-73⁹Lrl ①	1 ¹⁄₁₆ 1:45⅗fm	7½e	11²	8¹⁰	4⁵½	5⁷	4¹½	KurtzJ²	5000 76	ⒻSlide frMe111 T'oAnx's S'b'naL..
Nov12-73¹Lrl	6 f 1:13¾ft	11	112	8⁹½	7⁸	5⁴½	3¹½	Fel'noBM³	3000 79	ⒻAuntieJ'n105 Sum'rPl'n'g QuillP..

Feb 20 Bow 3f ft :38⅖b   Jan 17 Bow 5f ft 1:02⅖b

51 56 44

Doc's Line
113 Dk. b. or br. g (1970), by Roman Line—Honey Doc, by Martins Rulla..
Br., Dr. & Mrs. G. G. Meredith (Md.).
1974 3 0 0 0
1973 24 3 3 2
Owner, C. A. Faulkner. Trainer, L. W. Donovan. $3,000

Feb14-74⁹Bow	1 ¹⁄₁₆ 1:49⅕ft	17	113	9¹⁹	9¹⁴	9¹³	7⁸¼	MorenoO⁸	3000 50	Therapist114 Dean'sSister DizzyS..
Jan28-74⁸Bow	1 1:44⅖ssy	3-2	115	5⁵	5⁷	5⁸¹	4⁹	Bradf'rdB³	2500 63	Ca...7 DirectHit JackieJun..
Jan 4-74⁷Dov	1 1:42⅘gd	9-5	▲120	5⁵½	5¹⁰	5⁹½	5⁶½	MorenoO¹	2500 73 B	...ay112 Nipigon DivotApp..
Dec 4-73³Lrl	1 1:41	15	117	12¹⁷	12¹⁸	11¹⁸	8¹²	MorenoO¹	3000 56	Wha..er 20 Miessen Maxi M..
Nov26-73⁹Lrl	1 1-8 1:55⅖ft	4¼	119	5³½	5³	5²¾	5⁷	MorenoO²	3000 63	WingedC'rier112 BaronJet R'galBr..

Jan 27 Dov 4f sy :51⅖b   Jan 16 Dov 6f ft 1:17h   Jan 11 Dov 5f sy 1:06⅖b

49

Maryland Prince
119 B. c (1970), by Frankie's Nod—Tussy Bell, by Tuscany.
Br., W. T. Leatherbury & E. Wayson (Md.).
1974 3 1 1 0
1973 16 2 1 0
Owner, W. T. Leatherbury. Trainer, K. T. Leatherbury. $3,000

Feb 9-74¹Bow	7 f 1:26⅘sy	8-5	▲113	10⁷	10⁹¼	4⁴½	1¹½	WalshE⁷	3000 71	M'ryl'dPr'ce113 S'rdSw'l'o'r H'ds'eG..
Jan29-74²Bow	6 f 1:13⅘m	3½	114	4⁷	3⁵	5²	2¹½	WalshE⁸	4000 72	L'l...114 Maryl'dPrince Ruler..
Jan 7-74²Bow	6 f 1:14 gd	2	▲112	9⁵½	9⁶½	4²	4¹½	WalshE⁷	4750 71	L...'dRul..r 115 Pr...ngm...o..
Nov 2-73³Lrl	7 f 1:25 ft	4¾	112	5³	3⁴	3³½	3¹	WalshE³	7000 65	Blu.F...k110 Ri...beaugem...114..
Oct 9-73⁹Bow	1 ¹⁄₁₆ 1:48⅖ft	3½	114	4³	3³½	3¹	3nk	WalshE⁴	7500 66	Red'dic'te119 M'rnTilNite M'rvl'dP..
Sep28-73⁷Bow	7 f 1:26 ft	5¾	114	9⁴¾	9¹⁰	8⁸½	5³¾	P'ss'reWJ⁸	7500 71	NobleP'mise114 Jamb'lot S'aOutLo..

Jan 5 Bow 4f sl :50⅖b   Jan 1 Bow 3f m :39⅖b

57 59 63

Ambi Hula ✳
113 Dk. b. or br. g (1969), by Ambiopoise—Hula Hop, by Hill Prince.
Br., Mr. & Mrs. H. J. O'Donovan (Md.).
1974 3 0 0 0
1973 26 1 3 5
Owner, F. J. De Francis. Trainer, J. S. Clark. $3,000

Jan26-74⁹Bow	1 1-4 2:08⅖m	4¾	115	9¹⁰	7⁸½	7¹¹	6⁷	McC'nG⁴	H5000 74	Mendelson113 RapidTreat MintCo..
Jan19-74²Bow	1 1-8 1:55⅖ft	2¼	▲119	12²²	10⁸¼	3½	3½	Jimen'zC⁶	c5000 69	SpringHop113 Save theMaxi AmbiH..
Jan 2-74⁹Bow	1 ¹⁄₁₆ 1:48⅕ft	9-5	▲114	7⁹½	7⁹	6⁸½	3⁴½	HawleyS⁶	8500 62	W...114 H'Turb...le AmbiH..
Dec15-73⁹Lrl	1 1-8 1:53⅖ft	6-5	▲116	7¹¹	7⁷¼	4²½	1²	HawleyS⁷	6500 78	Amb..116 H'Turble AmbiH..
Dec 3-73²Lrl	1 1:38⅖ft	14	116	7⁸	9⁶½	6⁷	5³¼	McH'eDG²	8000 78	HuckPuppie116 O'kStone Sw..
Nov24-73⁵Lrl	1 1:38⅗ft	4¾	107½	6⁴¼	6⁴½	6⁹½	6¹¹	Minerv'iF⁴	7000 52	Octet 113 CharlieJr. UncAll..
Nov 5-73⁵Lrl	1 1:39⅗sy	5¾	116	10¹⁴	10¹¹	5³½	3¾	B'c'leVJr¹	8000 74	BoldLord114 SuperBuper AmbiH..

Feb 14 Pim 4f my :51h

70 77 81

Exclusive Helio
113 B. g (1970), by Exclusive Nashua—Hello Helio, by Helioscope.
Breeder, Buck Ridge Stable (Md.).
1974 5 0 0 0
1973 20 1 2 0
Owner, Buck Ridge Stable. Trainer, W. B. Hill. $3,000

Feb13-74¹Bow	6 f 1:12¾ft	13	113	5²¾	7⁶½	6⁸	7¹¹	AlbertsB⁴	3000 69	M'nsinger113 NightPrinc's Br'th'rL..
Feb 4-74⁹Bow	1 ¹⁄₁₆ 1:48⅕ft	17e	114	6⁵½	9⁸½	12¹⁹	12²⁰	AlbertsB⁹	4000 74	PrinceJ'k'r113 Br'k'sBest K'g ofFr..
Jan29-74²Bow	6 f 1:13⅘m	19	114	10¹⁵	9¹³	9⁸½	7⁵½	LeeT⁶	4000 68	L'l..Mary119 Maryl'dPrince..r..
Jan11-74²Bow	7 f 1:28⅕m	11	114	3³	4⁵½	6⁷½	6³½	LeeT¹⁰	4000 73	M...ck114 ...nt A...Frum..
Jan 4-74⁹Bow	1 ¹⁄₁₆ 1:50 m	11	114	1h	2³	3³½	4⁷½	LeeT³	4000 50	EasyFar114 PrinceJoker Pa..W..
Dec28-73²Lrl	1 1:44⅗shy	4¾	112	12½	2½	4⁷	7¹¹	StovallR⁷	3000 39	BobH'rse110 Save theMaxi S'ble1sl..
Dec 6-73⁹Lrl	1 1:40⅘ft	25	115	8¹²	9¹⁷	11⁸½	8⁹	Bel'lleEM⁶	5000 62	Bite theBul't112 Mend'lson Villiers..
Nov27-73¹Lrl	6 f 1:12¾ft	33	116	9⁷¾	9¹²	8⁹¼	7⁴½	Belv'leEM⁴	4000 81	VilliersLad117 AClearDay VegasHo..

Jan 26 Lrl 4f sl :50⅗b

52 32 50

lonel Jerry ✱ **116** Dk. b. or br. g (1967), by Martins Rullah—Sturdy Miss, by Unbreakable.
Breeder, Harford Stud, Inc. (Md.). 1974 2 1 0 $2,820
er, W. H. Wolfendale III. Trainer, W. H. Wolfendale III. $3,000 1973 34 5 5 7 $20,878

17-749Bow	1$\frac{1}{16}$ 1:48⅕ft	4	119	91⁷11¹⁵11¹⁹10¹⁶	B'v'leEM⁸	c3000	51	Adonis 113	Seychelles	Brook's Best 12
9-749Bow	1$\frac{1}{16}$ 1:50	sy	7-5 ▲119	6¹² 58¹ 2ʰ 12½	Belv'leEM²	3000	58			P'nc'yM'gin 12
5-747Pen	1 1:43⅖sm	5¾	116	46¼ 46 52½ 2¾	HedgeD⁶	HcpO	66			Jerry Magoni 6
7-739Lrl	1 1:40 ft	8¾	116	43 36½ 71¹ 71⁰	CanessaJ⁷	4000	61		116	DoubleDay 11
29-739Lrl	1$\frac{1}{16}$ 2:00⅜ft	5½	116	97½ 85¾ 6⁵ 43¾	CanessaJ⁵	4000	69	Mr. Janin 116	Big Vin	Potestas 12
14-739Lrl	1 1-8 1:55⅕gd	4	114	14 12 2ʰ 21½	Hi'j'aH¹²	c3000	80	ContentedCl'n116	ColonelJerry	Adonis 12

ven Never **113** B. g (1970), by Seven Corners—Prize Pet, by Little Reaper.
Breeder, M. E. Pellens (Md.). 1974 3 0 0 0 (——)
er, Mary E. Pellens. Trainer, W. G. Meyers. $3,000 1973 9 2 1 0 $7,125

14-749Bow	1$\frac{1}{16}$ 1:49⅘ft	2½	▲113	34½ 3² 3⁴ 67¼	Rowl'ndJ²	3000	51	Therapist114	Dean'sSister	DizzySag 9
4-745Bow	7 f 1:25 ft	19	108	96¼ 88½ 910¹0¹¹	Cusim'oG⁸	5000	69	L'ndR'l'r117	Sp'nishSt'm	M'dis'nStr't 12
25-745Bow	6 f 1:13⅘sm	11	108¼108½1112¹111¹181¼	VillonA⁸	5000	58	Hy	ple 115	Oto	Citrus Lad 11
18-734Pim	6 f 1:12 ft	19	114	63¼ 51¾ 67½ 58¾	CookeC⁶	13500	77			H le 6
6-736Pim	6 f 1:13⅕gd	8¼	114	43½ 3½ 3½ 51¾	†CookeC⁷	13500	78		x114	'l 9

†Placed fourth through disqualification.

17-733Pim	1$\frac{1}{16}$ 1:49⅘sm	18	114	34 12 2ʰ 3ʰ	CookeC³	1500	56	D'nnyAgain114	Bally forY'u	S'v'nN'v'r 9
23-737Bow	6 f 1:13⅕ft	26	114	99¼ 88½10¹⁰10⁵	CookeC¹¹	11500	72	What aTr'sure	Starkadder	AngelSkin 12
9-737Bow	7 f 1:27 m	15	114	58¼ 66¼ 86¾ 8¹²	CookeC⁶	13500	58	LandingGray114	Nepperham	C'tPl'ck 8

Jan 30 Pim 5f my 1:04⅖h   Jan 19 Pim 6f ft 1:17⅜b   Jan 12 Pim 5f st 1:05b

Ambi Hula, like Thayer, has figures that are consistently superior to those of the horses he is facing today. He should be an easy winner if he duplicates any of the ten races in his past performances. But will he?

Ambi Hula was running in $8000 claiming company for most of the season and was slightly overmatched. When he was dropped to $6500, he won convincingly. He was a solid $6500 animal. Yet despite this record his trainer entered him in a $5000 claiming race. Something had to be wrong with the horse, for neither trainers nor any other business-men give away $6500 merchandise for $5000. Ambi Hula couldn't even win that cheap race.

Henry Clark, an astute veteran horseman, claimed the supposed bargain for $5000 and ran him a week later. Ambi Hula confirmed that he did indeed have problems. He ran his worst race, and his worst figure, in months. So Clark wisely rested him for a month, trying to correct whatever ailed the animal.

If Clark had entered Ambi Hula for $5000 or thereabouts,

a handicapper might bet the horse because he respected the trainer's expertise and thought he may have revivified his new acquisition. But by entering Ambi Hula for $3000, Clark was practically announcing that the animal's problems were dire. Trainers do not give away $5000 merchandise for $3000. Dropdowns of this type do occasionally win — it is conceivable that Ambi Hula has enough left in him to be a decent $3000 horse — but generally they are the worst bets in racing.

Only three other horses in this field — Maryland Prince, Dean's Sister, and Bar Tab — have respectable credentials.

Maryland Prince, like Ambi Hula, is evidently a horse beset with problems. After running well for $7000 earlier in the season, he gradually descended to the bottom of the class ladder. He won his last start for $3000, which may suggest that he has found his proper level. But Maryland Prince won that race only because he was facing an extraordinarily weak field. His figure was 57, which will rarely win anything. Maryland Prince did rally strongly from tenth place in that seven-furlong event, a performance that might lead some handicappers to conclude that he will improve at today's distance of a mile and one-sixteenth. But his past performances seem to suggest that he prefers sprints. Like many fast-closing sprinters, he cannot sustain his rally at a longer distance.

Dean's Sister, a speed horse, earned a figure of 60 in her last start, over a track with a strong bias in favor of speed horses. In her previous race at Bowie on a more normal track, she tired badly.

Bar Tab won his next to last race in $3000 company, stepped up to $4000 where he was overmatched, and is dropped back to $3000 today. Whether winning or losing, he has displayed consistency of a sort, running figures in the

60s each time. He may not be an inspiring animal, but he is racing at the level where he properly belongs, and his usual figure should be good enough to win this race, assuming that Ambi Hula does not approximate his best form. Unless I were feeling very courageous, I would not make Bar Tab a prime bet. I prefer horses with stronger credentials and slightly sexier past performances. But Bar Tab does appear to have an edge in this field, and if his odds are reasonable he deserves a moderate bet.

NINTH RACE
Bow
February 26, 1974

1 1/16 MILES. (1:41⅗). CLAIMING. Purse $3,700. 4-year-olds and upward, registered Maryland-breds. Weight, 122 lbs. Non-winners of two races since Jan. 15 allowed 3 lbs.; a race, 6 lbs.; a race since Jan. 8, 9 lbs. Claiming price, $3,000. Value to winner $2,220; second, $814; third, $444; fourth, $222. Mutuel Pool, $35,584. Exacta Pool, $73,870.

Last Raced		Horse	EqtAWt	PP	St	¼	½	¾	Str	Fin	Jockeys	Owners	Odds to $1
-19-74⁹	Bow⁴	Bar Tab	b10 119	1	2	6⁴	6⁵	6³	3¹½	1¹	JRowland	Bear Creek Farm	5.20
2-14-74⁹	Bow²	Dean's Sister	4 105	2	1	1³	12½	11½	2¹½	2¹½	CJMcCar'n⁷†	J Eshelman	7.10
2- 9-74¹	Bow¹	Maryland Prince	b4 119	5	4	2ʰ	31½	2ʰ	2ʰ	3½	EWalsh	W T Leatherbury	2.10
2-26-74⁹	Bow⁶	Ambi Hula	b3 113	6	9	9	8²	7²	63½	42¾	GMcCarron	F J DeFarncis	1.90
2-14-74⁹	Bow⁶	Seven Never	b4 113	9	6	52½	52½	4¹	4¹	51¼	GCusimano	Mary E Pellens	14.90
2-21-74²	Bow⁹	Quill Pen	5 112	3	3	4ʰ	4ʰ	51½	51½	6⁸	JKurtz	Vin Lo Stable	11.20
2-13-74¹	Bow⁷	Exclusive Helio	b4 113	7	5	31½	2ʰ	31½	7⁴	7⁸	GVasquez	Buck Ridge Stable	72.40
2-14-74⁹	Bow⁷	Doc's Line	b4 113	4	8	7²	72½	8⁸	8¹²	8¹⁵	LGino	C A Faulkner	92.50
1-17-74⁹	Bow¹⁰	Colonel Jerry	7 116	8	7	8¹	9	9	9	9	CCooke	W H Wolfendale III	12.10

†Three pounds apprentice allowance waived.
OFF AT 4:48 EDT. Start good. Won driving. Time, :24⅗, :49⅘, 1:15⅘, 1:42⅗, 1:49⅖. Track fast.

$2 Mutuel Prices:

1-BAR TAB		12.40	5.80	3.20
2-DEAN'S SISTER			7.00	4.00
5-MARYLAND PRINCE				3.00

$2 EXACTA (1-2) PAID $76.40.

B. g, by Trojan Monarch—Tabarina, by The Yuvaraj. Trainer, J. N. Skinner. Bred by J. L. Skinner (Md.).
BAR TAB, unhurried while saving ground early, brushed with EXCLUSIVE HELIO when lodging his bid between rivals entering the stretch and finished determinedly to secure the lead and draw clear in the closing yards. DEAN'S SISTER sprinted to a clear lead, continued willingly when called upon for the drive, weakened in the final sixteenth. MARYLAND PRINCE, never far back, lacked a solid late response. AMBI HULA had a belated closing rally. SEVEN NEVER brushed EXCLUSIVE HELIO while making a mild bid into the stretch and hung. QUILL PEN saved ground to no avail. EXCLUSIVE HELIO raced forwardly placed, then was brushed between rivals when weakening into the stretch.
Overweight—Dean's Sister, 1 pound; Quill Pen, 4.
Maryland Prince claimed by J. L. Guthrie, trainer J. Gill. Ambi Hula claimed by W. H. Hardesty, trainer D. Gaudet.
Claiming Prices—All $3000.
Scratched—Sergeant Major, Rosaryville.

The betting public loves to lose its money on horses with spurious "class." The crowd at Bowie made Ambi Hula the 9-to-5 favorite, with Maryland Prince 2 to 1. Ignoring the one solid $3000 animal in the field, they allowed Bar Tab to pay $12.40.

2nd Saratoga

6 FURLONGS. (1:08). MAIDENS. SPECIAL WEIGHTS. Purse $9,000. Colts and gel ings. 2-year-olds. Weight, 119 lbs.

COUPLED: TRUMPETER SWAN and SHINING KNIGHT.

Office King   **119**   Ch. c (1971), by Vitriolic—Determine Gal, by Determine.
Breeder, Ocala Stud (Fla.).   1973 . 0 M 0 0   (—
Owner, D. Sturgis. Trainer, J. B. Cantey.
Aug 14 Sar 4f ft :46⅖h   Aug 10 Sar 6f ft 1:12⅖hg   Aug 9 Sar 3f ft :37bg

Attaboy John   **119**   B. c (1971), by Wind Driven—Diva's Girl, by Royal Admiral.
Breeder, J. W. Warner (Va.).   1973 . 0 M 0 0   (—
Owner, Mrs. C. MacLeod, Jr. Trainer, C. MacLeod, Jr.
Aug 11 Sar 5f 1:01hg   Aug 8 Sar 6f ft 1:15⅗h   Aug 4 Sar 3f gd :36⅗b

Bold and Fancy   **119**   B. c (1971), by Bold Hour—Khal Me Fancy, by Khaled.
Br., Mr. & Mrs. G. Grieger, Jr. (Cal.).   1973 . 1 M 0 0   (—
Owner, M. Vogil. Trainer, L. S. Barrera.
Aug11-73²Sar   6 f 1:11   ft   64   114⁰ 8³   89¾11151116 AmyJ¹²   Mdn 69 TakeByStorm 119 Hilo TheScotsman
Aug 6 Sar trt 3f ft :37b   July 25 Bel trt 4f ft :48⅖h   Aug 8 Sar 4f ft :49⅕bg

Royal Approval   **119**   B. c (1971), by Prince John—Recommendation, by Dark Star.
Breeder, C. E. Mather II. (Ky.).   1973 . 3 M 0 0   (—
Owner, Avonwood Stable. Trainer, G. P. Odom.
Jly 18-73³Aqu   5½ f 1:05⅗ft   16e 118   6⁶   76¾ 78¼ 77¼ Bal'zarC¹¹   Mdn 79 Pia'ccel18 Sh'tUp andD'l L'dFar'h
Jly 9-73³Aqu   5½ f 1:04⅗ft   12e 118   8⁶   7¹⁰ 7¹² 7¹⁴ VeneziaM⁸   Mdn 75 Lafevil18 LorEorso'n'r Fl'tChie
Jun27-73⁴Aqu   5½ f 1:04   ft   18   117   1023102610281024 VeneziaM⁴   Mdn 69 Casino Ace112 ThCroush Firs Road
Aug 17 Sar 3f ft :35⅖h   Aug 14 Sar 4f ft :50b   July 16 Bel 3f ft :37⅕b

Trumpeter Swan   **119**   Ch. c (1971), by Sea-Bird—Trumpery, by Tudor Minstrel.
Breeder, Greentree Stable (Ky.).   1973 . 5 M 1 1 $ 3,
Owner, Greentree Stable. Trainer, J. M. Gaver.
Aug 8-73²Sar   5½ f 1:06½ft   5¼   119   6⁵   67¾ 6⁹   75¼ VasquezJ⁹   Mdn 80 DingD'ngBell 119 Lea'sPass BuckHill
May26-73³Bel   5½ f 1:06   m   9-5 ▲117   88¼ 7⁷   5⁶   55¼ TurcotteR⁵   Mdn 88 Ground Bold 112 Bd JayCee'ss
May16-73³Bel   5½ f 1:05   ft   3¾   117   52¼ 41¼ 1½   2ʰ   TurcotteR⁵   Mdn 94 Es'cc'ss 118 Trip't'rSwa'n'd
May 7-73³Aqu   5f :58⅗ft   2 ▲117   68½ 67¼ 4⁸   49¼ TurcotteR⁴   Mdn 82 Rac Cup11? Trezheim B.D Boy
Apr23-73³Aqu   5f :59⅗ft   6-5 ▲117   52¼ 5⁵   44¼ 36¼ TurcotteR⁷   Mdn 81 WhoD'zit117 Jov'lJudge T'mp't'rSw'n
Aug 14 Sar 4f ft :46⅖h   Aug 6 Sar 3f ft :34⅗hg   July 31 Sar 4f ft :50⅖b

Right Pitch   **119**   Ch. c (1971), by Jaipur—Centrifuge, by Middleground.
Breeder, King Ranch, Inc. (Ky.).   1973 . 0 M 0 0   (—
Owner, King Ranch. Trainer, W. J. Hirsch.
Aug 11 Sar 4f ft :49hg   Aug 7 Sar 5f ft 1:03⅘g

Criterion   **119**   B. c (1971), by Sir Gaylord—Nature, by Nashua.
Breeder, R. N. Webster (Ky.).   1973 . 2 M 0 0 $5
Owner, R. N. Webster. Trainer, L. Laurin.
Aug 8-73²Sar   5½ f 1:06⅕ft   9½   119   7⁸   56¼ 5⁵   41¾ Turc'tteR³   Mdn 84 DingDngBell 119 Lea'sPass BuckHill
Jly 31-73¹Sar   6 f 1:11⅗ft   8½   119   41¾ 5⁵   8⁹   79¼ TurcotteR⁵   Mdn 73 Prddio R'son119 2ByBySt'm Lea'sP's
Aug 14 Sar 3f ft :37⅕b   Aug 6 Sar 3f ft :37b   July 29 Sar 3f ft :36⅖b

Bronze Express   **119**   Ch. c (1971), by Tobin Bronze—Nosey Body, by Tom Fool.
Breeder, D. A. Headley (Ky.).   1973 . 2 M 0 0   (—
Owner, Pastorale Stable. Trainer, G. T. Poole.
Aug 4-73²Sar   6 f 1:12½ft   48   119   7¹³ 7¹⁵ 7¹³ 7¹⁴ P'leGTlll¹   Mdn 65 T E'rount119 Ar.7 P'lli G'der'sGold
May16-73³Bel   5½ f 1:05   ft   35   117   9¹¹ 9¹² 9¹⁴ 9¹⁷ CardoneE⁹   Mdn 77 Es'cc'ss Tript'rSw'n E'rF'd
Aug 13 Sar 5f gd 1:02⅕h   Aug 9 Sar 4f ft :51b   July 31 Sar 5f ft 1:03⅘h

termined King 119 Blk. c (1971), by Determined Man—New Love, by Pardal.
r, H. Allen. Trainer, E. Jacobs. Breeder, Herbert Allen (Ky.).   1973 3 M 3 0 $2,680

```
4-733Bel  5½ f 1:05  ft   2½ 117  1½  2¹  3¹½ 2³½ BaezaB³   Mdn 90 Ev...17 Det'm'dK'g TakeBySt'm 9
-733GP   5 f :58⅕ft  4-5 ▲118  1½  1h  1h  2³½ RotzJL²   Mdn 91 J.R...118 DeterminedK'g Im'd'r'te 12
3-733Hia  3 f :33⅖ft  8-5 ▲120  2   2¹  2½       RotzJL¹⁴  Mdn 93 Vil...120 DeterminedK'g Ohmyl've 14
   Aug 17 Sar 3f ft :35⅖h        Aug 13 Sar 5f gd 1:01h        Aug 8 Sar 4f ft :49⅘b
```

gal Rolfe 119 Ch. c (1971), by Tom Rolfe—Princess Cloud, by Prince John.
r, Saron Stable. Trainer, S. E. Veitch. Breeder, W. L. Jones, Jr. & Claiborne Farm, Inc. (Ky.).   1973 . 0 M 0 0   (——)

```
   Aug 10 Sar 5f ft 1:04¾h        Aug 6 Sar 5f ft 1:04⅖b
```

ning Knight 119 Dk. b. or br. c (1971), by Round Table—Trophy Room, by Bold Ruler.
r, Greentree Stable. Trainer, J. M. Gaver. Breeder, Greentree Stud, Inc. (Ky.).   1973 5 M 1 1 $2,550

```
4-734Sar  5½ f 1:06  ft   9  119  8¹³ 7¹⁰ 79¼ 65¾ VasquezJ⁹   Mdn 81 SeaDee119 RedStr'k SparklingPl's're 9
-733Aqu  5½ f 1:05⅖ft  6-5 ▲118  76  65¾ 56¼ 54  MapleE⁴     Mdn 82 Pia'A...8 Sh...m'D'l L...or'... 11
-733Bel  5½ f 1:04⅖ft  6¾  117  3nk 1½  2½  25½ VasquezJ⁴   Mdn 91 B...Boy17 Shi...Knight ...ck... 8
)-733Aqu  5 f :59  ft  17  117  2¹  2h  2½  35  VasquezJ⁷   Mdn 85 K'...'tive117 B...Hill S... 7
5-733Aqu  5 f :59⅕ft  2½  117  65  78¼ 7¹⁰ 69½ Velasq'zJ²  Mdn 79 L'v'rJohn117 K't theN'tive R'seA Cup 7
   Aug 16 Sar 3f ft :34⅖h        Aug 6 Sar 3f ft :34⅖hg        July 30 Sar 6f ft 1:14⅖h
```

Two-year-old maiden races can be baffling because a handicapper must compare two types of horses that almost defy comparison: those who have shown promise in their brief racing careers and first-time starters who have shown promise in their workouts. As a general rule, the best bets in these events are horses who have raced only once or twice and have demonstrated some ability. First-time starters are at a disadvantage because of their inexperience. Horses who have raced several times have already proved themselves as losers.

In this race at Saratoga, four horses have shown signs of ability in actual competition. Trumpeter Swan ran very well on May 16 and finished second, but his only recent race was mediocre. He worked a half mile in a swift 46⅘ seconds since his last start, but he has worked well on previous occasions, and still has not been able to win in five tries.

Criterion has raced only twice, running poorly in his debut and then improving on August 8. Winners of two-year-old maiden races often have records like this, but there is one thing wrong with Criterion. His figure in his most recent start was a 75, which is not very good in New York maiden-special-weight company where the average winning figure is 93. Unless today's field is another unusually weak one, he must improve a great deal in order to win.

Determined King is already beginning to look like a sucker horse, finishing second in each of his three career starts. His figures are poor. He weakened at five and five and a half furlongs and is now running a longer distance. He has been laid off for two months, and his workouts are unimpressive. (A three-furlong work in 35⅗ seconds is not particularly meaningful for a horse whose record shows he possesses plenty of early speed. If Determined King had a strong workout at six furlongs, that would be significant.)

Shining Knight is a five-time loser whose most recent race is a poor one.

Because none of the horses with established form has convincing credentials, a first-time starter may win this race. There are four colts in the field who are making their debuts, but only one of them has ever worked fast. Office King's workout line shows a half mile in 46⅗ seconds and a six-furlong move in 1:12⅗. Seeing these signs of ability, a thorough handicapper should plow through the daily workout listings in previous issues of the *Racing Form* to get a more complete picture of the horse's preparation. This was Office King's training schedule:

July 27:	four furlongs in 47 seconds.
Aug. 1:	five furlongs in 1:04⅗.
Aug. 6:	five furlongs in 1:02.
Aug. 9:	three furlongs in :37.
Aug. 10:	six furlongs in 1:12⅗. (The clocker's footnotes said, "Office King acts sharp.")
Aug. 14:	four furlongs in :46⅗.
Aug. 17:	three furlongs in :37.

Office King had shown almost everything one could ask of a horse who had never raced. He was obviously fit, having worked seven times in three weeks. He had shown speed in his half-mile workout. He had covered today's distance in excellent time. He had a workout on the day before his debut (which the *Racing Form*'s past performances erroneously omitted), suggesting that the stable was trying to sharpen him for a winning effort at first crack.

Office King is the only horse in this field who has shown exceptional promise. There are not many times when a handicapper can bet seriously and confidently on a first-time starter, but this is an exceptional case.

<table>
<tr><td colspan="2">SECOND RACE
Sar
August 18, 1973</td><td colspan="9">6 FURLONGS. (1:08). MAIDENS. SPECIAL WEIGHTS. Purse $9,000. Colts and geldings. 2-year-olds. Weight, 119 lbs.
Value to winner $5,400; second, $1,980; third, $1,080; fourth, $540.
Mutuel Pool, $150,724. Off-track betting, $49,557.</td></tr>
</table>

Last Raced	Horse	EqtAWt	PP	St	1/4	1/2	Str	Fin	Jockeys	Owners	Odds to $1
	Office King	2 119	1	11	11½	14	13	11½	EMaple	D Sturgis	1.90
14-73³ Bel²	Determined King	b2 119	9	2	2¹	2³	2³	2²	BBaeza	H Allen	3.60
8-73² Sar⁴	Criterion	b2 119	7	5	6³	3⁴	3⁵	3ʰ	RTurcotte	R N Webster	2.60
8-73² Sar⁷	Trumpeter Swan	b2 119	5	6	9³	9²	4¹	4⁴	RCSmith	Greentree Stable	a-4.90
11-73² Sar¹¹	Bold and Fancy	2 119	3	3	4ʰ	4¹	5¹½	5¹½	MCastaneda	M Vogel	25.60
	Regal Rolfe	2 119	10	10	11	11	7½	6¾	TWallis	Saron Stable	48.20
8-73⁴ Sar⁶	Shining Knight	2 119	11	9	7½	5¹½	6¹½	7¹½	HGustines	Greentree Stable	a-4.90
18-73³ Aqu⁷	Royal Approval	b2 119	4	8	8³	7¹	8³	8³	EBelmonte	Avonwood Stable	20.40
4-73⁴ Sar⁷	Bronze Express	2 119	8	7	10²	10¹	9³	9⁴	CBaltazar	Pastorale Stable	55.80
	Right Pitch	2 119	6	4	5½	8½	10⁵	10⁸	RPineda	King Ranch	29.90
	Attaboy John	2 119	2	1	3¹½	6½	11	11	JVasquez	Mrs C MacLeod Jr	13.60

a-Coupled, Trumpeter Swan and Shining Knight.

Time, :22⅖, :46, 1:11⅘ (no wind in backstretch). Track fast.

$2 Mutuel Prices:			
2-OFFICE KING	5.80	4.20	2.80
9-DETERMINED KING		4.20	2.80
7-CRITERION			2.60

Ch. c, by Vitriolic—Determine Gal, by Determine. Trainer, J. V. Cantey. Bred by Ocala Stud (Fla.).
IN GATE—2:04. OFF AT 2:04½ EASTERN DAYLIGHT TIME. Start good. Won ridden out.
OFFICE KING, rushed to the front along the inside after breaking slowly, drew off around the turn and held TERMINED KING safe under good handling. The latter, a forward factor throughout, finished gamely while ing to get in during the late stages. CRITERION was going well at the finish. TRUMPETER SWAN rallied ately from the outside. BOLD AND FANCY, steadied behind ATTABOY JOHN at the turn, failed to seriously nace. SHINING KNIGHT was always outrun. RIGHT PITCH was through early. ATTABOY JOHN had brief ed.
Scratched—Covered Portage.

The virtues of Office King were not a well-kept secret. He received strong betting action, closing as the 9-to-5 favorite. Showing the early speed that he had displayed in his workouts, he raced to a four-length lead and won handily.

9th Saratoga

AUGUST 13, 1

1⅛ MILES SARATOGA

Start ⏴Finish

1⅛ MILES. (1:47). ALLOWANCES. Purse $10,000. 3-year-olds and upward w have not won a race other than maiden, claiming or starter. 3-year-olds, 116 older, 122 lbs. Non-winners of $5,400 at a mile or over since July 15 allowed 2 $5,700 at a mile or over since June 15, 4 lbs.; maidens, 6 lbs. 3-year-olds which never won at a mile or over allowed 3 lbs.; older, 5 lbs. (Winners preferred.)

COUPLED: GRAND SALUTE and CHINCHONA.

Clarion Sky — 114
B. g (1971), by Proud Clarion—Gibellina, by Ribot.
Breeder, J. W. Galbreath (Ky.). 1974 . 9 1 0 3 $4
Owner, Darby Dan Farm. Trainer, T. L. Rondinello. 1973 4 M 0 1 $

Aug 5-74⁹Sar	ⓉⒼ 1⅛ 1:48⅖fm	39	114	12²⁷12²⁵11¹⁷10¹⁶	Riv'aMA¹⁰	Alw 69	Whatawip 117 Haraka RoyalBounde
May18-74⁶Bel	Ⓣ 1¼ 2:03⅕fm	7½	113	8¹⁴ 8¹² 7¹¹ 7¹⁰	HoleM²	Alw 78	Consigl'ri112 J'ntAgreem't Br'zeExp
Apr13-74⁸Kee	1⅟₁₆ 1:44 ft	.6-5	▲117	7²⁴ 6¹² 5¹² 6¹¹	UsseryR⁴	Alw 75	TheGeneral 119 Trephine Alexande
Mar30-74⁹Hia	1 1-8 1:49 ft	6⅜e	122	10²⁰10¹⁸ 9¹⁸ 8¹⁶	Riv'aMA¹	ScwS 71	Bushongo 122 Hasty Flyer Judge
Mar22-74⁹Hia	Ⓣa1⅟₁₆ 1:42½hd	4½	122	10²⁰ 9¹⁹ 8¹³ 7⁴	RiveraMA⁵	Alw 95	LittleEcho115 Rule ofS'c's NewN'd¹
Mar 7-74⁶Hia	1 1-8 1:51⅗ft	1e²122		12²⁰ 9¹⁵ 4²½ 1¹	Riv'aMA¹¹	Mdn 74	Clarion Sky 122 Advisedly Wise Ric
Feb13-74⁴GP	1⅟₁₆ 1:43⅗ft	6	120	6¹⁰ 6⁵½ 4⁶ 3²¾	Cast'daM¹	Mdn 80	EmperorRex120 R'se theAxe Clar'nSk
Jan30-74⁴GP	1⅟₁₆ 1:46⅖ft	3½	120	12¹⁶10¹³ 6¹⁰ 3⁴	HoleM¹¹	Mdn 65	Maharajo120 BlueWonder ClarionSk
Jan23-74³GP	Ⓣa1⅟₁₆ 1:51¾fm	15	120	11¹⁵11¹⁵ 6⁴¼ 3¹¾	HoleM¹²	Mdn 53	Alexander120 SandyHill ClarionSk
Dec15-73¹Aqu	1 1 1:37⅖ft	15	122	14¹⁴12⁹ 12¹²10¹⁰	Casta'aM³	Mdn 70	Roger'sD'ndy122 Crit'rion Sp'nishL'r

Aug 12 Sar 3f ft :39b Aug 4 Sar 3f ft :37⅖b July 31 Sar 6f ft 1:19⅘b

*El Carrerito — 120
Ch. c (1970), by Aristophanes—La Chiflada, by Right of Way.
Breeder, Haras Ojo de Aqua (Arg.). 1974 17 1 2 3 $17
Owner, Camijo Stable. Trainer, J. Martin. 1973 6 1 0 1 $

Aug 2-74⁹Sar	ⓉⒼ 1⅛ 1:48⅖fm	6	112	6¹² 4⁶ 2³ 2¹½	SmithRC²	25500 84	G'dHorse116 ElCarrerito AmericanW
Jly 24-74⁷Aqu	1 1-8 1:51 ft	7¼	115	5¹⁰ 4⁶ 3ⁿᵏ 4¹¼†	Riv'aMA⁷	22500 78	Stick toReason113 BoldCrusader Gar

†Placed third through disqualification.

Jly 8-74⁷Aqu	Ⓣ1⅟₁₆1:42½fm	20	112	5⁸ 5⁵ 7⁶¾ 4³	SmithRC¹	24500 90	BoHatch 118 ...til II. BlackSpring
Jly 2-74⁴Aqu	Ⓣa1⅟₁₆ 1:57⅖fm	32	111	2⁴ 1½ 1½ 1½	Sm'hRC⁶	17000 83	ElC'r'rito111 R'd'es'd'r B'rkingSt'p
Jun24-74⁵Aqu	1 1:36½fm	19	113	5⁷ 4² 6⁵ 5⁷	Her'd'zS⁶	18000 79	St'k toR'son116 B'dCr's'd'r E'lySt'r
Jun17-74⁷Bel	Ⓣ 1 1:36⅕fm	28	115	5⁴½ 8¹⁴ 9¹⁹ 9¹⁵	Hern'ezS¹⁰	Alw 76	Jovial Judge 105 Camelford Pro
Jun 4-74⁴Bel	Ⓣ 1⅛ 2:03⅖fm	14	112	3¹½ 2¹½ 2³ 3³¾	Her'd'zS¹	27500 83	RoughPlace116 Volatil II. ElCarreri

July 22 Bel trt 4f ft :50⅖b

Group Plan — 113
B. g (1970), by Intentionally—Nanticous, by Nantallah.
Breeder, Eaton Farms, Red Bull Stable 1974 . 2 0 0 0
& Mrs. G. Proskauer (Ky.). 1973 . 6 1 1 1 $9
Owner, Hobea Farm. Trainer, H. A. Jerkens.

Aug10-74⁹Sar	6½ f 1:17 ft	4½	121	8⁵¼ 7⁷ 8⁵¾ 6⁶½	MapleE⁸	Alw 84	Plantagen't119 FaceM'k PokersBrus
Aug 3-74²Sar	6 f 1:11⅘fm	19	124	6⁸ 6⁸ 5⁵½ 4½	Cast'daM⁹	Alw 83	Lothario 119 Aquinas Hudsonia
Dec 8-73³Aqu	6 f 1:10 ft	6¾	122	1h 3¹½ 3⁵ 4⁸	Vel'quezJ¹	Alw 85	Spicyapple124 RightSchroc
Nov29-73³Aqu	6 f 1:11⅘sm	7	122	7⁶¾ 6¹¹ 6⁶½ 1²	BaezaB⁸	Mdn 84	GroupPlan 122 M...stic'tive Inv'stig't
Nov16-73⁴Aqu	6½ f 1:19½ft	6	122	7⁶½ 6⁵ 4²½ 3³¼	Vel'q'zJ¹⁰	Mdn 76	D...thM...2 Inv'tig't'n Gr'pPl
Nov 5-73²Aqu	6 f 1:13 ft	5¼	122	7⁸ 6⁷ 5⁵½ 5⁵¾	Velasq'zJ⁹	Mdn 72	SpanishDew112 Investigat'n JewelBa
Oct 9-73¹Bel	6½ f 1:17⅖ft	7-5	▲121	6³¼ 8⁵¼ 8⁷½ 8¹²	Velasq'zJ⁹	Mdn 77	G'tl'm'sW'd121 Inv'tig't'n D'mW'hM
Oct 1-73⁵Bel	6 f 1:11 ft	6	120	5³ 1½ 1¹ 2¾	VasquezJ⁷	Mdn 87	Downtown120 GroupPlan Investigatio

Aug 8 Sar 3f ft :36⅖b Aug 1 Sar 4f ft :47h

The Scotsman — 112
Dk. b. or br. c (1971), by Buckpasser—Fast Cookie, by Beau Gar.
Breeder, J. H. Adger & A. G. Clay (Ky.). 1974 14 1 2 3 $13
Owner, Saron Stable. Trainer, S. E. Veitch. 1973 6 M 0 3 $13

Aug 8-74⁹Sar	ⓉⒼ1⅟₁₆ 1:55⅕fm	9½	112	Lost rider.		TurcotteR³	Alw	Camelford 118 Prod BigBrownBea
Jly 29-74³Sar	1 1-8 1:49⅘ft	2½	▲113	4⁵½ 4³ 6⁶ 5⁵½	Turc'tteR⁶	Alw 87	Peleus 113 Pokers Brush War Reaso
Jly 7-74⁸Del	1⅟₁₆ 1:42⅖ft	29	110	5⁶ 6⁴¾ 5⁶ 5⁵½	McC'onG³	HcpS 90	Gold andMyrrh110 ParkGuard Sherb
Jun30-74⁶Suf	1⅟₁₆ 1:43⅗ft	4	116	4⁵ 4⁵ 5³ 3⁴¾	Ander'nP²	HcpS 81	Sp'r inMyW'b116 KinR'n TheSc'tsma
Jun22-74⁵Del	1⅟₁₆ 1:43⅖ft	5½	113	3ⁿᵏ 1h 2½ 2³	HoleM³	Alw 82	D'mWithMe11... ...n'n TheBigSam
Jun 5-74⁶Mth	ⓉⒼ1⅟₁₆ 1:44⅖fm	3¼	120	10⁹ 8⁹ 5⁹ 5²	AndersonP³	Alw 83	Assag'l 115 JovialJudge Br'zeExpr'
May25-74⁸Bel	1 1:35⅗ft	58	126	9⁸¼12¹⁰10¹³	W'dheR¹	ScwS 75	Accipiter 126 ...p of It Hosie
May18-74⁹Bel	6 f 1:10⅗ft	12	122	9¹² 8¹³ 8⁹¼ 6¹²	MapleE⁴	Alw 78	Q'nCityLad122 F'lyPhys'n Silv'rD'bl
Apr17-74⁷Kee	6½ f 1:17⅗ft	3½	117	8⁵¼ 8⁷½ 4⁴½ 2¹	UsseryR⁵	Alw 89	T.V.S'tan114 TheSc'tsm'n F'rB'seM
Mar14-74⁸SA	1 1-8 1:48⅖ft	20	120	5⁵½ 7⁹¾ 6¹² 6²¹	GrantH⁸	SpwS 69	Agitate 118 Ja Aglo Littlef
Feb17-74⁵SA	1 1:43 ft	12	118	5²½ 3¹¼ 3² 3⁶½	VasquezJ²	Alw 80	Agitate 116 BoldTalent TheScotsma
Feb 3-74⁴SA	1⅟₁₆ 1:44⅖ft	3¾	118	5³½ 2¹½ 1h 1¹	VasquezJ⁸	Mdn 78	TheSc'tsm'n118 Rudy'sPro'se ElSeet

Aug 12 Sar 3f ft :37⅘b Aug 6 Sar 4f ft :48b Aug 3 Sar 3f ft :36b

ar Reason 112 Gr. g (1971), by Warfare—Morning Calm, by Hail to Reason.
Breeder; M. Church III. (Va.). 1974 . 7 1 0 1 $4,332
1973 . 4 M 0 0 (——)
ner, Beverly R. Steinman. Trainer, P. R. Fout.

ld and Gallant 112 B. c (1971), by Gallant Man—Proved Bold, by Bold Ruler.
Breeder, E. P. Evans (Va.). 1974 . 9 1 2 1 $10,637
1973 . 2 M 0 0 (——)
ner, Buckland Farm. Trainer, J. P. Campo.

ark Encounter 112 Dk. b. or br. c (1971), by Cornish Prince—Karate Skill, by Cohoes.
Breeder, Tricorn Farms, Inc. (Ky.). 1974 . 5 1 0 1 $7,320
1973 . 2 M 0 0 $600
ner, F. G. Allen. Trainer, S. Watters, Jr.

g Moses ✳ 99 B. g (1971), by Raspberry Ice—Jane S., by High Lea.
Br., Mrs. J. Ellis & R. L. Dotter (S. C.). 1974 . 7 0 3 0 $7,500
1973 . 4 2 0 1 $10,260
ner, Mrs. J. Ellis. Trainer, R. L. Dotter.

ero Hour 109 Ch. c (1971), by Vertex—Desert Trail, by Moslem Chief.
Breeder, Mrs. V. Adams (Fla.). 1974 . 11 1 0 1 $5,950
ner, H. T. Mangurian, Jr. Trainer, T. F. Root, Sr.

(cont'd on next page)

Chinchona
109 Ro. c (1971), by Cyane—Chinchon, by Goya II.
Breeder, Pine Brook Farm, Inc. (Ky.).　1974 . 9 0 0 3　$5
　　　　　　　　　　　　　　　　　　　　　　1973 . 6 1 2 0　$4
Owner, Lillian F. O'Keefe.　Trainer, M. Miller.

Jly 29-74³Sar	1 1-8 1:49⅘ft	8½	113	8¹³ 8¹⁵ 8¹⁴ 7¹¹	Velasqu'zJ⁸ Alw 81 Peleus 113 Pokers Brush War Reaso
Jly 15-74⁷Aqu	1 1-8 1:50 ft	13	110	45½ 52¾ 55½ 44½	NemetiW⁵ Alw 80 J'ckSp't115 M'n't'ryPr'ciple J'geP'w
Jun29-74⁶Aqu	1 1:34⅖ft	20	111	6⁹ 59½ 5⁹ 39¾	NemetiW⁴ Alw 85 G'ntlem'n'sW'd117 L's'gton Chinchon
Jun 8-74³Bel	⊤ 1⅜ 2:15⅖fm	26	105	5¹¹ 75½ 64½ 42½	CardoneE⁴ Alw 94 BobbyMurcer112 Alexander Outst'din
May28-74⁶Bel	⊤ 1¼ 2:02 fm	17	110	5⁶ 9⁹ 99½ 8⁷	NemetiW⁹ Alw 87 Cr───110 E─'ce ─obl
May 8-74⁹Pim	⊤1 1/16 1:45⅗fm	3	112	2ʰ 2½ 3ⁿᵏ 32½	McC'r'nG¹¹ Alw 80 ClWilliam115 ─kpit Thre
Apr29-74⁷Pim	1 1/16 1:43⅗ft	6½	112	5⁵ 3¹ 33½ 3⁶	McCar'nG⁷ Alw 82 B─re112 J.C. sSh'd'w Ch'ch'n
Apr20-74⁷Pim	6 f 1:12⅕ft	5½	113	85¾108½ 7¹¹ 44½	Pass'reWJ⁵ Alw 81 Ise' Wild 112 On to Glory Pras
Apr13-74⁵Pim	6 f 1:12⅕sy	32	114	84¾ 8⁷ 6⁴ 42½	Pass'reWJ² Alw 82 Millfleet113 On toGlory DeB'rry'sT'k
Jly 20-73⁵Del	5½ f 1:06⅕ft	1	▲120	3¹ 1ʰ 2½ 1ⁿᵒ	WalshE⁴ Mdn 87 Chinchona120 Tex'sL'ger EarlC'rdig"

Aug 12 Sar 3f ft :38b　　July 25 Bel 6f sy 1:18b　　July 21 Bel 4f ft :50b

83 93 96

Judge Power
111 B. c (1970), by Traffic Judge—Just Fancy That, by Vertex.
Breeder, Danada Farm (Ky.).　1974 .14 4 2 1　$23
　　　　　　　　　　　　　　　　1973 .13 2 4 1　$11
Owner, Mrs. J. S. Nash.　Trainer, J. S. Nash.

Jly 29-74³Sar	1 1-8 1:49⅘ft	4½	119	59½ 5⁷ 5⁵ 4⁵	Bracc'eVJr⁷ Alw 87 Peleus 113 Pokers Brush War Reaso
Jly 15-74⁷Aqu	1 1-8 1:50 ft	8¾	120	3⁴ 4² 3² 33½	Bra'leVJr³ Alw 82 J'ckSp't115 M'n't'ryPr'ciple J'geP'w
Jly 9-74⁶Aqu	6½ f 1:16⅖ft	12	116	6⁷ 56½ 55½ 46½	Br'leVJr⁴ 32500 87 SpecialTex112 PassenMood N'seWin
Jun22-74⁵Bel	1 1/16 1:43⅖ft	3	120	5½ 5³ 6⁹ 6¹⁴	W'dh'seR² Alw 71 D'───'m'n──'s BgSw
Jun14-74⁷Bel	1 1:36 ft	33	120	95½ 66½ 48½ 4⁹	Cast'daM⁶ Alw 74 Judge Power 126 Algernon Thaye
May11-74⁴GS	1 1-4 2:05⅕ft	8-5	▲120	5⁵ 2ʰ 1³ 1⁸	BlumW⁶ H7500 74 Judge Power 120 Algernon Thaye
Apr27-74⁹Aqu	1 1-8 1:50 ft	6	119	64½ 3¹ 2ʰ 2½	Casta'daM³ Alw 84 Whickery 111 Judge Power Oilim
Mar23-74⁵Hia	⊤1 1/16 1:41⅖shd	8	122	44 4⁵ 58½ 6¹¹	W'dh'seR² Alw 80 St'ryKnight112 J'nGod'y P'p'r'dJabn
Mar13-74⁶Hia	1 1-8 1:49 ft	1	▲122	14 11½ 11¹ 1³	W'h'seR⁶ H7500 87 JudgePower122 G'l'ntExch'ge Olmec

Aug 8 Sar 6f ft 1:15h　　Aug 3 Sar 6f ft 1:14⅖h　　July 27 Bel 4f ft :49b

93 95 91

Hy Button Shoes
112 B. g (1971), by Misty Flight—Button My Shoe, by One Count.
Breeder, Hymill Stables (Va.).　1974 .11 1 1 2　$1
Owner, Hymill Stable.　Trainer, F. S. Schulhofer.

Aug 5-74⁹Sar	⊤ 1⅛ 1:48⅖fm	28	113	6⁵ 5⁸ 6¹⁰ 7¹²	MontoyaD³ Alw 73 Whatawip 117 Haraka RoyalBound
Jly 22-74⁴Aqu	⊤ 1⅛ 1:51⅖fm	40	115	2⁴ 3² 5⁵½ 6¹⁰	MontoyaD¹ Alw 73 Prod 115 Royal Bounder Harak
Jly 13-74³Aqu	6½ f 1:16⅖ft	13	117	43½ 66¾ 7¹² 6¹⁵	Cast'daM⁷ Alw 78 Quebec124 Knight ofHonor SharpD
Jun 5-74⁹Bel	1 1:35⅗ft	25	114	6⁶ 76½ 7¹⁶ 7²¹	VeneziaM⁶ Alw 69 HatchetMan114 G'tlem'n's'k─ak
May27-74⁷Bel	6 f 1:09⅖ft	27	121	9¹² 9¹⁴ 8¹¹ 6¹⁰	VeneziaM⁷ Alw 84 Fr'c'lyN'tive121 NileD'ita T'keLeadSh
Apr20-74³Aqu	1 1:37 ft	12	116*	2ʰ 44½ 3⁸ 3⁶	MontoyaD¹ Alw 76 Rule ofSuccess118 Capit─NoSh
Apr 5-74⁸Aqu	1 1:37⅘sy	5	116*	4⁵ 48½ 59½ 59¾	MontoyaD³ Alw 68 FirstSlice121 EmpireM'n B'ld a dF'c
Mar28-74⁴Aqu	1 1:38⅕ft	1	▲109*	66½ 3⁵ 34½ 1ʰ	MontoyaD² Mdn 76 HyB't'nSh's109 Tr'pic'lB'y M'nt'naH
Mar16-74⁵Aqu	6 f 1:11⅕ft	2½	117*	51¼ 3½ 3ⁿᵏ 2ⁿᵏ	Mont'yaD⁸ Mdn 87 FreeAssociat'n122 HyB't'nSh's Mr.B

Aug 11 Sar 3f ft :36h　　July 29 Sar tc 4f fm :48⅖h　　July 20 Bel 4f ft :47⅗h

62

War Reason has the best figure in this nondescript allowance race. He earned a rating of 98 on July 29 while he was beating several of the contenders in today's field — The Scotsman, Judge Power, and Big Moses.

On that day practically every race at Saratoga was won by

a speed horse with an inside post position. War Reason managed to come from far behind, circle the field, and finish a close third. It was an impressive performance. His subsequent defeat on August 5 can be ignored. That race was run on the grass, and War Reason's record shows clearly that he is not a grass horse. Back on the main track today, he should be ready for a top effort.

Most of his competition appears very weak. El Carrerito is a turf horse. Dark Encounter is a sprinter. Zero Hour's figure in his recent 5½-length victory was atrocious. Clarion Sky and Bold and Gallant are off form. But there is one horse in this field likely to improve dramatically.

Group Plan made a promising debut for the year on August 3, when he finished fast and lost a six-furlong race by half a length. After that race, trainer Boo Gentry sold him to Allen Jerkens. Wasting no time, Jerkens entered him in another sprint on August 10. Group Plan finished a lackluster sixth, 6½ lengths behind the winner, earning a figure of 85 that would not menace the horses he is facing today. Yet many indications are present that this is going to be another Jerkens training miracle.

Jerkens always does well with horses he acquires privately. In 1973 he bought Prove Out and within nine days transformed him from a nonentity into a star.

Jerkens wins often when he enters a horse within three or four days of his last start. In 1973 he brought Onion back after three days' rest and upset Secretariat at Saratoga.

Jerkens' greatest strength is his ability to convert sprinters into routers. He made his reputation in the early sixties when his sprinter Beau Purple beat the great Kelso three times.

A horseplayer could logically bet Group Plan on the basis of faith in Jerkens. Or he could logically bet War Reason because of his superior figures and established handicapping merits. There are no rules that govern the situation. This is one of the close, agonizing decisions that separate the winners from the losers.

NINTH RACE
Sar
August 13, 1974

1⅛ MILES. (1:47). ALLOWANCES. Purse $10,000. 3-year-olds and upward w have not won a race other than maiden, claiming or starter. 3-year-olds, 116 older, 122 lbs. Non-winners of $5,400 at a mile or over since July 15 allowed 2 $5,700 at a mile or over since June 15, 4 lbs.; maidens, 6 lbs. 3-year-olds which n never won at a mile or over allowed 3 lbs.; older, 5 lbs. (Winners preferred.)
Value to winner $6,000; second, $2,200; third, $1,200; fourth, $600. Mutuel Pool, $89,914.
Off-track betting, $110,144. Triple Pool, $102,090. Off-track betting Triple Pool, $219,582.

Last Raced	Horse	EqtAWt	PP	St	¼	½	¾	Str	Fin	Jockeys	Owners	Odds
8-10-74⁹ Sar⁶	Group Plan	b4 113	3	4	2¹½	1h	1h	1⁶	18½	EMaple	Hobeau Farm	
8- 8-74⁹ Sar	The Scotsman	b3 113	4	10	7½	5h	51½	4²	2h	RTurcotte	Saron Stable	
7-29-74³ Sar⁴	Judge Power	b4 118	12	8	9¹	8²	6⁴	3½	32½	MCastaneda	Mrs J S Nash	
8- 5-74⁹ Sar¹⁰	Clarion Sky	3 114	1	12	12	11½	10²	5h	43¾	MARivera	Darby Dan Farm	2
7-29-74³ Sar⁶	Big Moses	3 103	8	1	1h	2³	2³	2²	5⅜	MADotter¹⁰	Mrs J Ellis	1
7-29-74³ Sar⁷	Chinchona	b3 109	10	6	8½	7½	9²	9²	6no	ECardone	Lillian F O'Keefe	2
8- 5-74⁹ Sar⁶	War Reason	b3 112	5	9	10⁸	10⁶	8h	81½	7nk	BMFeliciano	Beverly R Steinman	
7-22-74⁴ Aqu⁹	Bold and Gallant	b3 112	6	11	11²	12	11⁵	10¹½	8²	VBraccialeJr	Buckland Farm	1
8- 2-74⁹ Sar²	El Carrerito	4 120	2	3	4¹½	4⁴	4h	6¹½	9no	RCSmith	Camijo Stable	
8-10-74⁹ Sar¹	Dark Encounter	3 113	7	2	3¹	3¹	3⁴	7½	10²	MHole	F G Allen	2
8- 5-74⁹ Sar⁸	Zero Hour	3 109	9	5	5h	6¹	7h	11¹¹	11¹³	JSLong⁷	H T Mangurian Jr	2
8- 5-74⁹ Sar⁷	Hy Button Shoes	b3 112	11	7	6¹½	9½	12	12	12	DMontoya	Hymill Stable	4

OFF AT 5:59 EDT. Start good. Won driving. Time, :23⅗, :47, 1:10⅘, 1:35⅘, 1:48⅘. Track fast.

$2 Mutuel Prices:

3-GROUP PLAN	7.00	4.20	3.8
4-THE SCOTSMAN		4.40	3.6
12-JUDGE POWER			3.8

$2 TRIPLE (3-4-12) PAID $256.00.

B. g, by Intentionally—Nanticious, by Nantallah. Trainer, H. A. Jerkens. Bred by Eaton Farm, Red Stable and Mrs. Proskauer.
GROUP PLAN saved ground while vying for the lead with BIG MOSES, put that one away approac the stretch and increased his advantage under pressure. THE SCOTSMAN rallied from the outside leaving far turn and continued on with good courage. JUDGE POWER split horses after entering the stretch finished well. CLARION SKY, void of early foot, rallied entering the stretch but failed to sustain his BIG MOSES was used up dueling for the lead. WAR REASON was always outrun. ELCARRERITO was thre after going three quarters. DARK ENCOUNTER, a factor to the stretch, had nothing left. ZERO HOUR through early. HY BUTTON SHOES had brief speed.
Overweight—The Scotsman, 1 pound; Dark Encounter, 1; Big Moses, 4.
Scratched—To The Tune, Grand Salute, Crag's Corner.

Group Plan supported the judgment of the many New York horseplayers who think Allen Jerkens is God. He won by 8½ lengths, earning a figure of 106, and went on to establish himself as one of the better horses in the country. War Reason was never close.

7th Pimlico Race Course
MARCH 20, 1974

6 FURLONGS. (1:09⅕). CLAIMING. Purse $5,500. Fillies. 3-year-olds. Weight, 122 lbs. Non-winners of two races since Feb. 7 allowed 3 lbs.; a race, 5 lbs.; a race since Jan. 30, 8 lbs. Claiming price, $7,500; for each $250 to $7,000, allowed 1 lb. (Races where entered for $6,000 or less not considered.)

COUPLED: GLITTERING GOLD and I'M DIANA.

Annie Oak   **107**   B. f (1970), by Rambunctious—Activation, by Prove It.
Breeder, Mrs. F. Biere (Md.).   1974   5   0   2   0 $1,620
Owner, E. M. Casey.   Trainer, G. W. Walters. $7,500   1973   4   1   1   0 $1,826

Mar11-747ShD	6 f 1:15⅕ft	10	114	2½	23	33	46	EspinosaV6	Alw 66 JetAppeal 118 WmRLewisJr Ch'sCh'r	7
Feb26-748ShD	5½ f 1:09⅖ft	4½	115	5³½	44½	66	88¾	EspinosaV6	Alw 70 H'rySt'p118 Ch'sCh'g'r En'gh'sEn'gh's	9
Feb14-747ShD	6 f 1:14⅗ft	6¾	114	1³	15	14	21½	EspinosaV8	Alw 79 JiggerMan118 AnnieOok En'gh'sEn's	8
Feb 1-749ShD	3½ f :41⅖ft	3¾	115	5	31½	43	42	EspinosaV5	Alw 86 DimmitCh'rg'r120 AvidC'rt R'ghP'der	6

March 9 CT 3f :37b   Feb 24 CT 3f ft :36b

Glittering Gold   **114**   B. f (1971), by Hedevar—Bob's Princess, by Selinsgrove.
Breeder, F. D. Vechery (Md.).   1974   4   2   0   0 $3,924
Owner, F. D. Vechery.   Trainer, K. T. Leatherbury. $7,500   1973   4   1   1   0 $1,780

Mar 8-743Bow	6 f 1:15⅗ft	5½	119	2¹½	1h	1¹½	12½	WalshE1	5500 65 ⑤Glit'ngGold119 S'c'ndS'a Sp'shC'f'e	7
Feb26-743Bow	6 f 1:14⅖ft	9	117	3½	32½	32	52¾	WalshE3	6000 68 ⑤Li'lBuy'r114 Sp'nishC'fee Dar'gD'nd	9
Feb13-744Pen	5½ f 1:05⅕ft	4½	113	54½	45½	43½	NobleJF2	Alw 89 Nell's B'l221 PrinceAr CrackR'g'nt	5
Feb 7-741Pen	5½ f 1:06⅕ft	14	118	41½	52½	44½	1h	N'leJF12	M3500 92 Glit'gG'ld118 Ap'cheW'dge D'lBr'h's	12

Feb 23 Bow 3f ft :37⅖b   Jan 31 Pen 4f sl :52hg   Jan 23 Pen 6f sl 1:19⅗bg

58 47

Tree Lace   **114**   B. f (1971), by Advocator—Rubber Game, by Reneged.
Breeder, K. C. Firestone (Ky.).   1974   6   0   3   2 $3,804
Owner, E. J. Wirth.   Trainer, R. Cartwright. $7,500   1973   12   1   1   1 $3,588

Mar11-746Bow	6 f 1:14⅕ft	5½	112	13	12	12	12½	KurtzJ4	7000 70 ⑤Banana 114 Tree Lace Inky B.	7
Feb 9-742Bow	6 f 1:13⅕sy	5½	114	3nk	2¹	1h	2¹	GinoL3	c5500 76 ⑤DaringDiamond119 TreeL'ce Nad'te	12
Jan30-742Bow	7 f 1:28¾gd	14	114	1½	1½	2½	36½	GinoL3	5500 56 ⑤HelloKim112 Dar'gD'm'nd TreeL'ce	12
Jan22-742Bow	6 f 1:14⅘ft	6¾	114	4½	4³	3nk	2h	GinoL3	5500 67 ⑤Dotty S'n'cki Tree L'ce	12
Jan10-746Pen	5½ f 1:08⅕sy	4½	114	2h	2¹	22	2¹	Reynl'dsR2	5500 62 ⑤Yest'ction TreeLace D'le Bi'ne	9
Jan 3-745Bow	6 f 1:14⅘ft	14	114	76¼	89	7101062	Pass'eWJ6	7500 62 ⑤S'Dec'n114 Mary'dQ'n F'leBillie	12
Dec16-734Pen	6 f 1:14⅗gd	2½	112	22	32½	51½	41½	DennieD4	5000 73 ArcticM'nd117 R'dheadD. CatfishJ'nh	10
Dec10-732Lrl	1 1:42 m	13	113	1¼	2¹½	67½	71³	CookeC2	7500 50 LottaJack120 SolarCircle DabneyR'd	9
Nov22-731Lrl	7 f 1:27⅕ft	12	116	1½	1½	2½	32	CookeC3	7500 73 BoldSq'w109 MissOverdrive TreeLace	9

March 3 Lrl 7f 1:30 ⅖b

67 58 40

Daring Diamond   **117**   Ch. f (1971), by Choker—Lordy Me, by Our Babu.
Breeder, Fellowship Farm (Fla.).   1974   6   2   1   1 $7,410
Owner, J. R. Whorl.   Trainer, T. C. Patterson. $7,000   1973   6   2   1   0 $6,320

Mar11-746Bow	6 f 1:14⅕ft	4	114	44	56	56	58¾	ShukN5	7000 63 ⑤Banana 114 Tree Lace Inky B.	7
Feb26-743Bow	6 f 1:14⅖ft	3-5	▲117	53	65	52½	32½	Cus'noG5	c5500 68 ⑤Li'lBuy'r114 Sp'nishC'fee Dar'gD'nd	9
Feb 9-742Bow	6 f 1:13⅕sy	3-2	▲119	74½	56	33	1¹	Cusim'oG1	5500 77 ⑤DaringDiamond119 TreeL'ce Nad'te	12
Jan30-742Bow	7 f 1:28¾gd	2½	▲119	53½	43½	33	2nk	Cusim'oG3	5500 67 ⑤HelloKim112 Dar'gD'm'nd TreeL'ce	12
Jan15-745Bow	6 f 1:26⅖ft	8-5	▲114	54½	45½	2½	1½	Cu'manoG1	8500 73 ⑤Daring'iam'119 TreeL'ce Ch'erL'k	10
Jan 2-747Lrl	7 f 1:27⅖ft	11	113	67	77	610	614	Cus'noG6	13500 54 G'r'l'sB'ty113 Chee'rM'n't F'M'n	9
Dec 7-734Lrl	6 f 1:13⅗ft	2	▲116	63½	54	54	52	Cus'noG5	12500 80 F'looM'chTime148 B'dSq'w D'deVe	9
Nov20-736Lrl	6 f 1:11⅘ft	4½	103*▲64½	67	511	511	Ber'diW6	15500 79 RedRamage115 Cheri'te M'ndat'rY'ct	9
Sep24-736Bow	6 f 1:13⅖ft	3-2	▲114	44½	31½	2h	1¹½	Haw'yS2	c12500 74 DaringD'md114 JigTimeR'se DiB'ss	9
Aug27-734Mth	6 f 1:11⅘ft	9-5	▲117	33½	34½	1½	1¹½	Us'ryR5	M10000 83 Dar'gDiam'd117 H'zyTr'th Pl'dLake	9
Aug17-734Mth	5½ f 1:07⅘gd	23	112*	64½	56½	65½	2¹	M'tinR5	M10000 77 ⑤M'l'caM'n'r117 D'r'gD'm'd O'sL'd'n	8

50 47 60

Sharp Nurse   **105**   B. f (1971), by Piercer—Special Nurse, by New Moon.
Breeder, J. E. Hughes (Md.).   1974   5   1   0   0 $2,520
Owner, J. E. Hughes.   Trainer, G. L. Ballenger. $7,000   1973   10   M   2   1 $2,344

Feb27-745Bow	6 f 1:13⅗ft	26	110	52¾	44½	35½	512	Jamtg'dW4	5000 63 B'c'pGary119 Br'veTonto F'rM'reY'rs	7
Feb 9-742Bow	6 f 1:13⅕sy	8½	110*	85	109¹¹011	88	Miner'niF2	5000 69 ⑤DaringDiamond119 TreeL'ce Nad'te	12
Feb 1-744Bow	6 f 1:13⅗ft	18	110*	78½	77	79	56½	Min'viniF5	7000 70 ⑤M'w'l'dQu'n114 InkyB. C'pp'rM'k't	10
Jan22-744Bow	6 f 1:12⅖m	21	108*	69½	615	614	618	Min'niF5	12500 61 M'm'ydC't'wh'ght Right L'dr'k	6
Jan11-741Bow	6 f 1:16⅕m	6½	112	66½	67½	55½	1nk	Min'niF6	M7500 62 ⑤SharpNurse125 Nadia Anton	12
Dec20-731Lrl	7 f 1:29⅕ssl	7½	112*	64	59	510	56½	M'niF12	M5000 59 ⑤CeWl'l 119 S't'n'sSq'w E'ma'sL'y	12
Dec 7-732Lrl	1 1:40⅖ft	21	108*	86½	910¹0141120	Min'niF1	M9500 52 Sam 'N H'bie120 V't'r'sD'cer B'c'pG'y	12
Nov29-731Lrl	6 f 1:28⅕gd	4	110*	69½	44½	23	23½	Min'niF4	M5000 67 C'zinsJimAndy120 Sh'pN'se L'stS'nd'l	12
Oct31-741Lrl	7 f 1:28⅗gd	15	110*	75¾	57½	45½	21½	M'iniF11	M5000 67 F'rM'reY'rs120 Sh'pN'rse D'ntotheS'a	12

March 16 Bow 4f ft :50bg   March 12 Bow 4f ft :51⅖b   March 5 Bow 3f ft :37⅗b

39 40 41

(cont'd on next page)

I'm Diana
114 Ch. f (1971), by I'm Nashville—Brutessa, by Dear Brutus.
Breeder, R. R. Bailey (Va.).　　　1974　5 0 0 0　　$67
Owner, C S W Stable. Trainer, K. T. Leatherbury.　　**$7,500**　　1973　6 1 0 0　　$2,3

Mar 7-74	6Bow	1 1/16 1:48⅕ft	6½	109	3 1½ 2½ 45½ 57½	WalshE⁴		7500 59 ArloFleet112 PrinceSwept NoNoAlvin 1
Feb26-74	4Bow	1 1/16 1:50⅖ft	7¾	109	4³ 3nk 2¹ 4¹	WalshE⁴		7500 55 PrinceSwept114 Br'kmoore CafeNoir
Feb14-74	7Bow	1 1/16 1:49⅕ft	12	109	9¹² 88½ 6⁷ 68½	WalshE⁵		11500 53 I'm InNeed113 DabneyRoad NineP'nts
Feb 1-74	3Bow	6 f 1:13⅘ft	7	112	8¹³ 8¹² 7¹¹ 7³½	WalshE⁷		9500 70 ⑤SilvrK'e114 Th'erone FriskieBillie
Jan15-74	5Bow	7 f 1:26⅖ft	17	114	43½ 56½ 64½ 44½	LeeT⁶		c7500 68 ⑤DancingDiam'd119 PalceWh'l C'prM't 1
Dec 5-73	1Lrl	6 f 1:14 sy	3½	119	54½ 4² 1² 1³	C'm'oG⁴		M5000 79 ⑤I'mDiana119 PalaceWhirl Sec'dSea 1
Nov 5-73	4Lrl	6 f 1:14⅗sy	16	112	66½ 69½ 68½ 65½	Fel'noBM⁷		5000 71 ⑤EvNCh't108 Reb'IM'l Q'nOfTheBB's
Oct17-73	3Bow	7 f 1:26 ft	33	117	8⁶ 79½ 79½ 78½	McC'nG⁵		M5500 64 Whispinder115 Alson TighmansIsle 1
Oct 4-73	1Bow	6 f 1:14⅕ft	30	119	8⁷ 87½ 66½ 66½	McC'nG⁶		M5000 66 ⑤Nadeete 119 Tree Lace Silver Jay 1

Gala Image
114 B. f (1971), by Dancer's Image—Brow Brook, by Lurullah.
Breeder, Glade Valley Farms, Inc. (Md.).　1974　4 0 0 0　　(—
Owner, Gert Leviton. Trainer, B. P. Bond.　　**$7,500**　　1973　9 1 1 1　$4,91

Mar 5-74	8Bow	7 f 1:25⅖ft	41	112	37½ 4¹² 8¹⁴ 8¹⁸	Felic'oBM⁸	Alw 60 ⑤Engag'd120 C'tiousMill St'tingVix'n
Feb 5-74	8Bow	7 f 1:23⅗fr	4¾	112	87½ 9¹⁰10¹⁶10¹⁹	HawleyS³	Alw 68 ⑤Esth'rDin'h112 B'ldSq'w L'dyM'rine 1
Jan29-74	7Bow	6 f 1:14⅕m	27	115	88½ 98½ 75½ 53½	McH'ueDG⁵	Alw 68 ⑤D'g'Prize120 M'sOverdrive Eth'rD'h'
Jan 7-74	7Bow	6 f 1:13 gd	48	116	9⁷ 75½ 5⁴ 5⁷	McCarr'nG⁶	Alw 71 ⑤Rel'tiv'e119 M'rDu'te M'cov're 1
Dec 5-73	7Lr!	6 f 1:12⅖sy	8¾	115	11131020¹⁰14¹07½	HawleyS¹¹	Alw 40 ⑤K'v't'114 Advis'ry Qu'n
Nov 3-73	5Lrl	6 f 1:26⅕ft	2½	114	3¹ 4² 5⁶ 5¹⁰	Feli'noBM⁷	Alw 70 ⑤NoiseD'114 B'sB'h'v'g T'cLen' 1
Oct26-73	7Lrl	6 f 1:13⅗ft	14	115	8⁴ 73½ 66½ 65½	Felic'oBM⁶	Alw 86 ⑤Nevsari 112 Maid At Sea Brash 1
Oct15-73	4Bow	7 f 1:25 ft	2¾	119	52½ 4²½ 33½	Bra'leVJr⁴	Alw 77 ⑤Groan 119 PleasureChest Gala:image
March 14 Bow 5f 1:04b					March 2 Bow 3f ft :37⅗b			Feb 25 Bow 6f 1:15⅘b

Copper Market
107 Ch. f (1971), by Hurry to Market—Azurita, by Rico Monte.
Breeder, W. H. Morgan (Ky.).　　1974　8 0 0 2　　$2,23
Owner, Larking Hill Farm. Trainer, E. D. Gaudet.　**$7,500**　1973　8 0 0 1　　$2,97

Mar 4-74	5Bow	6 f 1:12⅖ft	50	112	8¹³ 8¹⁸ 7¹³ 7¹⁰	BlackAS⁵	9500 69 ⑤FriskieBillie114 M'sTid'lW've Ch'te 1
Feb20-74	7Bow	7 f 1:27⅖ft	23	112	86½ 66½ 6⁷ 7⁵	WrightDR¹	9500 61 ⑤Libertine 117 FriskieBillie HiDottie
Feb13-74	3Bow	7 f 1:27⅖ft	4	113	9¹⁰ 85½ 64½ 51½	Br'leVJr²	c7000 64 ⑤D'g'rB'y117 Qu'nB'b B. Her'kin 1
Feb 4-74	3Bow	6 f 1:13⅖ft	3¼	112	10¹² 97½ 4⁶ 32½	Br'aleVJr⁶	7000 73 ⑤Rock'n'n112 R's'eF'e C'ppr't'n 1
Jan25-74	4Bow	6 f 1:14⅗m	3¼	112	7¹¹ 7¹⁰ 5⁸ 42½	Bra'leVJr⁷	7000 68 ⑤Reb'lMill114 Advis'ry IW've Jewel 1
Jan15-74	5Bow	7 f 1:26⅖ft	23	114	75½ 6⁷ 43½ 3⁴	Br'c'leVJr³	7000 69 ⑤DaringDiam'd114 InkyB. C'perM'k't 1
Jan 8-74	4Bow	1 1/16 1:49 gd	2½	▲114	1h 41½ 34½ 45½	BlackAS³	7500 58 DabneyR'd114 Bundy'sBoy Brookm're 1
Jan 3-74	5Bow	6 f 1:14⅗m	3-2e	▲114	97¾ 77½ 5⁶ 4²	BlackAS⁸	7500 67 ⑤Ly'sDec'n114 Maryl'dQ'n F'kieBillie 1
March 14 Bow 5f 1:06⅖b					Feb 28 Bow 6f 1:06⅖b			Feb 1 Bow 4f ft :50⅘b

Better Reason
114 Gr. f (1971), by Turn To Reason—Mabe Trader, by War Admiral.
Br., Mr. & Mrs. C. O. Goldsmith (Md.).　1974　3 M 0 0　　$64
Owner, C. O. Goldsmith. Trainer, J. P. Considine.　**$7,500**　1973　3 M 0 0　(—)

Mar 1-74	5Bow	6 f 1:12⅖ft	29	112	4⁶ 65½10¹³10¹⁶	StovallR⁵	7500 65 HelloKim109 Ch's'p'keB'g'ye D'lHimIn 1
Feb 4-74	3Bow	6 f 1:13⅖ft	5	107*	32½ 4² 3⁵ 4⁵	Lindb'gG⁷	7500 71 ⑤M'd'nQu'n11½ InkyB. C'prM'k't 1
Jan21-74	7Bow	6 f 1:13⅖sm	55	104*	53½ 43½ 53½ 44½	Lindb'gG¹⁰	7500 72 Not'llAsB's11½ J'tSp's'n F'kB'le 1
Dec29-73	2Lrl	6 f 1:17 sl	23	111*	85½ 66½10¹⁴10¹³	L'b'gG³	M10500 51 St'r'nd115 TopE'sTopHome 1
Dec 6-73	4Lrl	6 f 1:13 gd	8e	119	7⁶½ 69½ 7¹⁰ 9¹⁷	StovallR⁶	Mdn 67 ⑤Dance Prize 119 Sailingon Nalgana 1
Nov14-73	3Lrl	6 f 1:13 ft	31	116	4⁴ 56½ 5⁶½ 5⁶½	StovallR⁶	8000 74 ⑤Rus'eChris118 C'nt'rb'ry E'ma'sL'dy 1
March 16 Pim 4f ft :50⅘h					Feb 24 Bow 6f ft 1:16⅖½b			Feb 16 Bow 4f ft :50b

Scuttled
107 B. f (1971), by Salerno—Surfboard Betty, by Bold Commander.
Breeder, C. N. K. Church (Va.).　　1974　4 M 0 0　　$600
Owner, Mrs. R. Hutchinson. Trainer, C. R. Lewis.　**$7,500**　1973　2 M 0 0　　(—

Mar 2-74	5Bow	6 f 1:11⅗ft	10	119	99½ 9¹² 8¹⁹ 9²²	Hinoj'aH¹²	Mdn 63 ⑤Mamaloi119 SallyLev SirloinTip 12
Feb23-74	3Bow	7 f 1:27⅖ft	14	119	51½ 3½ 52½ 42½	Hino'osaH⁹	Mdn 65 ⑤H'r'119 High'T'p Top of the M're 12
Feb 6-74	5Bow	7 f 1:24⅗ft	15	119	4nk 52½ 4² 46½	Hinoj'saH²	Mdn 76 ⑤H'n'I T'p o' e F's't M're12
Jan 7-74	3Bow	6 f 1:12⅕gd	11	119	7⁵ 8¹¹ 8¹⁴ 8¹⁹	Hino'saH³	Mdn 63 ⑤Top H's't'rel115 Happy't'e 12
Dec28-73	4Lrl	7 f 1:31⅖hy	7½	119	1h 3¹ 4⁷ 7¹⁶	Hino'aH¹²	Mdn 38 ⑤BrightB'ndary119 Donetta Levanna 12
Dec 5-73	4Lrl	6 f 1:12⅘sy	37	119	31½ 1h 1h 5⁵	Hin'j'saH²	Mdn 81 ⑤Cauti'sMill 119 D'n'ta Castil'nRose 12
Feb 21 Lrl 3f ft :37b					Jan 30 Lrl 5f m 1:06b			

rak
112 B. f (1971), by Bold Ambition--Divali, by Royal Note.
Breeder, J. Krupnik (Md.).

er, J. Krupnik. Trainer, J. J. Lenzini, Sr.

$7,000 — 1974 4 1 0 0 $2,652 — 1973 1 M 0 0 (——)

```
7-7½²Bow    6 f 1:13⅕ft    4   115  11½ 13  11½ 1²  KurtzJ⁴  M5000 77 Jorak 115  Black Mo  A Poppy Formal 12
13-74³Bow   7 f 1:27⅖ft   39  105 ♠88¾ 96½ 76½ 76   McC'onCJ⁷ 7500 60 ⒻChesapeakeBy 14 InkyB.        10
4-74³Bow    6 f 1:13⅖ft   6¼  112  5³  53½ 68  67½ KurtzJ⁹   7000 68 ⒻMeryl'dQu'n       C'ppyM       10
11-74¹Bow   6 f 1:16⅕m     5  119  42½ 21  2¹  42½ KurtzJ¹¹  M7500 60 ⒻStarNurse11 MissNadia mu'on 12
19-73²Lrl   6 f 1:12⅖gd   24  119  8⁶  8⁸  9¹⁴ 9¹⁶ KurtzJ⁵   Mdn 71 ⒻR'd'sL'nd'g119 Cl'rM'd'te Mal'yM'd 11
```

March 16 Lrl 5f gd 1:03b   March 4 Bow 5f ft 1:02⅖b   Feb 27 Bow 5f ft 1:02b

Since the meeting began on March 18, almost every race at Pimlico was won by a speed horse who was able to get to the inside part of the track. The bias was so powerful that horses who did not have early speed or inside post positions could be eliminated almost automatically.

The fillies who drew the three inside post positions in this six-furlong race all have early speed and thus merit consideration. Annie Oak has been racing against males in allowance company at Charles Town, but the allowance tag is a bit deceptive. The horses in those fields probably weren't worth much more than $5000, and Annie Oak hasn't been able to win against them.

Glittering Gold has not run any glittering figures; her best effort is a 58. But she is lightly raced and is trained by the astute King T. Leatherbury, so she seems eligible for improvement.

Tree Lace has the best figure in this field, a 67, but her overall record is less than inspiring. She ran this good figure when she was able to break loose to a clear early lead, but there is no guarantee she will be able to do so again today, with two speed horses inside her. Tree Lace also seems to be developing sucker-horse tendencies, having finished second or third five times in a row without being able to win, even in $5000 company.

Since none of the horses favored by the track bias has awesome credentials, we must consider the other possible contenders in the field. Gala Image displayed some promise early in her career, but her form has deteriorated badly and she lost her last two starts by margins of 18 and 19 lengths. A drop in class from allowance company doesn't figure to help her enough to win today.

I'm Diana, the other half of Leatherbury's entry, has shown early speed in route races. But her figures are poor and her previous form in sprints suggests that she will be trying to rally from far behind — a nearly impossible task on this speed-favoring track.

Jorak has speed and opened a clear early lead to beat cheap maidens in her last start. But she will be severely

SEVENTH RACE
Pim
March 20, 1974

6 FURLONGS. (1:09⅗). CLAIMING. Purse $5,500. Fillies. 3-year-olds. Weight, 122 lb Non-winners of two races since Feb. 7 allowed 3 lbs.; a race, 5 lbs.; a race sin Jan. 30, 8 lbs. Claiming price, $7,500; for each $250 to $7,000, allowed 1 lb. (Rac where entered for $6,000 or less not considered.)

Value to winner $3,300; second, $1,210; third, $660; fourth, $330. Mutuel Pool, $49,373. Exacta Pool, $83,671.

Last Raced		Horse	EqtAWt	PP	St	¼	½	Str	Fin	Jockeys	Owners	Odds to
3-11-74⁷	ShD⁴	Annie Oak	3 114	1	4	1¹	1²	1³	1⁴	GMcCarron†	Eleanor M Casey	29.
3-11-74⁶	Bow²	Tree Lace	b3 114	3	3	2½	2ʰ	2¹	2ⁿᵒ	GCusimano	E J Wirth	2.
3- 7-74⁶	Bow⁵	I'm Diana	b3 114	6	9	1¹	7½	4¹½	3¹	AAgnello	C S W Stable	a-3.
3- 7-74²	Bow¹	Jorak	b3 112	11	5	3¹	3⁴	3³	4¹¾	JKurtz	J Krupnik	4.⁹
3-11-74⁶	Bow⁵	Daring Diamond	3 115	4	11	9ʰ	10¹½	6¹½	5¹¾	JDavidson	J R Whorl	6.¹
3- 4-74⁵	Bow⁷	Copper Market	b3 107	8	7	10²½	8¹	7½	6¾	CJMcCarron⁷	Larking Hill Farm	12.
2-27-74⁵	Bow⁵	Sharp Nurse	b3 105	5	10	7ʰ	9ʰ	8¹½	7³	SGraham⁷	J E Hughes	54.
3- 2-74⁵	Bow⁹	Scuttled	3 114	10	1	4½	6½	9¹½	8ⁿᵏ	HHinojosa†	Mrs R Hutchinson	11.
3- 1-74⁵	Bow¹⁰	Better Reason	3 114	9	2	6¹½	4¹	5½	9²¾	WJPassmore	C O Goldsmith	50.
3- 5-74⁸	Bow⁸	Gala Image	b3 114	7	8	8ʰ	11	11	10¹	BMFeliciano	Gert Leviton	6.
3- 8-74³	Bow¹	Glittering Gold	3 114	2	6	5¹½	5ʰ	10¹	11	EWalsh	F D Vechery	a-3.

Coupled: a-I'm Diana and Glittering Gold.   †Seven pounds apprentice allowance waived.
OFF AT 3:56 EDT.   Start good. Won driving.   Time, :24, :48⅕, 1:01, 1:14⅖. Track fast.

$2 Mutuel Prices:

2-ANNIE OAK	....	60.60	15.80	6.80
3-TREE LACE	....		4.40	3.00
1A-I'M DIANA (a-Entry)		..		3.20

$2 EXACTA (2-3) PAID $152.00

B. f, by Rambunctious—Activation, by Prove It. Trainer, Marlene M. Croy. Bred by Mrs. F. Bierer (Md.).
ANNIE OAK sprinted to a clear lead leaving the backstretch and gradually extended her advantag thereafter under vigorous handling. TREE LACE raced in closest attendance under a hustling ride ar continued gamely to hold on for the place. I'M DIANA lodged her bid from the outside entering the stretc and finished with good courage. JORAK gradually weakened. DARING DIAMOND passed tired horse SCUTTLED had only brief early foot. GALA IMAGE was through early, as was GLITTERING GOLD.
Overweight—Daring Diamond, 3 pounds.
Corrected weight—Daring Diamond, 112.
Scuttled claimed by Spartan Stable, trainer A. J. Hemmerick.
Claiming Prices (in order of finish)—$7500, 7500, 7500, 7000, 7000, 7500, 7000, 7500, 7500, 7500, 7500.

handicapped by her outside post today. With several speed horses inside her, it seems unlikely that she could break on top and get to the rail.

This race, like the majority of races, is one in which no horse seems clearly superior. If it were run five times, it might produce five different winners. But it is being run today over a track with a powerful bias, and since none of the horses has any great edge in ability over his rivals, the bias is likely to determine the outcome. The speed horses breaking from the three inside posts — Annie Oak, Glittering Gold, and Tree Lace — are the ones who will be helped by the bias. A logical way to play this race would be to combine these three horses in the exacta and hope for the best.

Annie Oak stayed on the lightning-fast rail from start to finish and won easily at 29-to-1 odds. Tree Lace, true to her sucker-horse tendencies, ran second all the way and completed a $152 exacta. The surprise of the race was I'm Diana, who managed to rally in the middle of the track and finish third. This strong performance against the track bias indicated that she was in sharp form; I'm Diana went on to win her next start and paid $8.40. When Annie Oak ran again, without a track bias to help her, she tired as usual and finished far out of the money.

7th Saratoga

AUGUST 25, 1973

6½ FURLONGS (chute). (1:15⅕). Sixty-ninth running HOPEFUL. SCALE WEIGHTS. $75,000 added. 2-year-olds. By subscription of $150 each, which shall accompany the nomination; $375 to pass the entry box; $375 to start, with $75,000 added. The added money and all fees to be divided: 60% to the winner, 22% to second, 12% to third and 6% to fourth. Weight, 121 lbs. Trophies will be presented to the winning owner, trainer and jockey. Closed with 25 nominations.

Take By Storm   **121**   B. c (1971), by Pronto—Great Achievement, by Bold Ruler.
Breeder, O. M. Phipps (Ky.).   1973.. 5 1 1 1 $10,080

Owner, O. M. Phipps. Trainer, R. Laurin.

Aug11-73²Sar	6 f 1:11 ft	3	119	1h	2h	1³	16½	TurcotteR¹	Mdn 85	TakeByStorm 119 Hilo TheScotsman 12
Jy 31-73¹Sar	6 f 1:11⅗ft	5¾	119	52¾	43	4²	2nk	Pin'yLJr¹⁰	Mdn 82	P...son119... ..t'm ...s... 11
Jy 4-73³Aqu	5½ f 1:04⅗ft	5	118	3²	3½¹	3²	33½	MapleE⁶	Mdn 86	M...A...18 Lea...as TakeB...rm 8
Jun14-73³Bel	5½ f 1:05 ft	7	117	3²	3¹	2¹½	3⁴	VasquezJ⁹	Mdn 90	Ev...117 D... ...g Ta... 9
Jun 6-73⁴Bel	5½ f 1:05⅗ft	3½	117	3²	2¹	2²	47½	VasquezJ⁴	Mdn 84	Gr'nGamb's117 DingD'gB'll OnHisOwn 9

Aug 21 Sar 4f ft :48b   Aug 17 Sar 4f ft :47⅖h   July 26 Bel 4f ft :48⅖b

(cont'd on next page)

Gusty O'Shay 121
Ch. g (1971), by Rose Argent—Stormy O'Shay, by Restless Wind.
Br., Mrs. G. T. Hopkins & Lola Peters (Md.1973). 6 3 1 1 $ 13,2

Owner, Mrs. G. T. Hopkins. Trainer, H. E. Johnson.

Aug 6-73⁷Sar	6 f 1:11 ft	20	117	14	14	11½	2½	Kot'koR⁷	AlwS 84 Az Igazi 117 Gusty O'Shay Lakeyille
Jly 18-73⁸Del	5½ f 1:05⅘ft	6¼	119	1³	11½	1⁵	1⁶	Kot'koR⁸	15000 89 G___'__y_19 Anot'rEpis'de B'dF'ble
Jun13-73⁷ShD	3½ f :41 ft	8-5	▲118	5	1¹	1²	1⁵	EspinosaV⁸	Alw 90 G___yO___118 Red'sBl'sing S'mC'rd
Jun 6-73³Del	5 f 1:00⅘ft	42	120	1³	1³	1³	13½	Kot'oR¹¹	M7500 87 G___y'y120 B'dFable G'd Lit'leG'l
May24-73⁴ShD	5½ f 1:10½ssy	6¼	118	6¹¹	6¹²	6¹³	3¹⁸	Esp'saV⁵	M5000 57 SoftN't115 P'lh'm'sPride G'styO'Sh'y

Aug 22 Sar 4f ft :50b

Green Gambados 121
B. c (1971), by Swaps—Cargreen, by Turn-to.
Breeder, Harbor View Farm (Fla.).   1973. 6 2 1 0 $14,5

Owner, Harbor View Farm. Trainer, J. W. Jacobs.

Aug15-73⁷Sar	6 f 1:10⅗ft	14	121	2¹	22	43½	47	Tur'tteR¹	ScwS 80 Azlgazi121ⁱ Prince ofReason Totheend
Aug 7-73⁵Sar	6 f 1:11⅖ft	7-5	▲118	3¹	1h	1h	1h	TurcotteR⁴	Alw 83 GreenG'mbados118 Totheend Pl'gAl'g
Jly 7-73⁴Aqu	5½ f 1:04½ft	5½	119	64½	45¼	46	24	BaezaB⁵	Alw 88 C'__'__dack___'__nG'b
Jun30-73⁴Aqu	5½ f 1:04 ft	2½	▲119	87½	67½	57½	54	Cast'daM⁷	Alw 89 A___'zi__7 Pl's__'c'd C'p'r__g
Jun 6-73⁴Bel	5½ f 1:05⅖ft	3½	117	53½	42½	3²	1³	Cast'daM⁵	Mdn 92 Gr__gamb's117 DingD'gB'll OnHisown
May16-73³Bel	5½ f 1:05 ft	3½	117	63¼	6⁴	65½	65½	VasquezJ⁷	Mdn 88 R'le ofS'cc'ss117 Tr'p't'rSw'n E'rF'd

Aug 24 Sar 3f ft :36⅖b   Aug 21 Sar 5f ft :59⅘h   Aug 13 Sar 4f gd :48⅗h

Sea Dee 121
B. c (1971), by Crackpot—Acean Love, by Panacean.
Breeder, C. D. Morgan (Va.).   1973 4 2 1 0 $13,3

Owner, Mrs. C. D. Morgan. Trainer, L. S. Barrera.

Aug16-73⁵Sar	6½ f 1:18⅖ft	3½e	119	11½	11½	1³	1½	Cast'daM⁷	Alw 86 Sea Dee 119 Mr. Sad Please Succeed
Aug 8-73⁴Sar	5½ f 1:06 ft	5½	119	1½	11½	1¹	12½	Cast'daM⁸	Mdn 87 S___D___119 Red___parkl___
Jly 26-73²Aqu	5½ f 1:04⅖ft	3½	118	3½	1h	2h	21½	Cast'daM⁸	Mdn 89 L___ofSr't11_B___d Spe___T'p'r
Jly 18-73³Aqu	5½ f 1:05⅖ft	5	118	1½	1h	4½	Cast'daM⁶	Mdn 85 Pia'sAce118 Sh'tUp andD'l L'dFord'y

Aug 23 Sar trt 4f ft :49b   July 17 Bel trt 3f ft :36h   July 6 Bel trt 4f m :50b

Az Igazi 121
Dk. b. or br. c (1971), by Time Tested—Fashionably, by Bald Eagle.
Breeder, B. P. Walden (Ky.).   1973.. 7 4 1 2 $52,

Owner, J. R. Straus. Trainer, H. C. Pardue.

Aug15-73⁷Sar	6 f 1:10⅗ft	3-5	▲121	1¹	1²	1³	1²	Ve'ziaM⁵	ScwS 87 Azlgazi121ⁱ Prince ofReason Totheend
Aug 6-73⁷Sar	6 f 1:11 ft	6-5	▲117	2⁴	2⁴	21½	1½	VenziaM⁵	Alw 84 Az Igazi 117 Gusty O'Shay Lakeville
Jly 27-73⁴Aqu	5½ f 1:03⅗ft	11	117	1½	1h	2½	V'n'ziaM³	AlwS 94 R___A Cup120 A___lgazi Big___m
Jun30-73⁴Aqu	5½ f 1:04 ft	2½	117	1¹½	1½	11½	11½	VeneziaM¹	Alw 93 A___y___Pl____'c'p'r___nd
Jun18-73³Aqu	5½ f 1:04½ft	3½	117	1¹	1²	1⁵	V'ziaM¹	M35000 92 Jz___azi 117 L___A. L___li
Jun 6-73⁴Bel	5½ f 1:05½ft	4½	117	2h	2h	2²	3⁵	V'ziaM²	M35000 88 CorporateHeadache115 Ham Azlgazi
May10-73³Aqu	5 f :59 sy	2½	117	3³	3³	43½	3²	Uss'yR⁷	M27500 88 Flip Sal 117 Mexican Onion Az Igazi

Aug 21 Sar 5f ft 1:00b   Aug 12 Sar 5f sy 1:01⅗h   Aug 3 Sar 5f sy 1:03b

Prince of Reason 121
Dk. b. or br. c (1971), by Hail to Reason—Home by Dark, by Hill Prince
Breeder, J. R. Gaines, J. J. Houlahan & 1973 6 1 1 3 $16,4
D. A. Headley (Ky.).

Owner, Saron Stable. Trainer, S. E. Veitch.

Aug15-73⁷Sar	6 f 1:10⅗ft	4	121	5³	5⁴	2³	2²	C'd'oAJr³	ScwS 85 Azlgazi121ⁱ Prince ofReason Totheend
Aug 6-73⁷Sar	6 f 1:11 ft	14	117	7¹⁰	79	46½	43½	Vel'q'zJ⁶	AlwS 81 Az___zi 117 Gusty O'Shay Lakeyille
Jly 31-73¹Sar	6 f 1:11⅗ft	2	▲119	3¹½	3¹½	2½	1ⁿᵏ	C'deroAJr¹	Mdn 82 P___'__'son1__9 B'dF'ble St'm
Jly 14-73²Aqu	5½ f 1:11⅗ft	2e▲113*	6³½	44½	34½	31½	WallisT⁶	Mdn 83 Wit__Apl__118 Ch__tofo__o Pr__R'__n
Jun20-73³Aqu	5½ f 1:05⅖ft	2½	117	87½	77	66½	33½	MapleE⁸	Mdn 82 Frozen117 Guider'sG__ld Prince ofR'son
Jun14-73⁴Bel	5½ f 1:04⅖ft	12	117	97¾	55½	55½	32½	MapleE⁷	Mdn 95 Ham 117 Cannonade Prince of Reason

Aug 24 Sar 3f ft :37⅕b   Aug 20 Sar 5f ft :59⅘h   Aug 14 Sar 3f ft :37b

Totheend 121
Dk. b. or br. c (1971), by Duel—Lady Patience, by Baybrook.
Breeder, Dr. Wallace S. Karutz (Fla.).   1973 8 1 2 1 $17,9

Owner, Mrs. M. Jolley. Trainer, L. Jolley.

Aug15-73⁷Sar	6 f 1:10⅗ft	7¾	121	31½	32½	33½	3⁷	Pin'yLJr²	ScwS 80 Azlgazi121 Prince ofReason Totheend
Aug 7-73⁵Sar	6 f 1:11⅖ft	2½	118	2½	2h	2h	2h	PincayLJr³	Alw 83 GreenG'mbados118 Totheend Pl'gAl'g
Jly 27-73⁴Aqu	5½ f 1:03⅗ft	17	114	74½	84½	7¹¹	7¹⁰	MapleE¹	Alw 89 Ra___A Cup120 Az Igazi Big Jam
Jly 9-73⁷Aqu	5½ f 1:05 ft	8½	116	1h	1h	1h	2ⁿᵏ	MapleE³	AlwS 88 W___h__Apl116__T___heend S__s__
Jun13-73⁸Mth	5½ f 1:05 ft	54	114	4¹	42½	41½	4³	Barr'raC⁵	AlwS 89 A___uzzit116 Irish__udiant Radiant
May28-73⁸Del	5½ f 1:04½ssy	24	116	2½	4¹¹	4¹¹	Impa'toJ⁷	AlwS 83 L___Sonn116 WhoDuzzit Sharpvote
Apr19-73³Aqu	5 f 1:00 ft	6	112*	2³	2²	2²	1½	Cas'aK⁶	M30000 85 Totheend 112 Flip Sal Native Dance
Jan30-73³Hia	3 f :33 ft	4	▲120	12	13¹³13⁹¾	VasquezJ⁹	Mdn 87 NearGale120 H'ds'nC'ty Am'c'nMys'y

Aug 23 Sar 4f ft :48½h   Aug 13 Sar 4f gd :49b   July 24 Bel 3f ft :34⅗h

A handicapper studying the past performances for the Hopeful Stakes at Saratoga might conclude that Az Igazi was the logical favorite because of his consistently good figures. Gusty O'Shay was a contender, but he had weakened in his last start at six furlongs and now was running six and a half. Take By Storm and Prince of Reason had been improving steadily and would be helped by the longer distance of the Hopeful.

But any observant horseplayer would have to revise his analysis after he saw how the early races on the Saratoga program were run. The inside part of the track was like a paved highway; horses with speed on the rail were winning everything. In two races run before the Hopeful, horses who looked like cinches on paper couldn't even manage to finish in the money because they were breaking from the No. 6 post position.

The track bias would wreck Az Igazi's chances of winning America's most prestigious race for two-year-olds. Breaking from the No. 5 post position with several speed horses inside of him, he was not quite fast enough to get to the lead and get to the rail. He figured to be bogged down in the middle of the track for the whole race. Prince of Reason, a stretch runner in the No. 6 post, would be hurt even more by the condition of the track.

Take By Storm had the good fortune to draw the inside post position, but he doesn't have enough speed to get the lead. He will probably be on the rail, within striking distance, during the early stages of the Hopeful. But when

he rallies, he may be forced to move to the outside for running room, and that will hurt his chances.

Gusty O'Shay, the Cinderella horse who started his career in $5000 maiden-claiming races, has blazing speed that none of his Hopeful rivals can match. He ran the first quarter of his most recent start in 21⅕ seconds. Gusty O'Shay should break quickly from the No. 2 post, hug the rail, and force the other horses to come outside him if they want to beat him.

Even if his credentials were modest, Gusty O'Shay might be a good longshot bet because of the track bias. But with a top figure along with the bias in his favor, he is clearly the horse to beat.

Gusty O'Shay went to the front, as expected, outrunning

SEVENTH RACE
Sar
August 25, 1973

6½ FURLONGS (chute). (1:15⅕). Sixty-ninth running HOPEFUL. SCALE WEIGHTS $75,000 added. 2-year-olds. By subscription of $150 each, which shall accompany the nomination; $375 to pass the entry box; $375 to start, with $75,000 added. The added money and all fees to be divided: 60% to the winner, 22% to second, 12% to third and 6% to fourth. Weight, 121 lbs. Trophies will be presented to the winning owner, trainer and jockey. Closed with 25 nominations.

Value of race, $84,000. Value to winner $50,400; second, $18,480; third, $10,080; fourth, $5,040.
Mutuel Pool, $232,769. Off-track betting, $114,265.

Last Raced	Horse	EqtAWt	PP	St	¼	½	Str	Fin	Jockeys	Owners	Odds to $
8- 6-73⁷ Sar²	Gusty O'Shay	b2 121	2	5	1¹¹½	1½	1¹½	1½	RKotenko	Mrs G T Hopkins	9.6
8-11-73² Sar¹	Take By Storm	2 121	1	7	4³	3h	2½	2²½	LPincayJr	O M Phipps	3.4
8-15-73⁷ Sar²	Prince of Reason	b2 121	6	1	6¹	6⁴	4½	3²½	PAnderson	Saron Stable	4.3
8-16-73⁵ Sar¹	Sea Dee	2 121	4	3	2²	2¹	3²	4²¼	MCastaneda	Mrs C D Morgan	10.6
8-15-73⁷ Sar⁴	Green Gambados	b2 121	3	6	5¹	5½	5¹	5³	RTurcotte	Harbor View Farm	10.1
8-15-73⁷ Sar³	Totheend	b2 121	7	2	7	7	7	6⁵½	JVelasquez	Mrs M Jolley	25.2
8-15-73⁷ Sar¹	Az Igazi	2 121	5	4	3½	4³	6³	7	HGustines	J R Straus	1.6

Time, :22⅕, :45, 1:09⅘, 1:16⅖ (with wind in backstretch). Track fast.

$2 Mutuel Prices:

2-GUSTY O'SHAY	21.20	7.00	4.80
1-TAKE BY STORM		5.60	4.20
6-PRINCE OF REASON			4.20

Ch. g, by Rose Argent—Stormy O'Shay, by Restless Wind. Trainer, H. E. Johnson. Bred by Mrs. G. T. Hopkins and Lola Peters (Md.).

IN GATE—4:48. OFF AT 4:48½ EASTERN DAYLIGHT TIME. Start good for all but AZ IGAZI. Won driving.

GUSTY O'SHAY, hustled to the front along the inside soon after the start, responded readily when challenged by SEA DEE midway of the turn, settled into the stretch with a clear lead while racing well out from the rail and was all out to turn back TAKE BY STORM. The latter, sent up along the rail after breaking slowly, was steadied along while continuing to save ground nearing the stretch, loomed boldly leaving the furlong grounds but wasn't good enough. PRINCE OF REASON, unhurried after breaking alertly, rallied leaving the turn and finished with good energy. SEA DEE prompted the pace, went after GUSTY O'SHAY approaching the stretch but gave way during the drive. GREEN GAMBADOS moved within striking distance after a half but lacked a further response. TOTHEEND was outrun after coming away in good order. AZ IGAZI stumbled following the start, recovered quickly to race forwardly to the stretch but had nothing left for the drive.

the other speed horses, Sea Dee and Az Igazi. But as he came into the stretch with a 1½-length lead, jockey Robert Kotenko unwisely allowed Gusty O'Shay to drift away from the rail. Laffit Pincay, Jr., saw the opening, drove Take By Storm along the inside, and got within a neck of the lead. Kotenko leaned to the left, trying to crowd and intimidate his rival, and Gusty O'Shay did the rest. He fought back gamely, held on to win by half a length, and paid a whopping $21.20.

th Aqueduct

JULY 20, 1973

INNER TURF COURSE

1 1-16 MILES. AQUEDUCT

START ♦ ♦ FINISH

1¹⁄₁₆ MILES (inner turf). (1:41⅕). CLAIMING. Purse $9,000. Fillies and mares. 3-year-olds and upward. 3-year-olds, 114 lbs.; older, 122 lbs. Non-winners of two races at a mile or over since June 9 allowed 2 lbs.; two such races since May 14, 4 lbs.; one such race since July 2, 6 lbs. Claiming price, $12,500; 2 lbs. for each $1,000 to $10,500. (Races where entered for $9,000 or less not considered.) 3-year-olds which have never won at a mile or over allowed 3 lbs.; older, 5 lbs.

retty Butterfly   100

B. f (1970), by Throne Room—Royal Lawn, by Royaumont.
Br., Clermont Farms of New York (N. Y.).   1973 13 1 0 5 $6,960
wner, Ges Stable. Trainer, J. Renick. $12,500

13-73⁴Aqu	7 f 1:24⅖ft	21	114	7⁶	7⁶	6⁹	7⁷¼	G'tin'sH¹⁰	15000 70	Ⓕ SelfDefense116 P'ficOc'n Gl'r'sA'f'r 11
3-73⁹Aqu Ⓣ	1¹⁄₁₆1:46⅗fm	10	108*	3³	3¹½	5¹½	3²	Cast'daK⁷	14000 71	Ⓕ M'sInt'n'ly105 D'pN'kline Pr'tyB'fly 8
n21-73¹Aqu Ⓣ	1 1:38½fm	10	108*	2⁶	3²½	4³¼	4⁶	Cas'aK¹⁰	15000 84	Ⓕ Tumb'gTo113 OurBestG'l MissN'b'y 10
n 4-73²Bel Ⓣ	1¹⁄₁₆ 1:43⅗fm	6¼	113	5⁵	4³	5⁸½	5¹¹	Turc'teR⁶	16000 73	Ⓕ JustC'rious113 FirstPitch T'blingTo 11
y 8-73⁹Aqu	1 1:38⅗ft	5½	114	1½	2ʰ	2¹½	3³½	Turc'teR⁴	14000 70	Ⓕ M.S.Star118 Ov'dueM'gic Pr'tyB'fly 6
y 4-73²Aqu	6 f 1:12⅗ft	6¼	116	7¹⁰	7⁹	7⁴¾	3¼	C'd'oAJr¹	10000 78	Ⓖ G'aBeF't116 D'l'gTime Pr'tyB'terfly 7
r25-73¹Aqu	7 f 1:25 ft	12	114	4²	5⁴	3⁶¼	3⁵¼	TurcotteR²	9500 71	Ⓕ MissCoh'n111 M.S.St'r Pr'tyB't'rfly 9
r30-73⁸Aqu	1 1:39⅛ft	7½	114	1¹½	2ʰ	2½	3²¼	TurcotteR¹	7500 69	Ⓕ SwiftSky116 AnneF. Pr'tyButterfly 7
r16-73²Aqu	6 f 1:11⅗ft	6¼	116	3⁷	3¹¹	3¹²	5⁹¾†TurcotteR⁷		7000 75	Ⓕ K'pthetune116 St'b'ryR'y'l G'aBeF't 8
†Dead heat.										
r 7-73¹Aqu	6 f 1:13⅗gd	15	114	4²	3¹	1⁴	1⁵	S't'goA²	M5000 75	Pr'tyB't'rfly114 TieltUp Ab'sIrishR'se 13
June 19 Bel trt 4f ft :50⅗b				May 29 Bel trt 4f sy :51b						

amily Princess *   103

Ch. f (1970), by First Family—Gala Girl, by Prince John.
Breeder, A. Rosoff (Fla.).   1973 11 1 2 1 $8,100
                                  1972 17 1 3 6 $13,220
wner, M. Gache. Trainer, J. T. Diangelo. $12,500

y 13-73⁴Aqu	7 f 1:24⅖ft	30	116	11¹⁶	11¹⁵	10¹³	9⁸¼	Bel'nteE²	15000 68	Ⓕ SelfDefense116 P'ficOc'n Gl'r'sA'f'r 11
n12-73⁸Bel	1¹⁄₁₆ 1:44⅝ft	12	118	9¹¹	9⁹¼	8⁸¾	7⁷¾	Vel'q'zJ¹	16000 75	Ⓕ l'pieE'p'r'r113 R'y'l Gig O'rd'eM'gic 9
n 4-73²Bel Ⓣ	1¹⁄₁₆ 1:43⅗fm	5½	111*	9¹¹	9⁶¼	9¹⁷	9¹⁷	WallisT³	16000 67	Ⓕ JustC'rious113 FirstPitch T'blingTo 10
y11-73⁶Aqu Ⓣ	1¹⁄₁₆ 1:48 yl	5¾	114	6⁶	5⁴	4³	8⁴½	Arel'noJ⁴	19000 62	Ⓖ Gr'nysD'l'g113 S'syC'ne Cr'meRh'da 9
r27-73⁵Aqu	1 1:38⅗sy	9-5	▲118	4⁴½	1½	1ʰ	2¹½	C'd'oAJr²	15000 71	Ⓕ M'tr'lC'se116 F'yPr'c's D'pN'ckl'ne 7
r21-73³Aqu	6 f 1:12⅗ft	9-5	▲118	5⁷½	6⁷¾	4⁷½	3²¾	C'd'oAJr⁴	17000 78	Ⓕ Cr'n ofSt'rs107 C'qu'r'gM's F'yPr's 7
r13-73⁶Aqu	1 1:39 ft	7½	114	7³¼	4³	5⁵½	5⁵¾	Arell'noJ⁷	22500 67	Ⓕ St'fC'p'tit'n115 M'gicSt'y S'syCy'ne 11
r 5-73⁶Aqu	1 1:39¹⁄₅gd	9-5	▲116	1½	2ʰ	1¹	1½	C'd'oAJr⁹	16000 71	Ⓕ F'milyPr'n's116 D't'dL've D'pN'kl'e 9
r28-73⁴Aqu	6 f 1:12 ft	3½	116	6⁵	5⁵	3³	2³	C'd'oAJr¹	16000 80	Ⓟ P'cificOc'n116 F'milyPr'c's Adv'c're 8
r20-73⁶Aqu	6½ f 1:20 ft	3¼	116	7⁷½	6⁵¾	6¹²	4⁵¼	C'd'oAJr¹	17500 72	Ⓕ M.S.St'r118 P'cificOc'n C'meRhoda 8
July 18 Bel 3f ft :35⅜hg				July 6 Bel 3f ft :35½h					May 29 Bel 7f sy 1:29b		

(cont'd on next page)

Madmoiselle Alice ✳ **111** Ch. f (1969), by Red Fox—Knuckles, by Hasty Road.
Breeder Mrs. W. C. Rigg & Brool: 1973   23   0   5   5 $13
Hill Farm (Va.).   1972   9   1   1   0 $3

Owner, L. Chang.   Trainer, O. S. Barrera. $12.500

Jly 18-73⁹Aqu	Ⓣ1¹⁄₁₆ 1:45	fm	2	▲112	45	2½	2½	32¾	MapleE⁶	15000 78	ⒻF'stT'keoff114 Pricelyn M'm'leAlic
Jly 10-73⁹Aqu	Ⓣ 1 1:36⅖fm		5½	112	68¼	6³	4³	3³	C'd'oAJr⁷	16000 96	ⒻS'ly leS'c120 Amb'rn'ka M'dm'eAl'
Jly 3-73⁶Aqu	Ⓣ 1¼ 1:52⅖fm		3¼	▲113	69¼	46	2³	2ⁿᵒ	C'd'oAJr⁷	13000 74ⒻW'gFl'ter114 Mad'sleAlice LasTr'p'
Jun25-73⁹Aqu	1 1-8 1:51⅘ft		7¾	103*	1ʰ	2¹	43½	58½	Cast'daK⁴	13000 68	ⒻD'pNeckline112 Pric'l'sJew'l Evyn
Jun20-73⁹Aqu	Ⓣ 1¼ 1:51	fm	7½	103*	3²	3²	3¹	3⁴	Cas'daK³	11500 76	PeterG.116 P'l'rTr'fic M'dm's'leAlic
Jun 7-73⁹Bel	Ⓣ 1¼ 2:03⅕hd		5	102*	7¹⁴	61⁰	58½	47½	C'st'daK²	20500 86	ⒻS'lly leSec112 Glor'sky MaryBeGoo
May31-73⁷GS	1¹⁄₁₆ 1:47⅖sl		3	110	3⁹	3⁹	3¹¹	41⁶	Bar'raC³	H5000 52	ⒻSmile 110 Brindabella Moon Stitc
May16-73⁹Bel	Ⓣ 1⅜ 2:18⅗ft		6¼	101*	75¾	53¼	2½	21¼	Cast'daK⁴	8500 81	LostIdol 118 M'dm'selleAlice Bagoos
May10-73²Aqu	6¼ f 1:19	sy	7	112	64¼	52¾	42½	32¾	Velasq'zJ⁷	7000 79	ⒻG'd'rSt'n102 M'yM'lc'y M'dm'leAl'
July 9 Bel trt 3f ft :37⅗h											

Deep Neckline ✳ **114** Dk. b. or br. f (1970), by Controlling—Social Plunge, by Toulouse
Lautrec. Breeder, R. C. Ellsworth(Cal.).   1973   16   2   3   4 $19
                                                  1972   13   1   2   4 $6

Owner, Little Lou Stable.   Trainer, J. Martin. $12.500

Jly 3-73⁹Aqu	Ⓣ1¹⁄₁₆ 1:46⅗fm		3½	118	8¹¹	63¾	4¹	2ⁿᵒ	MapleE⁴	14000 73	ⒻM'sInt'n'ly105 D'pN'kline Pr'tyB'f'
Jun25-73⁹Aqu	1 1-8 1:51⅘ft		10	112	52¾	44¼	2²	1²	MapleE¹	14000 77	ⒻD'pNeckline121 Pric'l'sJew'l Evyn
Jun18-73⁹Aqu	1 1-8 1:52⅖ft		6½	101	5²	3¹	1ʰ	1ʰ	Cast'daK⁶	9500 74	ⒻD'pNeckline101 Evyne Pricel'ssJ'w'
Jun 4-73²Bel	Ⓣ 1¹⁄₁₆ 1:43⅖fm		12	114	10¹⁹	10¹⁵	8¹⁵	6¹²	Cor'oAJr¹	14000 72	ⒻJustC'rious113 FirstPitch T'blingT
May30-73⁵Bel	1¹⁄₁₆ 1:44½ft		3¾	114	7⁹	71⁴	71⁷	41⁷	C'roAJr³	11500 65	ⒻInst'tC'h116 M'trim'n'lC'se P'cel'y
May 3-73⁴Aqu	1 1:37	ft	9	114	11¹⁶	101⁶	71⁰	6⁹	C'd'oAJr⁶	19000 73	ⒻBl'eSp'g108 M.S.St'r M'trim'n'lC's
Apr16-73⁶Aqu	1 1:38⅗ft		2	▲116	99¼	77¼	45¼	37	MapleE⁶	15000 66	ⒻM'tr'lC'se116 F'yPr'c's D'pN'ckl'n
Apr 5-73⁶Aqu	1 1:39⅕sgd		18	109	8¹	86¼	85¾	57	ClarkWC⁴	16000 65	ⒻF'milyPr'n's116 D't'dL've D'pN'kl'
Mar22-73⁶Aqu	1 1-8 1:52⅖ft		4	110	6⁸	6¹⁴	51⁷	52¹	VeneziaM⁵	Alw 53	ⒻD'rAn'e109 Ir'shR'm'ce R'ber'sH's
July 17 Bel trt 4f ft :49b								July 12 Bel trt 4m m :48⅗b			June 16 Bel trt 4f ft :50⅘b

Klondike Breeze ✳ **112** B. m (1968), by Persian Gold—Arctic Breeze, by Arctic Flyer.
Breeder, E. F. Schoenbern (N. Y.).   1973   15   1   1   3 $7
                               1971   12   1   2 $5

Owner, L. Calderon.   Trainer, F. Laboccetta. $10.500

Jly 5-73⁹Aqu	Ⓣ 1¼ 1:56½ssf		4¼	114	6⁷	2¹	3²	36½	Her'dezS⁵	8250 46	ⒻCount'sV.102 Indict'r Kl'ndikeBr'ze
Jun18-73⁹Aqu	1 1-8 1:52⅘ft		9	113	4²	2ʰ	59½	6¹⁷	He'dezS⁵	10000 57	ⒻD'pNeckline101 Evyne Pricel'ssJ'w'
May29-73⁹Bel	1 1-8 1:53	gd	3	▲116	79¼	3¹	42	42¼	Car'neE¹⁰	c5000 85	ⒻPric'l'sJ'w'l 113 T'lystar H'n'yG'l'
May21-73⁵Bel	1 1-8 1:52⅖ssy		10	111	85¼	5³	2¹	2ⁿᵒ	CardoneE⁴	7500 69	ⒻN't'eArt106 Kl'dikeBr'ze Pric'l'sJ'
May11-73⁹Aqu	1 1-8 1:51⅖ft		10	106	78¼	2½	1⁵	13¼	CardoneE⁶	5000 75	KlondikeBreeze106 M'terPiper MiTa
May 2-73⁹Aqu	1 1-8 1:52⅖ft		5¼	111	69¾	66¼	46½	36½	VeneziaM²	4500 65	ⒻGrapeJelly116 RedFog Kl'dikeBr'z
Apr18-73⁹Aqu	1 1-8 1:53⅖ft		6	112	6¹¹	57¼	3⁶	38¾	VeneziaM³	4500 40	ⒻK'pUp109 Sab'la'sN'se K'dykeB'z'
Apr13-73¹Aqu	6 f 1:11⅖ft		21	112	119¼	89¼	6¹¹	59½	VeneziaM³	6000 74	ⒻEl'n'sC'ce116 M'sC'pric's R'g'r'sR'
Mar27-73²Aqu	6 f 1:19⅖ft		11	116	85¼	8⁶	46	44	PinedaR⁶	5000 76	ⒻM'sC'pric's109 G'peJelly Sw'gDuc'
June 29 Aqu 6f ft 1:17⅖b								June 25 Aqu 5f gd 1:04b			Jne 13 Aqu 4f ft :48⅘h

Surf Queen **107** Gr. m (1968), by Native Rythm—El Senora byy I Am.
Breeder, Mrs. D. Coleman (N. Y.).   1973   5   2   1   1 $9
                                  1972   5   0   0   0   (—

Owner, Mary Lou Simmons.   Trainer, L. H. Hunt. $10.500

Jly 12-73⁸Aqu	Ⓣ 1 1:37⅘fm		6½	102	1²	1½	2½	33¾	Card'neE²	10500 88	Ifi116 PrimeAction SurfQuee
Jun28-73²Aqu	6 f 1:18½ssy		3½	112	2¹	1½	1³	1½	C'roAJr¹²	c5000 85	ⒻSurfQn'121 Ren'g'd'sD'gree C'tessV
Jun13-73¹Bel	6 f 1:11⅖ft		3	▲115	1½	1³	1¹	1ʰ	Cord'oAJr⁷	7000 88	ⒻSurfQu'n115 Sw'sPolicy GalaDance
May18-73²Bel	6 f 1:10⅖ft		12	111	1ʰ	2½	54	57½	Arel'noJ⁹	10500 84	Gl'dysII.113 R'stl'ssPro W't'ngAtH'm
May 1-73¹Aqu	6 f 1:11⅖ft		41	109*	2¹½	2½	1½	31†	AmyJ⁴	c6250 85	ⒻM'sC'precious109 M'ryM'chy S'fQ'
Mar 9-72⁷Bow	6 f 1:12	ft	31	112	4⁴	7⁶	8⁸	8⁶	Cusim'noG¹	Alw 80	ⒻCyamome113 G'nnysdeb Br'veP's'
Feb25-72⁸Bow	6 f 1:12½sm		33	112	43¼	2³	2⁴	5⁶	WalshE⁸	Alw 79	ⒻN'ma'sB'l'de112 Pr'm'rk Br'veP'p'
†Placed second through disqualification.											
July 18 Bel trt 4f ft :49⅘b								July 10 Bel trt 3f ft :36⅜h			July 4 Bel trt 4f ft :49b

Foxglow **111** Dk. b. or br. f (1969), by Besomer—How High, by Skyscraper.
Breeder, J. D. Archbold (Va.).   1973   5   M   0   0   (—
                             1972   3   M   0   0   (—

Owner, M. Brous.   Trainer, H. Hughes. $12.500

Jly 3-73⁶Aqu	Ⓣ 1¼ 1:52⅖fm		49	109	7¹¹	7¹¹	4¹¹	5⁷	RuaneJ³	12000 67	ⒻW'gFl'ter114 Mad'sleAlice LasTr'p'
Jun15-73⁸Bel	Ⓣ 1⅜ 2:16⅕fm		31	108	58¼	45	56¼	51¹	RuaneJ⁶	7500 83	GreekComedy116 SodaPop Harangue
Jun 7-73¹Bel	1 1:37⅛ft		36	119	97¼	89¼	71³	71²	R'aneJ²	M14000 74	ⒻArbeeEye113 C'b'l'sC't Dist'tTwil'
May 5-73¹Aqu	7 f 1:26⅗ft		21f	121	118¼	12¹¹	12¹⁴	11¹³	R'aneJ⁹	M8000 55	ⒻChefil 114 HenrysGal LovelyLance
Apr27-73²Aqu	6 f 1:12⅗ssy		32	119	8¹¹	71⁴	61⁵	61⁶	RuaneJ³	M8000 64	Nu Billing 113 Eulogy Joe Cement
Dec 1-72²Lrl	1 1:39⅗ft		21	116	86¾	8¹²	10²³	10²²	P'reWJ⁸	M5000 57	ⒻRoses ofAraby116 M'ch'nin K'g of T's
Nov24-72²Lrl	6 f 1:13⅕ft		29	117	10¹²	10¹⁰	9¹²	9⁸	P'reWJr⁹	M5000 76	ValiantWill 120 G'denM'nie Sh'ffJ'hn
July 19 Bel 3f ft :36⅖h							July 14 Bel 6f ft 1:17⅖bg			July 2 Bel 3f ft :36b	

ountess V. ✳ **107** Ch. f (1969), by Cyane—Libby II., by Court Harwell.
Breeder, Mrs. H. Obre (Md.).   1973 11 2 0 1 $8,400
ner, R. M. Harmonay. Traner, T. M. Miles.   **$11.500**   1972 16 2 2 2 $10,223

5-73⁹Aqu	ⓣ 1⅛ 1:56⅖sf	5	102∴33½	31½	1h	11½	MoonL¹	8000 53	Ⓕ Count'sV.102 Indict'r Kl'ndikeBr'ze 7
28-73²Aqu	6½ f 1:18⅕sy	12	113 111³	8¹⁴	66½	32½	VeneziaM⁵	5000 82	Ⓕ SurfQ'n121 Ren'g'd'sD'gree C'tessV. 14
19-73²Aqu	6 f 1:11⅖ft	5⅜e	106*109¾	79½	47½	43½	Cast'daK³	5000 82	Ⓕ Risha115 John'sPatrol SwissPolicy 12
13-73¹Bel	6 f 1:11⅕ft	21	114 7⁸	9¹⁰	7¹⁰	5¹²	RujanoM¹	6500 76	Ⓕ SurfQu'n115 Sw'sPolicy GalaDancer 11
30-73¹Bel	6 f 1:12⅖ft	22	113 9⁶	8⁶	65¾	75½	TurcotteR⁹	6500 76	Ⓕ MsC'pric's106 G'llaD'nc'r Divine L't 12
21-73⁸Bel	1 1-8 1:52⅖sy	10	114 107¼108¼	8¹²	8¹⁹	TurcotteR⁵	7500 50	Ⓕ N't'eArt106 Kl'dikeBr'ze Pric'l'sJ'l 12
•10-73²Aqu	6½ f 1:19 sy	33	114 5³	31½	52¾	53½	TurcotteR⁸	7000 78	Ⓕ G'd'rSt'n102 M'yM'lc'y M'dm'leAl'e 9
26-73¹⁰Hia	1 1-8 1:53 ft	4½	114 2²	8¹²	9¹⁴	8¹¹	Log'cioA²	7000 59	Ⓕ MaryPat108 LasTropas Amb'rPoint 11
20-73⁶Hia	1 1-8 1:54⅗sl	18	117 111⁶111³	77½	54½	Log'rcioA⁹	6500 58	Ⓕ M'yp'o114 J'l'sM's R'n'g'd's D'gree 12

June 6 Bel trt 5f ft 1:02h

iceless Jewel ✳ **114** Ch. f (1969), by Poppy Jay—Jewel's Dance. by Bolero. Br.. Dr.
W. S. Karutz & Dr. F. Milana (Ky.).   1973 12 2 2 3 $15,520
ner, N. Usdan. Trainer, J. A. Trovato.   **$11.500**   1972 7 2 1 0 0 $6,000

3-73⁶Aqu	ⓣ 1⅛ 1:52⅖fm	4½	114 43½	25	5¹¹	7¹²	Vel'q'zJ⁸	12000 62	Ⓦ W'gFl'ter114 Mad'sleAlice LasTr'p's 8
•25-73⁹Aqu	1 1-8 1:51⅖ft	3½	107* 4¾	1¹	1²	2²	WallisT⁵	12000 75	Ⓓ D'pNeckline112 Pric'l'sJew'l Evyne 8
18-73²Aqu	1 1-8 1:52⅖ft	2½	111 31½	42½	31½	3nk	MapleE¹	c9500 74	Ⓕ D'pNeckline101 Evyne Pricel'ssJ'w'l 6
7-73⁸Bel	1 1-8 1:51 ft	8-5 ▲117	4³	2h	2h	1³	Turc'teR⁷	c7000 76	Ⓕ Pric'l'ssJ'w'l 117 T'lyst'r H'n'yG'l're 8
•29-73⁹Bel	1 1-8 1:53 gd	3½	113 85½	51½	11½	1²	SantiagoA⁹	7500 66	Ⓕ Pric'l'sJ'w'l 113 T'lystar H'n'yG'l're 10
•21-73⁸Bel	1 1-8 1:52⅖sy	3½	113 64½	6⁴	3³	3³	San'goA¹¹	8000 66	Ⓕ N't'eArt106 Kl'dikeBr'ze Pric'l'sJ'l 12
•14-73⁸Bel	1¹⁄₁₆ 1:43⅗ft	6½	107 87¼	8⁷	9⁷	84½	Card'neE⁶	10500 80	Ⓕ Evyne 116 Swiss Policy Macaero 9
8-73²Aqu	7 f 1:25 ft	4	116 5⁶	56½	56½	56½	C'st'daM⁵	13000 70	Ⓕ Vellum111 Pr'yingM'ntis R'stl'ssPro 8
•26-73²Aqu	6 f 1:12 sy	4½	112 56½	5⁵	43½	31½	Cas'daM⁵	13000 81	Ⓕ Appear116 Mortally PricelessJewel 7

July 14 Bel trt 4f ft :51⅕b

The supreme handicapping factor in grass races is the established ability of the horses to run on the grass. Few of the entrants in this claiming event for fillies have displayed such ability. Only one of them, Countess V., has ever won on the turf. Two others, Madmoiselle Alice and Deep Neckline, have had near misses. The grass form of the rest of the horses in the field ranges from indifferent to abysmal.

Deep Neckline was beaten by a nose in $14,000 company on July 3, but she was racing against a weak group of three-year-olds. A studious handicapper who looked up that field would see that the winner, Miss Intentionally, had been soundly trounced in all four of her prior grass races. Pretty Butterfly, who finished third behind Deep Neckline, is in today's race, and her past performances reveal that she has never been a particularly adept turf runner. So Deep Neckline's second-place finish did not convincingly establish that she is a good grass horse.

Madmoiselle Alice has run well many times on the turf.

But she has never been able to win on the grass, not even at the $8500 level. In a total of twenty-two starts during 1973, she has zero victories, five seconds, and four thirds. She is the quintessential sucker horse.

Countess V., unable to win on the main track for $5000, was tried in an $8000 turf race and won by a length and a half. At a quick glance she looks a bit cheaper than the rivals she is meeting today. But the filly she defeated on July 5, Indicter, came back ten days later and won a $13,000 claiming race on the grass against males. Her victory implies that Countess V. is a legitimate $13,000 animal who was undervalued when she ran for an $8000 price tag and is entered at a proper level today. She couldn't have found an easier spot. All she has to beat is one chronic loser and a group of other horses who have minimal ability on the turf.

NINTH RACE

Aqu

July 20, 1973

1 1/16 MILES (inner turf). (1:41⅖). CLAIMING. Purse $9,000. Fillies and mares. 3-year olds and upward. 3-year-olds, 114 lbs.; older, 122 lbs. Non-winners of two races at mile or over since June 9 allowed 2 lbs.; two such races since May 14, 4 lbs.; one su race since July 2, 6 lbs. Claiming price, $12,500; 2 lbs. for each $1,000 to $10,50 (Races where entered for $9,000 or less not considered.) 3-year-olds which have nev won at a mile or over allowed 3 lbs.; older, 5 lbs.

Value to winner $5,400; second, $1,980; third, $1,080; fourth, $540. Mutuel Pool, $261,903.
Off-track betting, $158,988.

Last Raced	Horse	EqtAWt	PP	St	¼	½	¾	Str	Fin	Jockeys	Owners	Odds to
7- 5-73⁹ Aqu¹	Countess V.	4 107	8	5	3¹½	3h	4²	2²	1¹¼	LMoon	R M Harmonay	16.
7- 3-73⁹ Aqu²	Deep Neckline	b3 114	4	3	6³	5²	3½	3¹	2²	EMaple	Little Lou Stable	1.
7-12-73⁸ Aqu³	Surf Queen	b5 107	6	1	1⁷	1⁶	1³	1h	3¹½	ECardone	Mary Lou Simmons	4.
7-10-73⁹ Aqu³	Madmoiselle Alice	b4 114	3	4	7⁵	7³	6⁴	5²	4½	ACorderoJr	L Chang	3.
7-13-73⁴ Aqu⁷	Pretty Butterfly	b3 104	1	2	2⁴	2³	2½	4¹½	5³	KCastaneda⁵	Ges Stable	5.
7- 3-73⁶ Aqu⁷	Priceless Jewel	b4 114	9	7	4h	4¹½	5¹	6⁵	6²½	RTurcotte	N Usdan	10.
7- 3-73⁶ Aqu⁵	Foxglow	4 111	7	9	8½	9	8⁴	8¹⁰	7³	JRuane	M Brous	42.
7- 5-73⁹ Aqu³	Klondike Breeze	b5 113	5	8	9	8¹½	7²	7½	8¹⁰	SHernandez	L Calderon	19.
7-13-73⁴ Aqu⁹	Family Princess	b3 107	2	6	5¹½	6½	9	9	9	TWallis⁵	M Hache	13.

Time, :22⅖, :46⅖, 1:11⅖, 1:37, 1:43⅖ (wind in backstretch). Track firm.

$2 Mutuel Prices:

8-COUNTESS V.	34.40	11.60	6.20
4-DEEP NECKLINE		3.60	2.80
6-SURF QUEEN			3.80

Ch. f, by Cyane—Libby II., by Court Harwell. Trainer, T. M. Miles. Bred by Mrs. H. Obre (Md.).
IN GATE—5:12. OFF AT 5:12 EASTERN DAYLIGHT TIME. Start good. Won driving.

COUNTESS V. moved fast along the inside approaching the stretch, came out for the drive and, aft catching SURF QUEEN, held DEEP NECKLINE safe. The latter rallied from the outside leaving the far tur bumped with PRETTY BUTTERFLY near midstretch and continued on gamely. SURF QUEEN sprinted aw to a long lead early, made the pace to midstretch and faltered. MADMOISELLE ALICE rallied from t outside entering the stretch but failed to sustain her bid. PRETTY BUTTERFLY made a bid leaving the f turn but had nothing left for the drive. PRICELESS JEWEL had no excuse.

Overweight—Pretty Butterfly, 4 pounds; Family Princess, 4; Madmoiselle Alice, 3; Klondike Breeze, 1.
Claiming Prices (in order of finish)—$11500, 12500, 10500, 12500, 12500, 11500, 12500, 10500, 12500.
Scratched—Narso.

Countess V. won, as expected. But not even the most optimistic bettor could have imagined that she would pay the astonishing price of $34.40 in such a weak field. This is the sort of race that horseplayers dream about.

h Pimlico Race Course   MARCH 31, 1973

1 1-16 MILES
PIMLICO
▲Start ▲Finish

1¹⁄₁₆ MILES. (1:41). CLAIMING. Purse $6,500. 4-year-olds and upward. Weight, 122 lbs. Non-winners of two races at one mile or over since Feb. 17 allowed 3 lbs.; one such race, 5 lbs.; such a race since Feb. 10, 8 lbs. Claiming price, $9,500: 1 lb. for each $500 to $8,500. (Races where entered for $7,500 or less not considered.)

COUPLED: JALBE and GUNNER'S MATE.

---

here Am I   **114**   B. c (1969), by Mustato—Blanc de Chine, by Nashua.
Breeler: Mrs. T. M. Waller (N. Y.).   1973   1 0 0 0   (—)
 er, G. A. Freed. Trainer, H. F. Bowyer. $9.500   1972   13 3 1 3 $14,001

23-737GS	.6 f 1:14⅕ft	28	117	56½ 710 69½ 713	Tich'norW²	5000 60	Valtone112 CreoleWar'r Fant'sticEgo 10
2-725Del	⊤ 1 1:38⅗fm	7-5	▲114	3³ 11½ 11¹¹ 11	Jim'nezC¹	13500 82	WhereAmI 114 Killough Br'ne'leCh't'u 7
27-729GS	⊤ 1¹⁄₁₆ 1:43⅕fm	8¼	107	44 57 68 69	Iann'lliF⁶	H5000 80	Ray's Rebel 116 Fiendish Lad Petrous 9
8-725Pim	⊤ 5f :58⅖fm	13	112	98½ 67¼ 810 89½	JimenezC⁹	Alw 84	Mongo'sImage112 Verace Exhortation 9
28-729Pim	⊤ 1 1:41¾yl	21	112	11¹¹ 11 12 2½	Jim'ezC²	Alw 78	Tony'sLuck112 Octet Americ'nH'rit'ge 12
27-727Pim	1¹⁄₁₆ 1:44 ft	15	112	57½ 67½ 712 712	McCar'nG⁷	Alw 78	Tony'sLuck112 Octet Americ'nH'rit'ge 12
27-727Pim	1¹⁄₁₆ 1:44 ft	14	114	33½ 2h 1½ 1nk	Jim'n'zC⁸	10500 90	Wh'eAmI114 Am'r'c'nH''ge Vic'yRise 12
4-729Pim	1¹⁄₁₆ 1:46 sy	10	119	2½ 2½ 2½ 33½	T'c'teRL⁶	c7500 77	Circle ofLove 114 Midimin WhereAm I 8

March 29 Lrl 4f gd :49⅖b   Feb 26 Bow 3f ft :39b   Feb 22 Bow 7f ft 1:24b

---

oken Thumb ✱   **113**   B. g (1968), by Seven Corners—Mike's Gertie, by Colonel Mike.
Breeder, R. Kahoe (Md.).   1973   4 1 0 0 $3,480
er, R. F. Kahoe. Trainer, H. Ravich. $9,000   1972   5 1 5 2 $7,820

24-735Pim	1¹⁄₁₆ 1:47⅘ft	5¼	114	1212 77 51½ 53½	Br'aleVJr⁹	9000 65	BuffaloRun114 G'nner'sMate Surfac'd 12
5-736Bow	1¹⁄₁₆ 1:47⅕gd	5	112	55 57½ 2h 1³	Bra'leVJr³	7000 72	BrokenThumb113 ClaraFaye Goo'P'ce 7
23-739Bow	1¹⁄₁₆ 1:47⅗ft	6¼	114	69½ 811 67 58½	Cesp'desR⁷	7500 61	Col... Opened Das... itters 8
3-735Bow	1¹⁄₁₆ 1:49½sm	6	112	913 99½ 83¾ 64½	Cus'noG⁵	H4000 57	Wi... tt'TrainB...rum 12
3-724Lrl	1⅜ 2:04½sm	4	111	59½ 49½ 44½ 51½	PilarH⁴	H5000 62	Channeling119 VeryTouchy TacaroBoy 6
6-724Lrl	1 1-8 1:55½ssl	8½	110	43½ 43 22 22½	PilarH⁴	H5000 68	Channeling117 BrokenThumb Interw'd 7

March 29 Pim 5f ft 1:05b   March 21 Pim 4f ft :50⅖b   March 17 Pim 5f sy 1:04b

---

ssell's Rullah ✱   **113**   Ch. g (1966), by Martins Rullah—Hi Delight, by High Bandit.
Breeder, R. L. Buyck (Md.).   1973   2 0 0 0   (—)
er, R. Gallo. Trainer, D. H. Barr. $9,000   1972   3 0 0 0   (—)

24-735Pim	1¹⁄₁₆ 1:47¾ft	7½	114	98½ 97½ 84 74½	McC'onG¹¹	9000 63	BuffaloRun114 G'nner'sMate Surfac'd 12
2-737Bow	6 f 1:11⅕ft	20	112	814 817 813 79	KurtzJ⁴	13500 72	Bolero Supercut 8
25-726Pim	1¹⁄₁₆ 1:44 ft	4½	114	21½ 33 510 58	KurtzJ⁶	13500 77	Rhigo119 Shy M'ment Honey Taylor 6
24-729Pim	1¹⁄₁₆ 1:46 sy	5½	114	66 812 922 926	ShukN²	25000 54	PrivateTimes113 Blair El'tedPrince 10
10-726Pim	6 f 1:12⅖gd	7½	113	711 711 611 56	KurtzJ²	20500 76	Gs Silver A. 117 Gilzo Ground War 7
23-716Lrl	1 1:39⅘ft	4½	120	11¹¹ 11½ 14 12	McC'r'nG²	20000 80	R's'll'sR'll'h120 B'rkl'yC'rn'r Gr'y Id'l 7

March 19 Bow 1m gd 1:49b   Mar 1 Bow 3f ft :37⅖b   Feb 25 Bow 5f ft 1:03b

---

rmal Count ✱   **118**   Dk. b. or br. h (1968), by Count Amber—Formal Affair, by Frosty Mr.
Breeder, C. B. Fischbach (Ky.).   1973   4 1 0 1 $4,140
er, Audley Farm Stable. Trainer, J. B. Dodson. $9,000   1972   13 0 1 1 $3,205

22-734Pim	1¹⁄₁₆ 1:46⅖ft	8½	114	912 77½ 2h 12½	JimenezC¹	8000 73	FormalCount114 Templar Jandymar 9
22-734Pim	1¹⁄₁₆ 1:47⅕gd	5	114	79½ 69 53½ 55¾	Jim'nezC⁶	8000 66	Br...Thumb114 Cl...Faye... P'ce 7
10-739Bow	1¹⁄₁₆ 1:44⅘ft	7e	114	1114 916 712 78½	Jim'nezC¹⁰	7500 78	Cl...yC...t17 S'd...h'k'g ...Love 11
3-734Bow	1¹⁄₁₆ 1:46⅖ft	7½	114	710 73½ 22½ 3½	JimenezC¹	7500 75	Cl...yC...k114 S'...'nt... ount 7
4-729Lrl	1¹⁄₁₆ 1:46 gd	8½e	116	1018 914 76½ 69	BlackAS¹⁰	8000 74	Vic's Pick 116 Greybrook JoySmoke 12
20-725Lrl	1 1:40½sy	34	114	1217 62½ 44½ 55½	Jim'ezC¹¹	10000 79	StellarShot112 Jaipurll. ScotchBroth 12

March 21 Pim 4f ft :51b   Feb 24 Bow 5f ft 1:02⅖b   Jan 31 Bow 4f ft :50b

(cont'd on next page)

Stoneface, who has come to Maryland from Florida, ran well for $14,000 in January, but his form since then has been dismal. Where Am I made his only start of the year in New Jersey, where he was buried in a $5000 claiming race.

What is Where Am I doing in a $9500 race today? His record bears further scrutiny. The horse was a solid $10,000 campaigner last year. He was laid off for nearly a year, probably because of physical problems, which might explain the drop to $5000.

Where Am I was training steadily at Bowie, as his workout line indicates, but instead of running him in Maryland trainer Henry Bowyer went to the trouble and expense of vanning him to Garden State Park. Why? His six-furlong race there was probably just a prep since Where Am I is a router by nature. And there are plenty of $5000 races in Maryland.

There is one possible explanation for Bowyer's actions. When a horse runs once for $5000, he becomes eligible for starter-handicap races that are offered at all the Maryland tracks, and a solid $10,000 animal running in starter handicaps can win a lot of money. Perhaps Bowyer decided to take a gamble and enter his horse for $5000, figuring that he was less likely to be claimed at an out of town track where nobody knew him. Having gotten away with this gamble, he could return Where Am I to Maryland and run him where he belongs.

This interpretation may seem a bit too ingenious, but unless Bowyer is an utter madman it is the only way to explain his horse's past performances and his presence in a $9500 race. Proud of my brilliant deduction, I decided to bet Where Am I strongly, and my convictions were fortified when the horse received strong betting action that knocked his odds down to 5 to 1.

SIXTH RACE

Pim

March 31, 1973

1¹⁄₁₆ MILES. (1:41). CLAIMING. Purse $6,500. 4-year-olds and upward. Weight, 122
Non-winners of two races at one mile or over since Feb. 17 allowed 3 lbs.; one
race, 5 lbs.; such a race since Feb. 10, 8 lbs. Claiming price, $9,500; 1 lb. for each
to $8,500. (Races where entered for $7,500 or less not considered.)
Value to winner $3,900; second, $1,430; third, $780; fourth, $390. Mutuel Pool, $157,507.

Last Raced	Horse	EqtAWt	PP	St	¼	½	¾	Str	Fin	Jockeys	Owners	Odds
3-17-73² GP⁹	Old Stoneface	5 114	5	4	2³	2¹½	2³	1h	1nk	JBaboolal	G R Gardiner	
3-23-73⁷ GS⁷	Where Am I	4 114	1	1	1¹	1¹	1h	2³	2³	JKurtz	G A Freed	
3-24-73⁵ Pim⁷	Russell's Rullah	b7 113	3	2	3h	3h	5¹½	3¹	3¾	GMcCarron	R Gallo	
3-22-73⁴ Pim¹	Formal Count	5 118	4	5	8	7¹	7¹	6¹½	4no	WHartack	Audley Farm Stable	
3-24-73⁵ Pim⁷	Broken Thumb	5 113	2	3	6¹	6h	6¹½	5¹½	5¹	VBraccialeJr	R F Kahoe	
3-17-73⁹ Pim³	Curious George	4 114	6	6	5¹½	4½	3h	4h	6¾	WJPassmore	H Schifrin	
3-24-73⁵ Pim²	Gunner's Mate	b4 114	8	7	4⁴	5⁶	4½	7³	7²	RYork	Mrs J J Ries	
3-27-73⁷ Pim⁶	Tim	6 116	7	8	7¹½	8	8	8	8	BAlberts	A Adamopoulos	

Time, :23⅘, :48, 1:13⅕, 1:40, 1:46⅘. Track sloppy.

$2 Mutuel Prices:

5-OLD STONEFACE	25.00	12.20	8.*
1-WHERE AM I		9.00	6.2
3-RUSSELL'S RULLAH			5.4

B. g, by Lord Quillo—Rock Day, by Roc du Diable. Trainer, P. Buttigieg. Bred by Gardiner Farm Lir
(Can.).

IN GATE—3:30. OFF AT 3:30 EASTERN STANDARD TIME. Start good. Won driving.

OLD STONEFACE, hustled to the clubhouse turn, was rated in closest attendance to the pace and
down WHERE AM I. The latter set the pace under rating and continued gamely when tiring through
stretch. RUSSELL'S RULLAH showed an even effort. BROKEN THUMB passed tired rivals. CURIOUS GEO
possibly best, pulled his rider into a blind switch approaching the far turn, was taken up strongly a c
of times and then did not respond when clear. GUNNER'S MATE was through early.

Overweight—Tim, 2 pounds.

Old Stoneface claimed by Audley Farm Stable, trainer J. B. Dodson. Gunner's Mate claimed by J
Marsh, trainer J. Tammaro.

Claiming Prices (in order of finish)—$9500, 9500, 9000, 9000, 9000, 9500, 9500, 9500.

Scratched—Jalbe, Irish Tenor, Joy Smoke.

My reasoning had been correct, and Where Am I ran an
excellent race, beating all the logical contenders. But Where
Am I had the misfortune to be facing a horse who was
trained by a slightly sharper conniver than Bowyer. Old
Stoneface, the Florida invader who had been trounced in his
last four starts, came to life, battled Where Am I head-and-
head through most of the race, and won by a neck. Nobody
ever said this was an easy game.